Tacit Cinematic Knowledge

Tacit Cinematic Knowledge: Approaches and Practices

edited by Rebecca Boguska, Guilherme Machado, Rebecca Puchta, and Marin Reljić

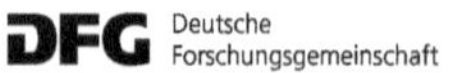

**Bibliographical Information of the
German National Library**

The German National Library lists this publication in the Deutsche
Nationalbibliografie (German National Bibliography); detailed
bibliographic information is available online at dnb.dnb.de

Published in 2024 by meson press, Lüneburg, Germany
www.meson.press

Design concept: Torsten Köchlin, Silke Krieg
Cover design: Mathias Bär
Cover image: Sequential Sequencing by Reto Togni, Demonstration:
Barbara Postolka, ETH Zurich (© CC BY-NC-ND 2.0: Reto Togni).
See page 9ff. in this volume for a detailed description
Copy editing: Dan J. Ruppel

The print edition of this book is printed by Lightning Source,
Milton Keynes, United Kingdom.

ISBN (Print):   978-3-95796-023-8
ISBN (PDF):   978-3-95796-024-5
DOI: 10.14619/0238

The digital editions of this publication can be downloaded freely at
www.meson.press.

Contents

Configurations of Film: Series Foreword

Scalable across a variety of formats and standardized in view of global circulation, the moving image has always been both an image of movement and an image on the move. Over the last three decades, digital production technologies, communication networks and distribution platforms have taken the scalability and mobility of film to a new level. Beyond the classical dispositif of the cinema, new forms and knowledges of cinema and film have emerged, challenging the established approaches to the study of film. The conceptual framework of index, dispositif and canon, which defined cinema as photochemical image technology with a privileged bond to reality, a site of public projection, and a set of works from auteurs from specific national origins, can no longer account for the current multitude of moving images and the trajectories of their global movements. The term "post-cinema condition," which was first proposed by film theorists more than a decade ago to describe the new cultural and technological order of moving images, retained an almost melancholic attachment to that which the cinema no longer was. Moving beyond such attachments, the concept of "configurations of film" aims to account for moving images in terms of their operations, forms and formats, locations and infrastructures, expanding the field of cinematic knowledges beyond the arts and the aesthetic, while retaining a focus on film as privileged site for the production of cultural meaning, for social action and for political conflict.

The series "Configurations of Film" presents pointed interventions in this field of debate by emerging and established international scholars associated with the DFG-funded Graduate Research Training Program (Graduiertenkolleg) "Konfigurationen des Films" at Goethe University Frankfurt. The contributions to the series aim to explore and expand our understanding of configurations of film in both a contemporary and historical perspective, combining film and media theory with media history to address key problems in the development of new analytical frameworks for the moving image on the move.

Tacit Cinematic Knowledge:
An Operative Term

Rebecca Boguska, Guilherme Machado,
Rebecca Puchta, and Marin Reljić

Since the development of moving-image technologies, cinematic techniques have been pervasive in many fields of cultural practice. Configurations of film have continuously appeared in unexpected locations, forms, and formats—far beyond what would eventually become the primary cinematic *dispositif* of the movie theatre. Today, airports, data centers, weather stations, laboratories of aerodynamics and fluid mechanics, corporations, military bases, and schools are just a few examples of sites where cinematic techniques routinely support a variety of procedures, processes, and social-material interactions. In all these sites of cinematic practice, the production and distribution of knowledge have been manifestly impacted by moving images.

Despite the ubiquity of cinematic techniques, film researchers interested in exploring non-theatrical cinematic *dispositifs* are still likely to encounter astonishment from the human actors engaged in shaping these various cinematic settings. For example, in our conversation with Barbara Postolka and Reto Togni, who, at the time of our conversation, were working at the Laboratory of Movement Biomechanics at the ETH Zurich and created the image we have chosen for the cover of this edited collection (see fig. 1), their surprise immediately surfaced: why would we, film scholars, be interested in their scientific practices? In turn, what has often surprised us is the deep awareness that such scientists—but also managers, architects, musicians, and others—have of the technical and historical commonalities between their *dispositifs* and more conventional forms of cinema. As our conversation progressed past their initial astonishment, this was clearly the case for Postolka and Togni as well.

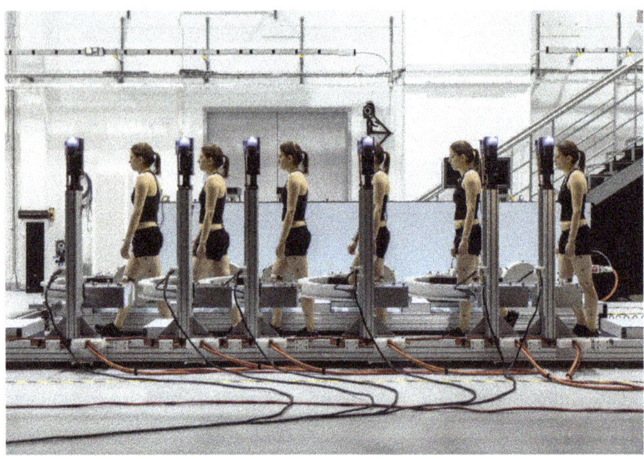

[Figure 1] *Sequential Sequencing* (Source: Postolka and Togni 2020)

Entitled *Sequential Sequencing*, the cover image consists of
a series of photographs, captured and edited into a single
composite image by Togni, which depicts Postolka as she demonstrates the use of a unique moving fluoroscope. The short
description that Postolka and Togni wrote to accompany their
submission of this picture to the Swiss National Science Foundation's *Scientific Image Competition* in 2020 shows that they are
perfectly aware of the historical ties that their *dispositif* has with
practices and technologies that are commonly considered to have
given birth to cinema:

> 142 years after Eadweard Muybridge's invention, the
> principle of chronophotography remains essential … [to]
> understanding human movement. The image not only
> builds on a rich cultural heritage of sequence photographs,
> nowadays best known in extreme sports, but also illus-
> trates cutting-edge scientific processes that reveal internal
> working principles of the human body. Shown is a gait trial
> using a unique moving fluoroscope that tracks and follows
> the movements of a study participant while taking a series of
> x-ray images to analyse bone kinematics. By merging a series

of six photographs taken during the trial, the image not only shows but also follows the maxim of novelty through continuous reinterpretation and repurposing of methods that are more than a century old. (Postolka and Togni 2020)

Togni and Postolka's awareness of the long history of their visualisation technique and its proximity to contemporary sports performance imaging devices did not seem sufficient to explain why film studies researchers were interested in their laboratory. The common origin and the similarity of the apparatuses did not obliterate what now appears to be a divide between cinema and scientific or utilitarian image practices, or between the feature-length theatrical film and various other configurations of film that have emerged over the past century.

While trying to explain our interest in cinematic practices outside of the movie theatre, we have often encountered difficulties posed by the increasingly problematic boundaries between filmic and non-filmic; theatrical and non-theatrical. Debates on marginal practices of cinema, and in particular on the "end (or death) of cinema" (Friedberg 2000; Gaudreault and Marion 2015), "expanded (or extended) cinema" (Dubois, Monvoisin, and Biserna 2010; Youngblood 1970), and "post-cinema" (Casetti 2015; Chateau and Moure 2020; Denson and Leyda 2016; Hagener, Hediger, and Strohmaier 2016; Shaviro 2010), have contributed to the plurality of perspectives within film studies and to the expansion of its fields of inquiry. However, the impact of these debates is still limited outside of the framework of film studies, which might explain the frequent surprise expressed by people involved in non-theatrical, cinematic settings when seeing film researchers like us interested in fields that are supposedly not "ours."

In this volume, we introduce the notion of "tacit cinematic knowledge," in order to account for the increasing ubiquity and the resulting ordinariness of cinematic conditions of knowledge. We also seek to provide an operative term that allows for engagement with cinema as a fluid *dispositif* of aesthetic and epistemic configurations. The following collection of essays draws on a number of historical and theoretical approaches to cinema that refuse to consider it as a field restricted to a privileged set of practices or *dispositifs* (Acland and Wasson 2011; Albera and Tortajada 2010; Casetti 2015; Eisenstein 2009; 1989; 2016; Elsaesser 2016; Farocki 2003; Hediger and Vonderau 2009; Virilio 1989; 2007). The notion of tacit cinematic knowledge thus aims to combine these approaches into a common perspective on cinema as a performative, transformative, and heterogeneous epistemic agent, which often assumes startling roles in the shaping of seemingly "non-cinematic" knowledge.

Our nomenclature draws critically on Michael Polanyi's (2013) concept of "tacit knowledge," which he identifies as a "personal," unformulated complement to any explicit (i.e., codified, enunciable) knowledge, underpinning practices of the body, perception, and communication. By inserting "cinematic," we attempt to shift the location of the knowledge his term describes, and therefore also to push against its anthropocentric character. The term tacit *cinematic* knowledge thus allows us to address the ways in which tacit epistemic operations based on cinematic forms, formats, and usages have been participating in education, art, science, politics, labor, and other fields of cultural practice— and continue to do so in ever-changing ways.

As the contributions to this volume show, tacit cinematic knowledge provides a framework for discussing film-based knowledge formations, while not restricting these inquiries to a single definition. Considering the constant metamorphoses of film throughout history, theorizing its epistemic agency requires a framework of analysis sufficiently extensive and adaptive to the singularity of particular cinematic *dispositifs*. Understood as an *operative term*, tacit cinematic knowledge suggests methods of investigation that elicit various aesthetic and epistemic operations, rather than being constrained by a specific definition limited to particular objects. The term thereby allows us

to explore expanded cinematic configurations while serving as a
unifying anchor for debates on the multiple epistemic potentials
of cinema.

While the authors featured in this edited collection propose ways
of engaging with this operative term that befit the analysis of
their objects, this introduction will present some examples that
will help the reader to situate tacit cinematic operations. Through
these examples and the variety of case studies discussed in the
following essays, the notion of tacit cinematic knowledge will
come to encompass multiple understandings of how implicit,
unspoken cinematic knowledge emerges from analytical gestures. Nevertheless, attending to tacit cinematic knowledge
does not dismiss or overlook the analysis of more conventional,
explicit forms of cinema. Rather, it opens up possibilities of
tracking cinematic objects across practices which—particularly in
the context of digitization—are increasingly dispersed (Alloa and
Cappelletto 2020; Denson 2020; Hagener, Hediger, and Strohmaier
2016; Rothöhler 2018), and seem to be fading into the background as they become the tacit infrastructure of contemporary
knowledge practices.

Cinematic Modes of Existence

The essays of this edited collection demonstrate the possibility
of reinstating cinematic features of processes and associations
that might not be, at first sight, particularly indebted to cinema.
This reinstatement reveals something substantial in our ways of
being, thinking, and acting. Insofar as the term tacit cinematic
knowledge aims at unearthing the cinematic qualities of practices
involving human actors who are potentially unaware of their
relevance, this notion designates ways of documenting—and
claiming—cinematic *modes of existence*.[1]

1   As Henning Schmidgen shows, the term "mode of existence" has under-
     gone a series of re-appropriations, shifting from phenomenological to
     ontological orientations, including in film theory (2016, 325). What we

Cinematic configurations of knowledge, wherever they operate, are worthy of study for their own sake. Such research is crucial in the face of contemporary concerns about forms of mediation that shape our societies (Akrich, Latour, and Callon 2006; Galloway and Thacker 2007; Kember and Zylinska 2012). Accordingly, we argue that cinematic mediation is productive of the social, meaning that our societies are inevitably affected by modes of cinematic existence whose complexity remains largely ungrasped. Thus, in order to give a series of *figurations*—to use Bruno Latour's (2005) terminology—to cinema, we need to track the cinematic traces of the social. We need to consider the ways in which cinema operates across practices and environments, imparting its operational modes.

But this raises the question of what allows us to designate certain forms of knowledge as "cinematic"? In other words, how can we recognize cinema outside of cinema? How can we argue for a similarity between these tacit cinematic knowledges outside of the movie theatre and practices and *dispositifs* that have so far been treated as explicitly cinematic?

There is no need to engage in the debate on medium specificity. We will not even restrict the "epistemic domain" of cinema to the generic presence of moving images displayed on screens, and thus associate the cinematic with the *"kinetic"* or the *"screenic"* (Casetti 2015, 112). Rather we would like to take up examples in which artists and theorists have claimed that cinematic modes of existence extend beyond the technological and temporal boundaries of what we intuitively (still) put under the sign of "cinema."

propose here is to take up the term in a sense close to Gilbert Simondon's (2017) and Bruno Latour's (2018) interpretations, i.e., in a sense "not limited to a phenomenological or ontological characterisation of a specific type of object, but rather [open to] a consideration—grounded, ultimately, in sociology and/or history—of how the object is embedded in particular modes of thought and action" (Schmidgen 2016, 325).

Among the authors who have thoroughly examined tacit
cinematic forms of knowledge, there is one for whom such forms
could hardly be restricted to specific sets of practices and *dis-positifs*. For Sergei Eisenstein, cinematic operations of meaning
production were already present at the end of the 16th century, in
the way that El Greco envisaged the composition of his paintings
as blocks of shapes that could be reassembled in different
ways—resulting in various compositions—while keeping their
inner structures unaltered (similar to filmic shots in montage
sequences) (Eisenstein 1980). The way children construct their
drawings, ignoring the laws of perspective in favor of a hierarchy
of pictorial elements whose dimensions correspond to their
narrative importance, mirrors the use of variation of shot sizes in
films (Eisenstein 1989, 111). Eisenstein further argues that prose
composition may be compared to the process of filmic montage
and the gesture of emphasizing objects through close-up shots.
He explains how orators compose their speeches in a "cinematic
way," seeking to meaningfully connect the stages of a thought,
and conferring on each sentence the power to alter the meaning
of the preceding one. Finally, he borrows a definition of the art
of oratory from Thomas de Quincey to conclude that, like films,
orators extract from the truth its most striking aspects in order
to bring them to the attention of an audience (Eisenstein 1980,
32).

In short, Eisenstein suggests that what has come to be "cinema"
are operations of meaning production present across the arts
and in various social practices. Moreover, these operations
embody knowledge as well as affects.

According to Eisenstein, El Greco's *View of Toledo* (1596–1600) (see
fig. 2), which is not concerned with the realistic spatial relation-ship between the different elements of the landscape, demon-strates the relationship between that painter's work and the
affective potential of cinematic montage. The painting is not
simply an interpretative narrative of the city where the painter
lived, but also a "fugue on the theme of the Last Judgment"

[Figure 2] El Greco's *View of Toledo* (1596–1600) (Source: Wikimedia Commons 2022).

(Eisenstein 1980, 28)—a landscape under a storm raised to the status of an ecstatic figure. Various elements drawn from real life are set up within the painting in order to render the conflict of passions that the painter was experiencing in the face of his imminent death, expressing his state of existence through a conflicting montage embracing all his suffering and anguish. Thus, for Eisenstein, the cinematic is a broad and long-standing operation of *thinking*, which does not dismiss *feeling*.

Perhaps Eisenstein's richest example of tacit cinematic knowledge is his famous interpretation of the Acropolis of Athens as "the perfect example of one of the most ancient films" (1989, 117). In his text "Montage and Architecture," based on the descriptions of the historian of architecture Auguste Choisy, Eisenstein put forward the idea that the layout of the Acropolis' buildings does not respect geometric symmetry from an over-arching perspective because it was designed to compose a sequence of points of view whose perfection can be perceived only through the idea of montage. The monuments that made

up the sanctuary of the Athenians were arranged in such a way
that the view of each one is juxtaposed with that of another.
By avoiding the simultaneous view of several buildings, the
architectural ensemble never takes away the uniqueness of each
individual monument, placed for a moment in the center of the
visitor's attention and offering an impression of unity of composition. Moreover, the Acropolis' buildings were arranged in a
manner that the visitor always comes to contemplate the monuments first in their most privileged angles of view. This prompted
Eisenstein to claim that "the Greeks have left us the most perfect
examples of shot design, change of shot, and shot length" (1989,
117).

Even the rhythm of this composition is designed by the
movement, not of the "film" itself, but of its spectators:

> [I]t is hard to imagine a montage sequence for an architec-
> tural ensemble more subtly composed, shot by shot,
> than the one which our legs create by walking among the
> buildings of the Acropolis. … [The] length of these montage
> sequences is entirely in step with the rhythm of the building
> itself: the distance from point to point is long, and the time
> taken to move from one to the other is of a length in keeping
> with solemnity. (Eisenstein 1989, 117 and 121)

Eisenstein's extensive genealogical project of writing—as Antonio
Somaini puts it—"the history of all the media and all the forms
of representation that had explored, *before cinema*, the same
'expressive means' that cinema would later employ" (Somaini
2016, 20)[2] is thus a key reference for thinking tacit cinematic
knowledge today.[3] In particular, it allows us to grasp cinematic
configurations that have never been rigidly fixed in specific

2   All translations by the authors.
3   Other prominent authors who proposed enlarged conceptions of cinema
      include Gilles Deleuze, who, drawing on Henri Bergson, speaks of "the uni-
      verse as cinema in itself, a metacinema" (1986, 59), and Jean-Luc Nancy, who
      posits cinema as a particular condition of existence (2004, 188).

settings or *dispositifs*. On the contrary, referring to objects as "post-cinematic" considers that these long-standing and diffuse cinematic means of expression have now been tamed, cultivated, and developed by the many kinds of film practices and technological configurations throughout the last century. The various configurations of cinematic knowledge today and their effects on social production are inevitably affected by film cultures.

Image Operations

On a different note, contemporary tacit cinematic knowledge may also be considered as an aspect of "invisible visual culture" (Paglen 2016), wherein the majority of image operations take place away from human eyes. Recent media theories account for a cinematic situation unimaginable at the time of Eisenstein's work. The advent of digital images has rendered images machine-readable, and has thus fostered a vast automation of sight (Virilio 2007). Images no longer need to have a human-readable form in order to operate and impact our everyday lives. As Trevor Paglen puts it: "Invisible images are actively watching us, poking and prodding, guiding our movements, inflicting pain and inducing pleasure. But all of this is hard to see" (2016). Cinematic technologies combined with machine learning technologies become tools for managing massive volumes of data used for military, government, and law enforcement practices, as well as for commercial management of large-scale sensorial experiences. As Mark B. N. Hansen argues:

> The self-propagating, self-escalating increase in non-perceptual sensible data generated by twenty-first-century media profoundly affects the economy of experience, such that our (human) experience becomes increasingly conditioned and impacted by processes that we have no direct experience of, no direct mode of access to, and no potential awareness of. (Hansen 2015, 8)

Most digital cinematic operations take place in a tacit domain,
from which they distribute visibilities and invisibilities, controlling experiences and attentional flows (Citton 2017; Rosa 2018; 2019). Knowledge itself calls for new definitions in the era of big data, when institutional practices of knowledge production are intimately linked to techniques of tracking digital traces and large-scale processing (boyd and Crawford 2013). All these new technological configurations raise aesthetic, epistemological, ethical, political, and ontological problems that are just beginning to be unraveled. Significantly, the hidden nature of digital operations cannot be elucidated with the traditional tools for investigating cinematic images, which primarily address human perception. The automated operations that precede (or pre-organize) sensibility are also becoming a topic of film research, as infra-empirical cinematic operations that embed practices and modulate human agency.

The work of video artist and film theorist Harun Farocki captures and reflects upon the implications of digital cinematic processes in a variety of institutional settings. In his video *War at a Distance* (see fig. 3), for example, Farocki (2003) shows how digital technologies and machine vision have simultaneously reshaped industrial modes of production and military strategies of visualization and destruction. He highlights the fact that, today, images are used not only as indexical testimonies of events, but also as indispensable operational units in processes of production and destruction, in which the human gaze itself is replaced by machine vision and relegated to marginal functions.

Perspectives on the diverse operations of images, in the Farockian sense, have multiplied in the last two decades, revealing a variety of relationships between the functions of digital images and processes in the military, pedagogical, economic, and legal spheres (Eder and Klonk 2017; Hoel 2018). Such work has also prompted retrospective examinations of non-digital cinematic techniques, proving that such techniques already had an active part in shaping the operation of these

[Figure 3] Film still from Harun Farocki's video *War at a Distance* (Source: Farocki 2003, 52:47; © Harun Farocki GbR).

spheres (Acland and Wasson 2011; Hediger, Hoof, and Zimmermann 2023; Hediger and Vonderau 2009). Aud Sissel Hoel argues that the growing literature on images as operational agents shows that "we are currently standing on the verge of an emerging, operational paradigm of media theory" (2018, 27), wherein digital technologies produce new types of images, questioning the very concept of the image itself and the assumptions that underlie it. The autonomous, active character of digital images unleashes the power of the tacit epistemological agency of media.

In the midst of such upheaval of contemporary visual culture, in which cinema—no less than the image itself—is hardly self-evident, the compelling new perspective opened by the term tacit cinematic knowledge helps to navigate through disparate domains in search of traces of cinema. As we evolve within digitally controlled spheres of sensibility, it is of great interest that we find the means and tools to track down the implicitly cinematic aspects of our experiences. This applies to both visual and acoustic fields (at least), insofar as sonic configurations have also always been largely relegated to the background of cinematic experiences, although they are powerful evocators of the universe of cinema outside of its classical *dispositif*. In the age of high-speed file sharing, the modes of semiotic production and of designing affective ambiences are constantly reviving, recombining, and translating visual and sonic configurations drawn from cinematic archives (Steyerl 2008). When these configurations become frameworks of experience, operations, gestures, associations, and moods, they carry the imprint of our cinematic knowledge cultures far beyond the movie theatre and filmic diegeses.

Tacit cinematic knowledge is thus potentially related to all kinds of cultural practices, historical periods, visual and sonic *dispositifs*. It arises from human as well as non-human knowledges (Braidotti 2019; Haraway 1988; 2007) and is directly or indirectly bound to the explicit universe of cinema. Just as Karin Knorr Cetina suggests that knowledge practices in a "knowledge society" take place primarily outside of academia (2002, 333), in times of "post-cinema," cinematic practices take place most often outside of the traditionally privileged sites of cinematic knowledge.

Tacit Cinematic Knowledge: Approaches and Practices

This volume brings together essays from scholars who participated in the international conference *Histories of Tacit Cinematic Knowledge,* organized by the Graduate Research Training Program "Configurations of Film" at the Goethe University Frankfurt (September 24–6, 2020), and from authors who were invited to follow up on the questions raised at the conference. Coming from different backgrounds, the authors propose distinctive approaches to the term tacit cinematic knowledge.

We have chosen to arrange the essays so as to allow the reader to move from technological, social, and environmental approaches to tacit cinematic knowledge to more object-oriented ones. Theoretical, conceptual, or practice-related points of articulation mark the intervals between the essays. We hope that this structure will help to map out not only the growing diversity of cinematic practices but also the theoretical and conceptual tools that are currently being developed to investigate them. While the essays gathered here are not intended to provide a conclusive account of tacit cinematic knowledge or a single definition thereof, they each attest to the way this notion operates within a multiplicity of cinematic settings, highlighting how each of these sites can benefit from further research into the subtle cinematic operations at work.

Benoît Turquety's "'Implicit Conceptual Structures': The Non-human Dimension" opens the discussion of tacit cinematic knowledge by inviting us to contrast Polanyi's anthropocentric understanding of tacit knowledge with the French tradition of technical epistemology, following in the footsteps of Georges Canguilhem and Gilbert Simondon. By reviving the notion of "implicit conceptual structures," Turquety proposes a way to think about cinematic knowledge as knowledge which circulates tacitly "from the device to its user," exemplified by human gestures prompted by cameras and projectors.

Henning Schmidgen's "Minoring Machines: René Laloux, Félix Guattari, and the Cinema of Animation" focuses on animations Laloux made in collaboration with Guattari, and with the help of the patients of the psychiatric clinic of La Borde. He proposes in his essay a revisitation of the concept of "minor cinema," separating it from questions of national origin and criteria of authorship by considering the interplay between the cinematographic machine, the body, and human subjectivity. The "technology of cinema," as Schmidgen suggests, can "itself ... be conceived as an environment imbued with tacit knowledge."

Veena Hariharan's "Bio-Logs and Non-Humans" discusses cinematic apparatuses designed to capture animal behavior and

turn tacit animal knowledge into cinematic images. She takes
up the case study of a Swedish slow-TV show, *The Great Elk Trek*
(Erhag and Edlund 2019–23), that records the migration of the
Swedish moose. She demonstrates how visual tracking of animal
movement, which has been one of the historical drivers of new
cinematic technologies, continues to inform our knowledge of
non-human worlds. As she argues, such tracking now enables
a global community to share a mode of contemplating distant,
vanishing wild realms.

Felipe Soares' "Old Modes, New Moods, or How Soundtracks
Can Experiment" opens a perspective on the long history of the
association between musical modes and particular moods, dominated by conservative industrial cinematic interests, but also a
source for new cinematic experiments. He considers mode-mood
associations as "memory move[s]" i.e., collective tacit knowledge
stemming from different temporalities and presenting count-
less possible reconfigurations. Specifically, Soares' case study
considers how the composer Sergei Prokofiev—notably in his collaborations with Eisenstein—drew extensively on Russian musical
heritage.

In "From the Construction Site via the Highway to the Guided
Tour," Rebecca Boguska reports on her research trip to the Large
Wave Flume, a coastal research facility located in Hanover, Germany. Building on Eisenstein's conception of cinematic montage,
Boguska explores the visualization apparatuses and the material
infrastructure of this research facility as multiple sites of hidden
cinematic performance, ranging from scientific measurement
to didactic activities. Her contribution reveals the degree to
which cinematic operations are embedded in everyday research
practices.

Guilherme Machado's "Scripting Organizations: How Labor Is
Becoming Cinematic" provides an account of the increasingly
generalized uses of cinematic apparatuses for recruitment,
training, and management of labor-related knowledge. He shows

how the scripting of learning environments gives rise to tacit epistemic conditions for self-discipline. As productive efficiency results from the apprentices' sensorial, cognitive, and affective activity within cinematically and algorithmically programmed environments, staging practices that have long been associated with cinema are now extensively shaping the performance of labor.

Claire Salles' "'When Pregnancy Becomes a Moving Picture': Negotiating Tacit Cinematic Knowledge in Fetal Ultrasonography" analyses how ultrasound studios produce images of fetuses that inform the political debates around the fetuses' ontological and legal status. She discusses the various uses of prenatal images and the diversity of meanings given to them, invoking feminist positions on the epistemological stakes of modes of visibility related to pregnancy, showing how the political operations of fetal images are themselves configured by diverse forms of tacit cinematic knowledge—from the settings in which echography takes place to family viewing practices.

Shifting scales, Jelena Rakin's "Phantasms of the Sun and Venus: Tacit Cinematic Knowledge in Astronomy" looks at visual *dispositifs* tracking and visualizing astronomical phenomena. She explores the cinematic configurations—such as time-lapse, chromatic rendering, and other forms of image processing—that give perceptible shape to celestial events and their temporalities. Rakin shows that photographic and filmic technologies and the aesthetic knowledge they embody are consistently involved in the "crafting" of astronomical realities and scientific knowledge, thereby allowing us to speak of "aesthetics as a form of cinematic episteme."

Bettina Paul's and Larissa Fischer's essay entitled "Iconic Materiality, or the Ambivalent Fascination of Cinematic Lie Detection Depictions (in Germany)" considers the numerous filmic representations of lie detection practices and machines — particularly in Hollywood—as constituting a widely disseminated

knowledge field that supports practices of law, policing, and
research in the US and Germany. By incorporating perspectives
on tacitness from social science and analyzing interviews with
experts, the authors argue that tacit cinematic knowledge gains
its epistemic significance through iterative representations and
the retelling of popular imaginaries of lie detection.

Moving from the institutional to the private realm, Andrea
Mariani's "Crafty Cinephilia: The Scrapbook and Film History as
Media Anamorphosis" lets us discover a practice of reconfiguring
the cinematic experience into a form of knowledge set out on the
pages of a cinephile's scrapbook. By emphasizing the agency of
the materialities at play in the process of mediating knowledge
between the films and the scrapbook, and through the scrapbook
maker's gestures, Mariani addresses tacit cinematic knowledge in
terms of a performance of material and technical configurations
transcending, as he claims, the symbolic and the discursive
realms.

R. Haritha's "New Media(tions): Audience's Engagement in Contemporary Malayalam Cinema" revisits narrative cinema via its
digital forms, formats, and reception devices, which facilitate
various modes of spectatorial engagement, from the production
of freeze-frames to practices of copying and recycling images.
Focusing on the ways in which users engage with each other
in online discussion about filmic details, she argues that the
reconfiguration of audiences fueled by social media eventually
transforms spectators into permanent producers of collective
knowledge about cinema, i.e., tacit volunteers contributing to the
digital economy of cinema.

As a closing reflection on tacit cinematic knowledge, Vinzenz
Hediger's and Felix Simon's "Unauthorized Fictions: Political Conflict as Spectacle and Conceptions of Trust in the Age of Trump"
provides a view on the part played by film in contemporary US
democracy (and potentially beyond). Drawing on Donald Trump's
election campaign and tribute videos, the authors show how

 these videos rely on a tacit collective knowledge of the movie-trailer format to promote a dramatized spectacle of politics and popular sovereignty and show that in an "ocular democracy," popular empowerment is grounded in spectatorial affects.

Literature

Acland, Charles R., and Haidee Wasson. 2011. *Useful Cinema*. London: Duke University Press.

Akrich, Madeleine, Bruno Latour, and Michel Callon, eds. 2006. *Sociologie de la traduction*. Paris: Les Presses des Mines.

Albera, François and Maria Tortajada. 2010. *Cinema Beyond Film: Media Epistemology in the Modern Era*. Amsterdam: Amsterdam University Press.

Alloa, Emmanuel, and Chiara Cappelletto, eds. 2020. *Dynamics of the Image. Moving Images in a Global World*. Boston: Walter de Gruyter.

boyd, danah, and Kate Crawford. 2013. "Big Data als kulturelles, technologisches und wissenschaftliches Phänomen: Sechs Provokationen." In *Big Data: Das neue Versprechen der Allwissenheit,* edited by Heinrich Geiselberger and Tobias Moorstedt, 187–213. Berlin: Suhrkamp.

Braidotti, Rosi. 2019. *Posthuman Knowledge*. Cambridge: Polity Press.

Casetti, Francesco. 2015. The Lumière Galaxy: 7 Key Words for the Cinema to Come. New York: John Belton.

Chateau, Dominique, and Jose Moure, eds. 2020. *Post-Cinema: Cinema in the Post-Art Era*. Amsterdam: Amsterdam University Press.

Citton, Yves. 2017. *The Ecology of Attention*. Translated by Barnaby Norman. Cambridge: Polity Press.

Deleuze, Gilles. 1986. *Cinema 1: The Movement-Image*. Translated by Hugh Tomlinson and Barbara Habberjam. Minneapolis: The University of Minnesota Press.

Denson, Shane. 2020. *Discorrelated Images*. London: Duke University Press.

Denson, Shane, and Julia Leyda, eds. 2016. *Post-Cinema: Theorizing 21st-Century Film*. Falmer: REFRAME books.

Dubois, Philippe, Frédéric Monvoisin, and Elena Biserna. 2010. *Extended Cinema: Le cinéma gagne du terrain*. Pasian di Prato: Campanotto.

Eder, Jens, and Charlotte Klonk, eds. 2017. *Image Operation: Visual Media and Political Conflict*. Manchester: Manchester University Press.

Eisenstein, Sergei. 2016 (1947–8). *Notes for a General History of Cinema*. Edited by Naum Kleiman and Antonio Somaini, translated by Margo Shohl Rosen, Brinton Tench Coxe, and Natalie Ryabchikova. Amsterdam: Amsterdam University Press.

Eisenstein, Sergei. 1989 (1937–40). "Montage and Architecture." Translated by Michael Glenny. *Assemblage* (10): 111–31.

———. 1980 (1939). "El Greco y el cine." In *Cinématisme. Peinture et Cinéma,* edited by François Albera, 15–104. Bruxelles: Complexe.

Elsaesser, Thomas. 2016. *Film History as Media Archaeology: Tracking Digital Cinema.* Amsterdam: Amsterdam University Press.

Friedberg, Anne. 2000. "The End of Cinema: Multimedia and Technological Change." In *Reinventing Film Studies*, edited by Christine Gledhill and Linda Williams, 438–52. London: Arnold.

Galloway, Alexander R., and Eugene Thacker. 2007. *The Exploit: A Theory of Networks.* Minneapolis: University of Minnesota Press.

Gaudreault, André, and Philippe Marion. 2015. *The End of Cinema? A Medium in Crisis in the Digital Age.* Translated by Timothy Barnard. New York: Columbia University Press.

Hagener, Malte, Vinzenz Hediger, and Alena Strohmaier, eds. 2016. *The State of Post-Cinema: Tracing the Moving Image in the Age of Digital Dissemination.* London: Palgrave Macmillan.

Hansen, Mark B. N. 2015. *Feed-Forward: On the Future of Twenty-First-Century Media.* Chicago: University of Chicago Press.

Haraway, Donna. 2007. *When Species Meet.* Minneapolis: University of Minnesota Press.

———.1988. "Situated Knowledges: The Science Question in Feminism and the Privilege of Partial Perspective." *Feminist Studies* 14 (3): 575–599.

Hediger, Vinzenz, and Patrick Vonderau. 2009. *Films that Work: Industrial Film and the Productivity of Media.* Amsterdam: Amsterdam University Press.

Hediger, Vinzenz, Florian Hoof, and Yvonne Zimmermann. 2023 (forthcoming). *Films that Work Harder. The Global Circulation of Industrial Cinema.* Amsterdam: Amsterdam University Press.

Hoel, Aud Sissel. 2018. "Operative Images: Inroads to a New Paradigm of Media Theory." In *Image-Action-Space: Situating the Screen in Visual Practice,* edited by Luisa Feiersinger, Kathrin Friedrich and Moritz Queisner, 11–27. Berlin: Walter De Gruyter.

Kember, Sarah, and Joanna Zylinska. 2012. *Life after New Media: Mediation as Vital Process.* Cambridge: MIT Press.

Knorr Cetina, Karin. 2002. *Wissenskulturen: Ein Vergleich naturwissenschaftlicher Wissensformen.* Frankfurt am Main: Suhrkamp.

Latour, Bruno. 2018 (2012). *An Inquiry into Modes of Existence: An Anthropology of the Moderns.* Translated by Catherine Porter. Cambridge: Harvard University Press.

———. 2005. *Reassembling the Social: An Introduction to Actor-Network Theory.* Oxford: Oxford University Press.

Nancy, Jean-Luc. 2004. "Cinéfile et cinémonde." *Trafic* (50): 183–190.

Paglen, Trevor. 2016. "Invisible Images (Your Pictures Are Looking at You)." *The New Inquiry.* Accessed February 12, 2022. https://thenewinquiry.com/invisible-images-your-pictures-are-looking-at-you/.

Polanyi, Michael. 2013 (1966). *The Tacit Dimension.* Chicago: The University of Chicago Press.

Rosa, Hartmut. 2018. *Unverfügbarkeit.* Wien/Salzburg: Residenz Verlag.

———. 2019. *Resonanz: Eine Soziologie der Weltbeziehung.* Berlin: Suhrkamp.

28 Rothöhler, Simon. 2018. *Das verteilte Bild. Stream | Archiv | Ambiente*. Paderborn: Wilhelm Fink Verlag.

Schmidgen, Henning. 2016. "Modes d'existence: Memoirs of a Concept." In *Reset Modernity!*, edited by Bruno Latour, 320–7. Cambridge: MIT Press.

Shaviro, Steven. 2010. *Post-Cinematic Affect*. Winchester: O-Books.

Simondon, Gilbert. 2017 (1958). *On the Mode of Existence of Technical Objects*. Translated by Cecile Malaspina and John Rogove. Minneapolis: Univocal Publishing.

Somaini, Antonio. 2013. "Généalogie, morphologie, anthropologie des images, archéologie des médias." In *Notes pour une histoire générale du cinéma*, edited by François Albera and Antonio Somaini, 237–91. Paris: AFRHC.

Steyerl, Hito. 2008. "Politics of the Archive: Translations in Film." *Transversal*. Accessed February 16, 2022. http://www.documnt.net/hito-steyerl-politics-of-the-archive.

Virilio, Paul. 2007 (1988). *The Vision Machine*. Translated by Julie Rose. Bloomington: Indiana University Press.

———. 1989 (1984). *War and Cinema: The Logistics of Perception*. Translated by Patrick Camiller. London: Verso.

Youngblood, Gene. 1970. *Expanded Cinema*. New York: Dutton.

(Audio)Visual Material

El Greco. 1596-1600. *View of Toledo*. Oli on Canvas. *Wikimedia Commons*. Accessed August 10, 2022. https://commons.wikimedia.org/wiki/File:El_Greco_View_of_Toledo.jpg.

Erhag, Johan, and Stefan Edlund. 2019–23. *Den stora älgvandringen*. Slow TV, Sweden.

Farocki, Harun. 2003. *War at a Distance*. Video, color, 58 min., Germany.

Barbara, Postolka, and Reto Togni. 2020. *Sequential Sequencing*. Digital Photograph. *Flickr*. Accessed August 8, 2022. https://www.flickr.com/photos/snsf_image_competition/49725501732.

TECHNOLOGY

LUMIÈRE CINÉMATOGRAPHE

GILBERT SIMONDON

GEORGES CANGUILHEM

HISTORICAL EPISTEMOLOGY

[1]

"Implicit Conceptual Structures": The Nonhuman Dimension

Benoît Turquety

In a foundational text, Jacques Guillerme and Jan Sebestik described technical operations as being ruled by what they called an "implicit conceptual structure" (1968): they only work when done in a certain way. "Implicit" strikingly echoes Michael Polanyi's "tacit" dimension of knowledge, but there is a difference: the "conceptual structure" lies in the operations, not in the subject. It is not a personal knowledge. These "implicit conceptual structures" describe precisely the kind of knowledge that, according to Gilbert Simondon, is archived in technical objects through a process he calls "concretization." This process implies a continuous exchange of knowledge between humans and

machines. The study of machines shows how cinematic technical objects and gestures systematically involve a nonhuman dimension in the circulation of knowledge.

In the first pages of *The Tacit Dimension*, Michael Polanyi defines his ground-breaking notion of "tacit knowing" through a simple but ambitious statement: "I shall reconsider human knowledge by starting from the fact that *we can know more than we can tell*" (2009, 4). As he comments just after, the apparent simplicity of that sentence can be misleading: "This fact seems obvious enough; but it is not easy to say exactly what it means" (ibid.). To clarify his claim, he goes on to present a number of examples of what it can mean to *know* without being able to tell. The first is recognition: we can recognize one person's face among a thousand, or interpret their moods, without being able to describe with words the distinctive features we base our judgement on. From this point on, Polanyi moves to descriptive sciences that "study physiognomies that cannot be fully described in words," and then to "the art of the expert diagnostician" (2009, 5 and 6). This art involves "both practical and theoretical knowledge," and here Polanyi makes another important theoretical gesture in announcing that he "shall always speak of 'knowing'" (2009, 7) as covering *both* these kinds of knowledge. For the argument that I will develop in this chapter, this is a major intervention.

The example of the diagnostician entails a decisive shift. Their work is grounded in descriptive science, but their observation is active, involving "skillful testing" (Polanyi 2009, 7), not only a distanced gaze. It is technical work. It belongs "in the same class [as] the performance of skills, whether artistic, athletic, or technical" (Polanyi 2009, 6). Technical expertise is thus an aspect of *knowing*, and more particularly, *tacit knowing*.

This move from what first appears to be a problem of language—
not all knowledge can be translated in words—to the integration
of technical as well as scientific knowledges under the single
notion of *knowing* has been central to the status of technology
within the philosophy of science and the development of the concept of "technics." "Tacit knowing" may not have been primarily
about technics; but it was clearly a major tool to think even the
most informal, everyday forms of practical expertise. Know-how
becomes knowing—a kind of knowing inscribed within the body
and surrounded by secret.

This chapter will outline the implications of Polanyi's model
of "tacit knowledge" for the study of technics in general, and
for cinematic technics in particular—"technics" including here
both technical gestures and technical objects, techniques, and
machines. To this end, I will present another technological model,
elaborated at about the same time as the publication of *The
Tacit Dimension*, but coming from a totally different background:
the French tradition of historical epistemology. This may lead
us to question what could appear as the most indisputable part
of Polanyi's initial definition, namely, that what is at stake is
essentially *human* knowledge.

Technics and the Implicit

As several scholars have noted (Sebestik 1992), the position of
technics within the history of epistemology in France has been
somewhat overlooked. One of the fundamental places for the
development of French epistemology, the Institut d'histoire des
sciences, created in 1932 and headed successively by Abel Rey
(1932–40), Gaston Bachelard (1940–55), Georges Canguilhem
(1955–71) and others, was renamed as early as 1933 the "Institut
d'histoire des sciences et des techniques."[1] Renowned as a

---

1   It is now the "Institut d'histoire et de philosophie des sciences et des
     techniques" (IHPST).

34 philosopher of medicine and biology and as an epistemologist, Canguilhem was in fact, during his time as the director of the Institute, a major proponent of "technology," the term being understood as the discipline that studies technics. This was not separate from his major philosophical preoccupations— in his 1943 dissertation, Canguilhem defines medicine as "a technique or art at the intersection of several sciences," and more particularly as "a technique for establishing or restoring normalcy" (2009, 7–8). This directly echoes Polanyi's description of diagnosis as an "art" (Polanyi 2009, 6–7), as much "technical" as it is "scientific."

During two academic years, between 1963 and 1965, Georges Canguilhem led a research seminar at the Institute on the "Beginnings of Technology," "technology" referring here again to an academic discipline. The collective work examined Western literature since the Middle Ages, from engineering manuals to philosophical texts, in order to investigate "the constitution of the discourse on technical operations as a scientific discourse" (Guillerme and Sebestik 1968, 1).[2] It was not a history of technics, but rather a history of meta-technics. The results gathered by the seminar were published in a ground-breaking essay in *Thalès*, the journal of the Institute, written by two of the participants, Jacques Guillerme and Jan Sebestik.

Among the important discoveries of the seminar was the importance of Christian Wolff's 1728 *Philosophia rationalis sive Logica*, whose introductory chapter on the classification of sciences presented the project of a "philosophy of the arts" (Guillerme and Sebestik 1968, 29) ("arts" here in the general sense of *technè*, as still used in Polanyi's quote) that he named *technology*. "*Technology* is thus the science of the arts and of the works made with art, or, if one prefers, the science of the things produced by persons through the work of bodily organs, mainly with the hands" (Wolff 1963, §71, 38). It was to be the first and for

2   All translations by author.

a long time the only attempt to express the possibility—and the
ambition—of expounding "a philosophical and mathematical knowledge" of technical operations. As summarized by Guillerme and Sebestik, "the aim is to gather within a coherent body of doctrine the *implicit knowledge* that manifests in the operations of an art and to inscribe them on the intellectual map of the academic system" (1968, 28; italics added).

The discipline of technology encompasses the analysis of laws that explain the possibility of operations performed by craftspersons, and the rules that govern the development of these operations. Cutting wood, for instance, is subject to certain specific rules: "there is a reason why one can cut wood, and why it can be done with a wedge, and then also with an axe" (Wolff 1963, §39, as cited in Guillerme and Sebestik 1968, 28). "The forces involved with the wedge and with the attack pushing it can be demonstrated mathematically" (Guillerme and Sebestik 1968, 28), claimed Wolff, which implied that for him technology was to be a mathematical discipline as well as a philosophical one. But the very understanding that "there is a reason why" a given technical operation or gesture can work in certain ways and not in others has major implications. As Guillerme and Sebestik formulate it, "Even a manual art as menial as cutting wood puts into play an implicit conceptual structure that governs the execution of the operations" (1968, 28). The philosophical task involved in technology thus relies on the establishment of these "implicit conceptual structures" by which operations are ruled, and which can be formalised mathematically.

The Tacit and the Personal

In the context of this edited collection, these "*implicit* conceptual structures," which follow the "*implicit knowledge*" embodied within human operations and which technology should integrate within the scientific system of the time, echo the "*tacit*" dimension of knowledge first described by Polanyi in his 1966 publication.

 But I think that the differences are no less striking than the commonalities.

Both these conceptual frameworks describe nonverbal forms of expertise. They both can be used to analyse technical know-how, and to examine the fact that a technical gesture is done in a certain way, without anyone having explained, formulated, verbalized why and how. But the major difference to me lies in the fact that Polanyi's framework is fundamentally subjectivist. Tacit knowledge is a form of what he had called, in an earlier book, "personal knowledge" (Polanyi 1958). As is well known, Polanyi fought for the recognition that the "declared aim of modern science … to establish a strictly detached, objective knowledge" was absurd. "Tacit knowledge" then became a step within this larger project. As he wrote, "But suppose that tacit thought forms an indispensable part of all knowledge, then the ideal of eliminating all personal elements of knowledge would, in effect, aim at the destruction of all knowledge" (Polanyi 2009, 20).

Tacit knowledge is thus at the heart of all personal knowledge. It is, to Polanyi, the most radically and obviously personal of all kinds of knowledge. I may not be able to *describe* how to cut wood, but I know, my body knows, and I can make the right gestures: this is my personal knowledge. In a way, Guillerme and Sebestik's account reverses the perspective. The "implicit conceptual structure" designates an arrangement of concepts, so it *is* knowledge, but it lies within the operations. It belongs to an objectivist epistemology, just as there is an objectivist aesthetics where beauty lies in the objects and not in the observer's gaze. A gesture or a machine do not contain concepts per se, but they materialize knowledge in the form of "implicit conceptual structures." The operation "cutting wood" can be done in various ways, but these ways are not infinite, and each of the possible techniques imposes on the operator its own internal coherence, a certain set of gestures and precisely conceived tools. Should these requirements be neglected, the operation just won't work. Technical laws do exist, which may not be theorized, formulated,

or understood by the operators, nor by science in general, but
which apply nevertheless. The specific assemblage of rules
governing a particular operation thus does not materialize in
theoretical discourse, but in the operator's succession of gestures and choice of tools. The correct execution of the operation
manifests the knowledge contained within the technicity of that
operation, within the structure of the machines or the precision
of the gestures. The technical process realizes the implicit conceptual structures inscribed within the operation. If I know how
to cut wood, it is because I have first adapted my actions to the
technique's implicit conceptual structure. *It rules me; I learn from
it.*

The learning process, I argue, defines technical knowledge as
such. In "Techniques of the Body," Marcel Mauss claimed that a
technique is "an action which is *effective* and *traditional*" (1973,
75): transmission is an essential, defining feature. Techniques are
fundamentally *what can be learned.* However, the Polanyi and the
Guillerme/Sebestik models imply different modes of transmission, different models for the circulation of knowledge. The latter
allows for the consideration of a nonhuman kind of knowledge,
and of its circulation from the device to its user. Unsurprisingly,
these "implicit conceptual structures" describe precisely the kind
of knowledge which, according to Gilbert Simondon, is archived
in machines—unsurprisingly, since the philosopher participated
in the "Beginnings of Technology" seminar after completing his
1958 doctoral thesis, *Du mode d'existence des objets techniques,*
under the supervision of Canguilhem *(Simondon* 2017). The "concretization" process described by Simondon implies a form of
evolution of the technical object wherein the progressive understanding of the machine's inner structural interactions, of its
objective internal coherence, generates the production of new,
improved forms (Simondon 2017, 25–29). Invention is thus not an
act of human imagination imposed on a machine, but an effort
toward a deeper understanding of the machine's own "implicit

[Figure 1] Turning the crank of the Debrie camera in *Man with the Movie Camera* (Source: Vertov 1929).

conceptual structure." The human operator's task is to become attentive to the kind of knowledge embodied in the machine.

Implicit Cinematic Conceptual Structures

Mediatic technical objects and gestures systematically involve this nonhuman dimension in the circulation of knowledge. A smartphone will teach you how you should use it: you do not need any user manual; all you have to do is follow the machine's instructions. You can even ask it questions and experience that human-machine learning relation within a reassuringly anthropomorphic model.

In film history, the art of turning the crank in a silent film camera or projector was similarly a form of tacit knowledge (see fig. 1).

Handbooks stated that the speed of rotation should be maintained at the "correct" rate, or—if it was a projector—that some expressive variations were allowed, but to be used with care, according to the situations. Then again, they gave little more

[Figure 2] Charles Moisson turning the crank of the Lumière Cinématographe (Source: Gay 1895, 216).

than basic advice as to how this should be done—singing a song to keep a basic rhythm not being really efficient and not possible in all situations... But what I discovered when I actually got to turn a camera crank myself was that to a large extent, the crank guides you. Its material shape, its radius, and its mechanical resistance participate actively in teaching you the right movement (see fig. 2).

The rate that the mechanism teaches one to turn it is not absolutely precise, of course, but it would be physically difficult to have the crank move much slower or faster than the "correct" speed. If I remain attentive to the machine, it will teach me how I should use it.

These examples, the smartphone and the crank, have this teaching capacity because they were designed that way by human beings. But if the camera's design is effective, it is pre-cisely because the designers understood the implicit conceptual structure of the operation "turning the crank" and adapted the form of the machine to its gestural, dynamic requirements. The operation's internal coherence dictated the structure of the

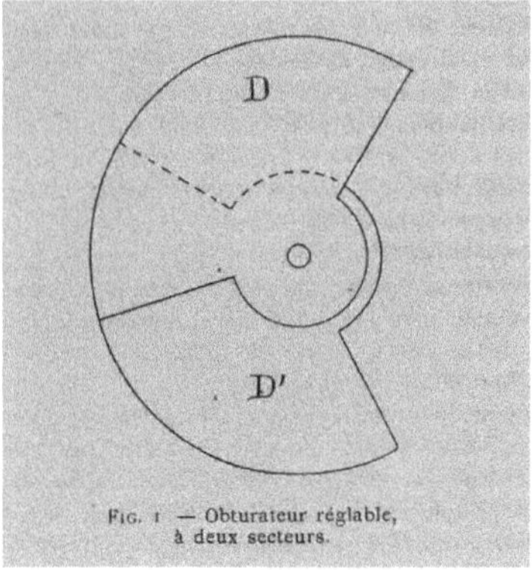

[Figure 3] The Cinématographe's adjustable shutter (Source: Sée 1896, 6).

machine which, in turn, tacitly informed the user's movements as well as their relation with the apparatus.

In fact, the initial concretization process of the "cinema" machine was already based on such a nonverbal circulation. As I discussed in my book *Inventing Cinema* (2019, 176–80), Louis Lumière's correspondence with the chief engineer Jules Carpentier shows that Lumière originally wanted his invention, the Cinématographe, to provide very short exposure times. Therefore, the shutter's opening had to be very thin (see fig. 3). Lumière thought that the animation effect relied on obtaining sharp, instantaneous photographs. This idea—or this bias—came from the framework of the Cinématographe's conception. As it appears in the original patent (Lumière 1895), Lumière initially considered his new machine to be a version of the Chronophotographe developed by the physiologist Étienne-Jules Marey. For Marey, the Chronophotographe was a scientific instrument conceived to analyse human and animal bodily motion. As he explained many times in various texts,[3] Marey believed the sharpness of the image to be crucial, because the photographs were produced for

3   The most important synthesis was Marey (1894).

measurement and analysis. Any blurring would invalidate the entire experimental protocol. Therefore, Lumière's knowledge of his own machine included sharpness as an obvious feature.

However, Carpentier found this to be a problem: employing a narrow shutter opening necessitated that it be adjustable.

The reason was that the Cinématographe was a reversible machine: it could be used both to capture images (i.e., as a camera) and to share or distribute them (as a projector or printing apparatus). When used as a camera, only a narrow shutter opening could produce sharp images. On the other hand, when used to project images, a narrow opening would reduce the amount of light passing through and thus interfere with the clarity of the projection.

Adjustability was therefore the only solution, but it engendered technical difficulties. Firstly, the requirements on the material used for the two superimposed, adaptable blades were more demanding, resulting in a more fragile instrument and higher costs. Secondly, adjustability would complicate the operations for the future users by requiring them to correctly set the shutter before each use. Was that really necessary? In fact, it was not. As a letter from February 6, 1896 shows (Lumière 1995, 115), *while testing the apparatus* Lumière suddenly realized that he was wrong: the Cinématographe worked just as well if the exposure time was slightly longer. In fact, it was even better visually if the frames included a bit of motion blur, so it was best to simply leave the shutter as wide open as possible.

This moment is a typical example of Simondon's concretization process: the internal coherence of the machine governs its evolution, beyond the will or resistance of its designers. The seeming simplification of the device in fact corresponds to a better understanding of how the Cinématographe actually works. The theoretical, even epistemological lesson of this is that technically and conceptually, a cinematic frame is *not* an instantaneous photograph. The Cinématographe had tacitly taught its inventor what its technical structure should be, and that cinematography's "implicit conceptual structure" was deeply different from chronophotography. Having learned from his machine, Lumière abandoned the idea of a variable shutter.

The Tacit and the Implicit

The notion of "tacit knowledge" encompasses more than technics. Still, its importance to technology is undeniable, as it allows for the description of skill and know-how as forms of knowledge on par with scientific, theoretical knowledge. The craftsperson, the user of an instrument or of a tool and the expert in a practical art, can be recognized as *knowing* something, even though we may not be able to *tell* what exactly that "something" is. Guillerme's and Sebestik's "implicit conceptual structures" entail a reversal of perspective, since suddenly the focus turns from the human individual to the operation: to the apparatus and the gestures that surround it. The human has not disappeared from their concept; the human element manifests in the *intentions* that inform the operation as such. Still, the consideration of implicit conceptual structures in a technological analysis, echoing Simondon's "concretization" process, encourages us to move our attention to the demands of the non-human. It also makes us realize that apparatuses, too, contain and materialize knowledge. They are knowing beings. They receive knowledge and communicate it, as humans do. To understand the circulation of knowledge, its transmission, one must take them into account as active participants within networks that they, in part, shape. That circulation is indeed tacit: it is based on examination and gestures, on combining "skillful testing with expert observation," as Polanyi described the "art of knowing" (2009, 7) when discussing the diagnostician.

In the case of cinema and media more generally, I contend that the role of apparatuses within the construction of cinematic knowledge must be recognized in order to understand the full scope of what this knowledge represents. Cinematic machines, from the Cinématographe to smartphones, are not only the recipients or the archives of human knowledge: they have also participated in constituting the vast aggregate of knowing and cultural practice that is "tacit cinematic knowledge." Thus, "tacit cinematic knowledge" is not exclusively *human* knowledge.

Literature

Canguilhem, Georges. 2009. *Le Normal et le Pathologique*. Paris: Presses universitaires de France.

Guillerme, Jacques, and Jan Sebestik. 1968. "Les commencements de la technologie." *Thalès* 12 (1966): 1–72.

Lumière, Auguste and Louis. 1995. *Letters: Inventing Cinema*. Edited by Jacques Rittaud-Hutinet. Translated by Pierre Hodgson. London: Faber and Faber.

———. 1895. "Appareil servant à l'obtention et à la vision des épreuves chronophotographiques." French patent 245'032, February 13.

Marey, Étienne-Jules. 1894. *Le Mouvement*. Paris: Masson.

Mauss, Marcel. 1973 (1935). "Techniques of the Body." Translated by Ben Brewster. *Economy and Society* 2 (1): 70–88.

Polanyi, Michael. 2009. *The Tacit Dimension*. Chicago and London: The University of Chicago Press.

———. 1958. *Personal Knowledge: Towards a Post-Critical Philosophy*. Chicago: The University of Chicago Press.

Sebestik, Jan. 1992. "Le rôle de la technique dans l'oeuvre de Georges Canguilhem." In *Georges Canguilhem: Philosophe, historien des sciences*, edited by Étienne Balibar et al., 243–50. Paris: Albin Michel.

Simondon, Gilbert. 2017 (1958). *On the Mode of Existence of Technical Objects*. Translated by Cecilia Malaspina and John Rogove. Minneapolis: Univocal.

Turquety, Benoît. 2019. *Inventing Cinema: Machines, Gestures and Media History*. Amsterdam: Amsterdam University Press.

Wolff, Christian. 1963 (1728). *Preliminary Discourse on Philosophy in General*. Edited and translated by Richard Blackwell. Indianapolis: Bobbs-Merrill.

(Audio)Visual Material

Gay, M. A. 1895. "Fig. 3—Production des nègatifs" (Charles Moisson turning the crank of the Lumière Cinématographe). In "Le Cinématographe de MM. Auguste et Louis Lumière." *La Nature* 1161 (August 31): 215–18.

44 Sée, Armand. 1896. "FIG. 1—Obturateur réglable, à deux secteurs." *Repro-duction analytique et synthétique des scènes animées par la Photographie: Le Cinématographe de MM. A. et L. Lumière.* 6. Graphics. Lille: Le Bigot Frères.

Vertov, Dziga. 1929. *Man with the Movie Camera.* Feature-length film, 68 min., Soviet Union.

MINOR CINEMA

RENÉ LALOUX

FÉLIX GUATTARI

GILLES DELEUZE

ANIMATION

TECHNOLOGY

Minoring Machines: René Laloux, Félix Guattari, and the Cinema of Animation

Henning Schmidgen

Following Gilles Deleuze, the concept of *minor cinema* is often discussed with respect to questions of authorship, nationality, and *fabulation*. This essay highlights the specificity of Félix Guattari's contributions to defining minor cinema, emphasizing the transversal connections between machine, body, and subjectivity. The essay focuses on animations that the French graphic artist, puppeteer, and filmmaker René Laloux (1929–2004) made at the psychiatric clinic of La Borde in the mid- to late 1950s with the active participation of Guattari and the clinic's patients. Drawing on Laloux's *Tic tac* (1957) and *Les dents du singe* (eng. *The Teeth of the Monkey*, 1960), it argues that the

 technique and aesthetic of his animations confront us with cinematography in its minor state in the sense of Guattari, i.e. before becoming overloaded with faces, texts, and meanings.

René Laloux was a French graphic artist, puppeteer, and filmmaker. Born in 1929 and deceased in 2004, Laloux is best known today for the feature-length animated films he made in the 1970s and 1980s in collaboration with graphic artists such as Roland Topor and Jean Girard (aka "Moebius"). In particular, two science fiction animations, *Fantastic Planet* and *Time Masters,* have received recognition and distribution (Laloux 1973; 1982). *Fantastic Planet* even obtained a special prize at the 1973 Cannes Film Festival, and both films have been shown many times on television. They are also now available in digital form and have become widely acknowledged as authoritative works of their genre. With *The Snails*, which he made with Topor in 1966, Laloux also set a benchmark for artistically sophisticated animated short films that is still recognized today.[1]

Less well known is the role that Laloux played at the beginning of his career at the psychiatric clinic of La Borde. Inspired by the radical movement of "institutional psychotherapy," the La Borde clinic was founded by the psychiatrist Jean Oury in Cour-Cheverny near Blois in 1953. Two years later, Félix Guattari began working at this clinic, with which he remained affiliated throughout his life, both before and after his collaboration with Gilles Deleuze. From 1956 to 1960, Laloux also worked in this clinic, first as a trainee (*stagiaire)*, then as a supervisor (*moniteur)*. His task was to stimulate and direct the artistic work of the patients—mostly

---

1   On Laloux in general see Blin (2004) as well as Keller (2012); see also *Laloux sauvage* (Dauman 2003); on *Fantastic Planet* see, for example, Stiglegger (2018).

drawing and painting, but also working with puppets as well as silhouettes, and, finally, making films.[2]

During his time at La Borde, Laloux made three films. The first is *Tic tac,* from 1957, a seven-minute 16mm black-and-white film. Using silhouettes, this film tells the surreal story of a woman who lives in a world where things gradually take on a life of their own. In this world, she starts to fly, being carried away by balloons. A living clock, a lamp, and another person accompany her. These beings are eventually eaten by a dragon, but the woman continues to fly, ultimately changing her silhouette from black to white (see fig. 1).

Tic tac was created in collaboration with the patients of La Borde. According to the opening credits, "This film was conceived, drawn, and filmed by a group of patients at a psychiatric hospital under the direction of René Laloux" (Laloux 1957, 00:12–20).[3] Laloux was responsible for directing the film along with Jacques Brissot, who at the time headed the "Image Research Group" at the French broadcaster *Radiodiffusion-Télévision Française* (RTF). In turn, the "Image Research Group" was affiliated with the "Research Service" of RTF, which was then headed by Pierre Schaeffer (Robert 1999-2002).

The second film Laloux made during his time at La Borde was *Les Achalunés (1958).* For this five-minute experimental film, Laloux again collaborated with Brissot, as well as the composer Henk Badings, a pioneer of electronic music. In this case, however, there seems to have been no direct collaboration with the patients of La Borde. The black-and-white film shows a series of visual phenomena—light reflections and refractions—that are reminiscent of organic forms and functions, of individual organs such as eyes, but also of the throbbing and pulsating of entire

2   For the history of institutional psychotherapy, see Dardy et al. (1976), Polack and Sivadon-Sabourin (1976), Tosquelles (1991); see also Ayme (2009), Hofmann (1985), and Robcis (2021).
3   All translations by author.

[Figure 1] ...a world where things gradually take on a life of their own. Still from *Tic tac* (Source: Laloux 1957, 06:25).

organisms. Badings' music adds a strikingly futuristic character to these abstract images.

The third film was *The Teeth of the Monkey*, completed in 1960, an eleven-minute 32mm animated film in color. This film tells another surreal story of a poor man who goes to the dentist to have a tooth pulled, but does not know that this dentist is stealing the teeth of the poor to give to the rich. A "magic monkey" gets wise to the dentist and makes amends: he pulls the dentist's teeth, thus returning them to the man from the beginning.

The Teeth of the Monkey makes clear that, and how, the film was made in La Borde through a short opening documentary shot in black and white. Not only is Jean Oury explicitly mentioned as a counsellor; we also get a glimpse of the painting workshop at La Borde. We witness the young Guattari as well as the young Laloux as they work on the film with the patients in the painting studio (see fig. 2).

In an interview, Laloux retrospectively described the work on the screenplay for *The Teeth of the Monkey* as a "collective

[Figure 2] Félix Guattari (front left, sitting at the table) and René Laloux (back right, standing at the table) work together with patients in the La Borde painting studio. A still from *Les dents du singe* (eng. *The Teeth of the Monkey*) (Source: Laloux 1960, 02:35).

improvisation" that was carried out by a group of about 15 patients in a kind of "association test" inspired by C. G. Jung. Words chosen as randomly as possible were expanded spontaneously first into sentences and then into a story (Ciment 1994). Simplifying the concept, the film itself says: "It was like a game, an improvisation, where they all looked for a story and invented heroes. Slowly, a theme emerged from these discussions. They had to meet up frequently to think up a scenario and a setting. Everyone had their own character and they finally chose the ones that they liked" (Laloux 1960, 02:34–03:02). Based on the original designs, drawings for the film were made by Julien Pappé, who would later become famous for, among other things, the trailer for Truffaut's *Shoot the Piano Player* (1960).

Minor Cinema

I would like to return to these early films by Laloux in order to discuss the concept of *minor cinema* associated with the work of Deleuze and Guattari. Deleuze, in particular, is famous for his remarks on a *cinema of minorities*, found in his two volumes on cinema from the 1980s (1989; 1997). In the second half of the second volume, when reflecting on the relationship between film and thought, Deleuze refers primarily to what he calls "third world cinema" the cinema of "minorities" and of "oppressed and exploited nations," which he sees as exemplified by the work of the Filipino filmmaker Lino Brocka (Deleuze 1989, 220 and 217).

As is well known, Deleuze argues that cinema conceived in this sense participates in a complex expressive task, "not that of addressing a people, which is presupposed already there, but of contributing to the invention of a people" (1989, 217). Similarly, a few years earlier, Guattari states that cinema can be conceived of as a "minor art," an *art mineur*, but only if it is an art "that serves people who constitute a minority" (2009a, 271).

As Deleuze and Guattari note in *A Thousand Plateaus,* the crucial reference for this idea of a minor cinema is Paul Klee, who said in a 1924 Jena lecture regarding his difficult situation at the Weimar Bauhaus, "We still lack the ultimate force... We seek a people" (Klee quoted in Deleuze and Guattari 1993, 337–38). Deleuze and Guattari also refer to Franz Kafka, who as they describe in *Kafka: Toward a Minor Literature*, developed the concept of *littérature mineure* in an effort to open up the dominant German-language forms to the expressive forms of the Jewish minority, especially by opposing "the oppressed quality of this language to its oppressive quality" (Deleuze and Guattari 1986, 27).

In the years since Deleuze and Guattari's initial development of the concept, *minor cinema* has been discussed primarily in terms of the origins and authorship of films, e.g. by David E. James (2005), Dudley Andrew (2000), and David Rodowick (1997). In this vein, *minor cinema* is understood as the cinema of the "Third World" and of minorities: the cinema that emerged independently from major US film companies and draws on non-Western, and especially post-colonial, discourses.

This does not mean, however, that the concept is entirely clear.
As David Rodowick explains, on the one hand, "[a] minority discourse must affirm its becoming in images by struggling to define itself through the forces of domination and exclusion that occlude it. The defining characteristic of a minority is in fact philosophical: to become-other as an affirmative will to power" (Rodowick 1997, 153).

On the other hand, in addition to this philosophical process of becoming-other, Rodowick refers to the "postcolonial cinemas in the 1960s and 1970s, both narrative and documentary" (1997, 158) and cites African filmmakers such as Hale Gerima and Ousmane Sembene. To what degree and in what way these filmmakers actually meet the previously stated philosophical criteria, remains, however, unclear.

With regard to the question of the tacit knowledge of cinema, I would like to recall that this already ambivalent definition is still only *one* possible way of reading *minor cinema*. Instead of referring to the questions of origin, authorship, and the problem of fabulation—as Deleuze, and later Rodowick, do—the questions raised by *minor cinema* can also be directed, via Guattari, to *cinematography as technology,* to cinema not as a medium but as a machine—or more precisely, to the relationship between the cinematographic machine, the body, and subjectivity.

There are at least three arguments in favour of such a reading. First, it has become clear in recent years that Guattari—unlike Deleuze—was involved in media practice to a considerable extent. Notably, he was involved with the "Free Radios" in Italy in the 1970s and set up of his own radio station (*Radio Tomate*) in Paris in the 1980s. Meanwhile, his critical collaborations with artists such as the photographer Keiichi Tahara and the painter George Condo; or the exhibition on Kafka that he set up with Yasha David for the Centre Pompidou in 1984 (Guattari 2016a; Prince and Videcoq 2005) demonstrate his commitment to tying media theory and practice together. Guattari's media activities also included theatre work (Garcin-Marrou 2011) and a number of film projects, including the draft for a miniseries published as "Project for a *Film by Kafka*," as well as the impressive screenplays Guattari co-wrote with Robert Kramer in the 1980s for a microbiological science fiction film titled *A Love of UIQ* (Guattari 2016b).

Second, Deleuze's and Guattari's references to Gilbert Simondon's philosophy of technology further encourage a reconsideration of minor cinema. Simondon is an important source for the theoretical work of Deleuze and Guattari, particularly in their two-volume study, *Capitalism and Schizophrenia* (1983; 1993). As early as the mid-1960s, Deleuze paid tribute to Simondon's book on individuation in an extended review (Deleuze 2004). However, the fact that this engagement concerns not only the question of individuation and hylemorphism but also extends to the problem of minor technology has often been overlooked.

In his treatise on the *Mode of Existence of Technical Objects*, Simondon (2017) indeed distinguishes between the "major" and the "minor" modes of interacting with technology. Similar to how Claude Lévi-Strauss contrasts the thinking of the engineer and the tinkerer in *The Savage Mind* (1966, 1–33), Simondon distinguishes a rationalistic way of relating to technical objects from an intuitive one. In this context, the term "major" is used to describe an attitude towards technology based in science and rational reflection. This attitude corresponds to technical knowledge that is based on descriptive analysis and geometric representations of technical objects, including measurement and calculation. Here, Simondon has in mind the *Encyclopedia* of Denis Diderot and Jean-Baptiste le Rond d'Alembert, but also engineers in 19th-century industrial societies (Simondon 2017, 109–111).

In contrast, the minor approach to technology is characteristic of agriculture and mining in the 17th and 18th centuries. It is based on a culture of technology that spreads essentially through the acquisition of locally rooted knowledge, physically grounded gestures, and intuition. According to Simondon, it is based on "a kind of co-natural relation" (2017, 107), a *connaturalité of* man with his environment. In other words, it implies an "implicit" or "tacit" knowledge of technology (Polanyi 1966). As we will see, however, the technology of cinema in itself can be conceived as an environment imbued with tacit knowledge.

In their appendix to the second edition of *Anti-Oedipus*, "Balance-Sheet for Desiring Machines," Deleuze and Guattari (2009) take up Simondon's categories in order to argue for the minor use of technology as an emancipative re-appropriation thereof, effected under the conditions of individual and collective desire. Key ideas in this regard are "the most extensive utilization of machines by the greatest possible number of people, the proliferation of small machines and the adaptation of large machines to small units, [and] ... the destruction of the specialization of knowledge and of the professional monopoly" (Deleuze and Guattari 2009, 107).

If as early as this publication, Deleuze and Guattari are already connecting minor uses of technology and "tinkering" both to Ivan Illich's programmatic attempt at "retooling society" (Illich 1973), and in the same breath, Buster Keaton's machine films, then it is no surprise to find this double reference—to Illich *and* Keaton— in Deleuze's cinema books as well, precisely at the point where he mentions the process of "minoration" of machines (Deleuze 1997, 176).

Deleuze describes the principle of *minorer* as "taking the biggest machine in the world and making it work with the tiniest elements, thus converting it for the use of each one of us, making it the property of everyone" (1997, 176). Unfortunately, he fails in this case to refer to cinema as such a machine. Such a reference could have been established comparatively easily via Keaton, if one considers the minoration the protagonist of his films performs not only on machines such as a locomotive (*The General* (Bruckman and Keaton 1926)) and a ship (*The Navigator* (Crisp and Keaton 1924)), but in *Sherlock, Jr.* (Keaton 1924) on the cinema itself though the hybridization of film and dream, the "getting into" the projected film, and the resulting change of its action. As we will see, it is precisely this process of minoration, which can be described, following Deleuze, as a direct transition "from the great, real machine to its reproduction as a toy" (1997, 176), which can be observed in the cinematographic practices associated with Laloux's early films.

The third argument for revisiting the concept of *minor cinema* is the increasing interest in the connection between cinematographic machine, body, and subjectivity in film and media studies, as well as in the history of science. I refer here to the work of Benoît Turquety (2019), who has examined the "machines" of cinema within a Simondonian framework, to the observations of Adam Szymanski (2020) on cinema as a psycho-therapeutic medium, and finally to the investigations of Elena Vogman (2018), who, starting with her meticulous studies of Eisenstein, has shown increasing interest in the connection between "madness, media, and milieus," in which context she also refers to Guattari.[4]

Laloux and Guattari

In order to understand Laloux's early films as minor cinema, I propose not to analyse them closely in terms of content, but to look at them in terms of form. Nevertheless, I will not view them as sweeping reflections on the medium of film *per se*, but as rather concrete interventions that disassemble and reassemble the cinematographic apparatus into its individual parts. In other words, I suggest looking at Laloux's films similarly to how Deleuze looks at "experimental film" in his books on cinema (though these include remarkably little work on animation) (Deleuze 1989; 1997).

At the same time, I suggest drawing a parallel to the scientific practices of early 20th-century cinematography. As the example of biological cinematography shows, these practices

4   See Vogman 2022.

also disassemble "the black box of the 'basic cinematographic apparatus,' in order to redistribute its elements—the 'movement image' (Deleuze 1997), the projector, the screen, the seat rows, and so on—without making any claim to be complete" (Schmidgen 2011, 60; see also Leyssen and Rathgeber 2013).

Such work with and on the machinery of film is also characteristic of Laloux's early works. The shadow-play of *Tic tac*, for instance, makes reference to the basic fact of projection. The film is reminiscent of the Platonic cave as well as the long tradition of Asian shadow theatre or—to choose an anachronistic but quite appropriate comparison—of the shadow processions in the video installations and theatre pieces of William Kentridge.

Les Achalunés alludes to the lenses in both the projector and the camera with its staging of light and glass. The film dramatizes games with light and glass in a manner similar to Man Ray's *L'étoile de Mer* (1928). It is reminiscent, on the one hand, of the depictions of surface textures in the water films of Joris Ivens, Laszlo Moholy-Nagy, and Ralph Steiner, and, on the other hand, recalls the later sequence about "Paris of the future" from *La Jetée* (Marker 1962).

In Laloux's film, these undulating and quivering light structures are staged in such a way that they draw attention to the process of seeing itself. What the film makes clear is that this process is not only human, based on the eye, but also a technical, lens-based process. The pulsating reflexes point to a new kind of life, as it were. The cinematic eye appears not only as an element of a machine that takes in images, but also as part of a yet unknown organism that produces them.

The Teeth of the Monkey makes the materiality of the "movement image" (Deleuze 1997) tangible through the technique of cut-out drawings and the animation of successive shots. Through this method of making, the film continually reminds us of how movement images are created: by gradually transforming one image into another. This viewing experience is extended and

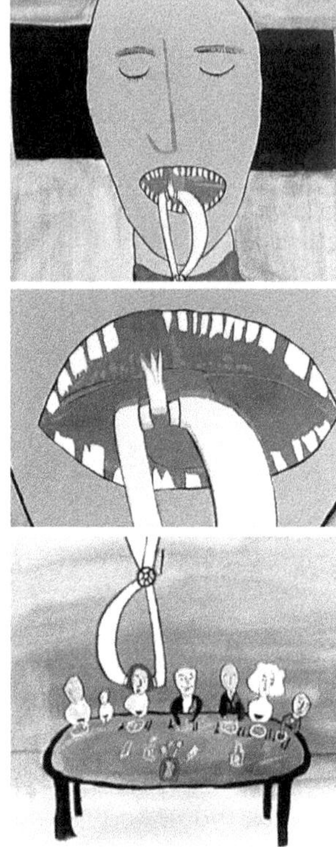

[Figure 3] People are transformed into teeth. Sequence of stills from *Les dents du singe* (Source: Laloux 1960, 05:03–45).

enhanced by the fact that the film shows an abundance of fantastic metamorphoses. People transform into things or into animals, but people also transform into other people, who are alive or dead, or they are transformed into teeth, as in other sequences (see fig. 3).

In addition, all three films combine their self-reflexive play on their constructed, technical nature with a contemplation about language. In *Tic tac* this is effected through an endless strip of the words "*tic tac tic tac*," which appear in the opening credits in

typewriter fashion, accompanied by the sound of a ticking clock.
Les Achalunés contains a pun in its title that oscillates between
the French words *achaler* (*to get on one's nerves*), *lune* (*moon*), and
allumer (*to set on fire*). In *The Teeth of the Monkey*, whose story—as
already mentioned—came about in a kind of random process
of collective association, the original French title (fr. *Les dents du
singe*) can be read not only as *The Teeth of the Monkey,* but also as
a pun: *The Gifts of the Sign* (fr. *Les dons du signe*).

Thus, we can say that Laloux's early films stage implicit
knowledge about the production of cinematographic images,
in particular their anchoring in a complex machine, which on
the one hand encompasses the relationship between image,
sound, and language, and on the other contains the camera, the
projector, the lenses, the screen, and similar equipment.

The self-reflexivity of Laloux's films is no coincidence. It spells
out the fact that cinema appears here as a minor art. On the
one hand, this is due to the relative simplicity of the production
conditions, which allowed for a far-reaching artistic freedom,
an autonomy that Laloux explicitly emphasizes in an interview
from 2003 (Dauman 2003, 11:24–14:30). On the other hand, it
reflects the conception of the cinematographic machine that
Laloux developed as an artist who came to film from drawing and
puppetry. The films in question retrace this path through artistic
media, leading from silhouettes, reflections of light, and drawings
to movement images.

In his 1996 book *Ces dessins qui bougent* (*These Drawings that
Move*), Laloux makes the conception of cinema thus outlined
explicit. A history of animation which is at once an autobiography
and a kind of manual for budding filmmakers, the book refers
to shadow theatres, puppets, and the magic lantern as "distant
ancestors" of what has become established as a "twin brother" of
"normal" cinema under the name of "animation" (Laloux 1996, 24).

In this context, Laloux explicitly sets himself apart from the
commercially successful model of industrially produced

animations à la Walt Disney. The technique he prefers is not *dessin en phases*, but rather—and this is what the films discussed in this essay make clear—the cutting out, mounting, combining, and recombining of drawings and other materials. As a result, it is not Walt Disney or Tex Avery, but Lotte Reininger, Berthold Bartotsch, and Jan Svankmajr who are the benchmarks of the tradition to which Laloux has committed himself.

Laloux characterizes this tradition by its emphasis on the importance of a wide variety of materials for the creative practice of cinematographic animation: "[t]he shadow figure, cut-out papers, the puppet, modeling clay, ink, charcoal, the pastel, the gouache, the oil painting, the crayon, powder, sand, and likewise all the objects that man makes, all the products that he consumes or uses, without forgetting humans as lively details, have been vectors of interesting creations" (Laloux 1996, 61).

Laloux thus not only outlines a history of cinema, highlighting the "vectors" of materials, but also formulates the program for a cinematography grounded in the heterogeneity of media, a kind of sculptural animation.

The flip side of this program is a view of "normal" cinema that has striking similarities to that of Guattari. In his statements on cinema as a minor art, Guattari frequently uses cinema's heterogeneous past to illuminate its homogenized present. From his perspective, for example, it is a mistake to think that the silent film of the 1910s and 1920s represents a poorer or more limited assemblage of expressive materials than today's film. On the contrary, according to Guattari, silent film "succeeded in expressing the intensities of desire in relation to the social field in a way that was much more immediate and authentic than that of the talkies" (2009b, 243). This, he continues, was because film was not yet structured like a language to the extent that it is today, i.e. *because the signifying script had not yet taken possession of the image*" (ibid.).

Laloux expresses similar scepticism about the fixation on
language and meaning in today's cinema when, in the aforementioned interview, he comments polemically on the dominant
forms of cinema (apparently referring back to his early work in La
Borde): "Today's films reveal more and more, it's the film-making
of paranoid dictators. But they say less and less. We'd be better
off with films made by schizophrenics. But there aren't any films
made by schizophrenics. Except for animation, perhaps" (Dauman
2003, 26:18–32).

What both authors ultimately favour is a cinema that—in
Guattari's words—turns against the "complete saturation" of the
audience, against a "stuffing full of images and meanings," as is
"increasingly becoming a fact in major contemporary cinema pro-
ductions" (1995, 144); a cinema, in other words, that—positively
speaking—brings to bear the heterogeneity of cinematic signs
and matters. For Guattari, this means helping the "asignifying
semiologies"—gestures, rhythms, colours, moods—find expression alongside "semiologies of signification" (2011, 59) like
language. Laloux's early films respond to this intention by relying
from the outset on a minor, heterogeneous ensemble creation
with rather simple materials.

The Cinematographic Unconscious

The convergence between Laloux and Guattari is not a mere
coincidence of preferences and tastes. It is due to their shared
experience of filmmaking in a psychiatric context—a recourse,
so to speak, to the "tacit knowledge" of filmmaking (Polanyi 1966;
from the point of view of the history of science, see Olesko 1993).

This implicit dimension of knowledge entails considerable effects,
especially in Guattari's work. While Laloux turns to cooperation
with artists (Topor, Moebius, etc.), in which knowledge also
remains implicit in artistic virtuosity, the presence of a tacit
knowledge of cinema can be discerned in Guattari's writings
whenever he criticizes, from his radical psychiatric point of view,

a type of psychoanalysis that fits into his perspective on the late capitalist economy of demand and prefabricated response, i.e., one that is part of the saturation-compensation system of the developed consumer society.

Guattari criticizes Freudian psychoanalysis for making the antiquated world of tragedy the frame of reference, basing its interpretative framework in the Oedipus myth. In contrast to the theatre, cinema refers to a mechanized world that, precisely because of its artificiality, represents a more authentic frame of reference for therapeutic interpretation and intervention. Relying on the dynamic visual and auditory experiences of cinema, Guattari thus criticizes the structuralism of Lacanian psychoanalysis for its old-fashioned fixation on language, which can be traced back to basic pairs of signifiers. To this fixation on language, cinema forms a rather complex, quasi-multimedia alternative.

It should be noted that the first drafts of Guattari's semiotics of the unconscious were written around the same time that he was cooperating with Laloux. These drafts reveal that in order to position himself in relation to Lacan's approach, Guattari not only theorizes the relatively passive consumption of cinematic products, but also the active, productive handling of film technology. As shown in his early essay "D'un signe à l'autre" (1966), Guattari had been trying to describe the emergence and development of heterogeneous sign matter since about 1960, and this is precisely the material he had to deal with while working on *The Teeth of the Monkey.* The unconscious described in "D'un signe à l'autre" includes above all images that are superimposed, shifted, and thus set in motion, but then also fragments of language, on the one hand, and gestures as well as movements, on the other (Watson 2009).

The primal scene of this theoretical sketch is based on a fundamental principle of cinematography. The signs of the unconscious no longer operate through pairs of signifiers, as they did in Lacan's understanding. According to Guattari (1996), they meet in a "black night," in a "fog of meaning," in which "spots" overlap and superimpose in such a way that characteristic lines emerge from their blurred contours—as in the flickering succession of film images in the movie theatre, or more precisely, as in the serial arrangement of drawings in different positions during the production of an animation.

It is only when, after *Anti-Oedipus*, Guattari sets out to further elaborate this sketch into a full-fledged semiotics of the unconscious that the reference to film becomes explicit. One of the lectures he delivered in 1973 is tellingly entitled "Cinémachines désirantes" (2009c), thus reaffirming the importance of cinematography to the dynamic, material-semiotic theory of unconscious desiring machines that Guattari formulates in ever-new attempts. At this point, he turns to the film theory of Christian Metz (1974) to bring the polyphony of a veritable machinery of moving signs to bear against the one-dimensional structuralism of the Lacanian linguistic unconscious.

Guattari distinguishes among four layers of meaning in film. The "significant semiology" in his terminology corresponds to the "linguistic tissue" of film as analysed by Metz, i.e. *grosso modo* the spoken word. Meanwhile, Guattari's "a-significant semiotics" is juxtaposed with the "sonic but not linguistic tissue" in Metz's frame, including, for example, instrumental music. This is followed by the "mixed semiotics," which correspond to the painterly, colourful dimensions of film as well as its photographic, black-and-white aspects. The final layer is constituted by the gestures and movements of the human body, which Guattari calls "symbolic semiologies" (2011, 42 and 72).

Similar layer-models of expressive material recur in Guattari's writings, as in the "machinic genealogy" of the components of the unconscious he sketches in *The Machinic Unconscious* (2011, 199), moving from points, icons, and indexes, to codes, as well as in the literal multiplicity of "energetic semiotics" that he captures and outlines in *Schizoanalytic Cartographies* (2013).

Overall, then, it can be said that Deleuze was not the only authentic philosopher of cinema. Perhaps Guattari was even more of one than Deleuze himself. While the latter went to the cinema to encounter an unheard-of range of signs and tried to taxonomize them; the former came out of the projection room, as well as the studio and the editing room, using the tacit knowledge of filmmaking to discover overlapping signs of the most diverse kinds in each of these places.

Conclusion

Guattari never referred to Laloux's films or Laloux's activities at La Borde in his writings, and Laloux does not appear in the double biography by François Dosse (2010) devoted to the "intersecting lives" of Deleuze and Guattari. Apart from a few interviews and some commentaries in DVD and Blu-ray editions of his films, there seems to be little research on this filmmaker to date.

This does not mean, however, that Laloux's films went unnoticed in their time. The contrary is the case. Through the intervention of Frédéric Rossif, *Tic tac* was shown on RTF's television program, as was *Les Achalunés*, presumably, because both were supervised by RTF's "Service de la Recherche." In addition, *The Teeth of the Monkey* received the *"Filmdukat"* for the best animation at the International Film Festival in Mannheim in 1960 and the Emile Kohl-Award for the best French animation in 1961.

The question of precisely when, how, and why Laloux came to La Borde to make animations with the patients there remains unanswered, however. Given the current state of research, this can only be stated here in general terms. Laloux's activity in La Borde can be understood in the particular context of a psychiatric reform movement that became known in France as institutional psychotherapy. Grounded in the work of the Spanish- or rather

Catalan-French psychiatrist François Tosquelles—a crucial figure for Guattari—institutional psychotherapy has advocated for a more active treatment of psychiatric patients since the its emergence in the 1940s (Guattari 2015).

Drawing on an eclectic mix of Gestalt theory, psychoanalysis, and Marxism, Tosquelles recommended giving patients access to artistic materials and practices, which in his eyes included the creative use of media. The Saint-Alban clinic, where Jean Oury completed his psychiatric training, included a patient newspaper and a print shop, as well as photography and film. Such media practices were also cultivated at La Borde, and where Guattari was responsible for organizing corresponding activities, from theatrical plays and puppetry to writing workshops, painting, and filmmaking (Dosse 2010, 55–75).

Ever since Tosquelles, the insight that underpins these activities lies in the question of the environment in which psychiatric patients live—more precisely: the environment they continually create for themselves. On this point, Tosquelles, Oury, and Guattari himself followed the work of neurologist Kurt Goldstein, who had already insisted prior to World War II, and certainly with a socio-critical intention, that the actions of physicians must not only apply to the body of a sick person, but to his or her environment as well (Schmidgen 2019). The fact that Goldstein also used film to illustrate this point of view by showing patients in their everyday environment very much belongs to this context (Geroulanos and Meyers 2014).

In institutional psychotherapy, however, environmental action was not limited to physicians, biologists, and psychiatrists. It also included psychiatric patients. According to Tosquelles, Oury, and Guattari, by relying on a wide variety of artistic and media practices, these patients are constantly in the process of constructing and reconstructing themselves and their world. This is ultimately the claim of cinema as *art mineur*. Through Laloux's films, cinema appears as a machine that creates specific environments and corresponding subjectivities.

The technology of cinema itself becomes a kind of environment. It constitutes an apparatus, an assemblage whose materialities and modes of operation can be appropriated not only in order to express one's own subjectivity, but to produce it in the first place. The crucial movement associated with this assemblage is the transition *from one sign to another*, from one image showing a particular material in a particular state and position to another image showing that material in a changed state and position—or to a different material.

As in Kentridge's cinematographic work, this kind of cinema-machine uses technical and physical means to explore the space between the represented and the representation. In addition, however, the existential territory of this machine is the space between different kinds of representations, or rather materials: the wandering back and forth between drawing, filming, and erasing, or, as in Laloux's case, between drawing, filming, and moving—a virtuoso dance of images, sounds, and gestures, of drawings, puppets, and lights.

By virtue of these movements in and through the interstices among images, cinema becomes minorized. Just as Keaton transforms the locomotive and the ship, Laloux makes the great machine of cinema "work with the tiniest elements," as we can conclude with Deleuze (1997, 176). Laloux thus adapts the cinema-machine to the potential use of each of us, "making it the property of everyone" (ibid.). Alongside authorship, origin and fabulation, this form of *retooling*, this re-appropriation of technology through its subjective as well as collective use, is an essential aspect of the concept of minor cinema.

Literature

Ayme, Jean. 2009. "Essai sur l'histoire de la Psychothérapie Institutionelle."
Institutions 44: 111–53.

Blin, Fabrice, ed. 2004. *Les mondes fantastiques de René Laloux: Avec des témoignages
de Topor, Moebius, Caza.* Chaumont: Le Pythagore.

Ciment, Gilles. 1994. "Entretiens sur le cinéma d'animation: René Laloux." *Cinéma
d'animation.* Accessed July 5, 2021. http://gciment.free.fr/caentretienlaloux.htm.

Dardy, Claudine, Gérard Grass, Numa Murard, Georges Préli, and Michel Rostain,
eds. 1976. *Histoires de La Borde: 10 ans de psychothérapie institutionnelle à Cour-
Cheverny 1953-1963.* Paris: Recherches.

Deleuze, Gilles. 2004. "On Gilbert Simondon." In *Desert Islands and Other Texts,
1953-1974,* edited by David Lapoujade, 86–9. Translated by Michael Taormina.
New York and Los Angeles: Semiotext(e).

———. 1997. *Cinema 1: The Movement Image.* Translated by Hugh Tomlinson and
Barbara Habberjam. Minneapolis: University of Minnesota Press.

———. 1989. *Cinema 2: The Time-Image.* Translated by Hugh Tomlinson and Robert
Galeta. Minneapolis: University of Minnesota Press.

Deleuze, Gilles, and Félix Guattari. 2009. "Balance-Sheet for Desiring Machines." In
Félix Guattari, *Chaosophy: Texts and Interviews 1972-1977,* 90–115. Edited by Sylvère
Lotringer and translated by David L. Sweet, Jarred Becker, and Taylor Adkins. Los
Angeles: Semiotext(e).

———.1993. *A Thousand Plateaus: Capitalism and Schizophrenia.* Translated by Brian
Massumi. Minneapolis: University of Minnesota Press.

———.1986. *Kafka: Toward a Minor Literature.* Translated by Dana Polan. Minneapolis
and London: University of Minnesota Press.

———.1983. *Anti-Oedipus: Capitalism and Schizophrenia.* Translated by Robert Hurley,
Mark Seem, and Helen R. Lane. Minneapolis: University of Minnesota Press.

Dosse, François. 2010. *Gilles Deleuze & Félix Guattari: Intersecting Lives.* Translated by
Deborah Glassman. New York: Columbia University Press.

Andrew, Dudley. 2000. "The Roots of the Nomadic: Gilles Deleuze and the Cinema
of West Africa." In *The Brain Is the Screen: Deleuze and the Philosophy of Cinema,*
edited by Gregory Flaxman, 215–49. Minneapolis: University of Minnesota Press.

Garcin-Marrou, Flore. 2011. "Le théâtre de Félix Guattari: Une fausse note au sein de
son parcours philosophique?" *Littératures* 65: 77–91.

Geroulanos, Stefanos, and Todd Meyers. 2014. *Experimente im Individuum: Kurt Goldstein und die Frage des Organismus.* Berlin and Cologne: August.

Guattari, Félix. 2016a. *Schriften zur Kunst.* Translated by Ronald Voullié, Horst Brüh-
mann, and Caroline Gutberlet. Berlin: Merve.

———. 2016b. *A Love of UIQ: A Screenplay.* Translated by Silvia Maglioni und Graeme
Thomson. Minneapolis: Univocal.

———. 2015. "Introduction to Institutional Psychotherapy." In *Psychoanalysis and
Transversality: Texts and Interviews 1955-1971,* 60–75. Translated by Ames Hodges.
South Pasadena: Semiotext(e).

68

——. 2013. *Schizoanalytic Cartographies*. Translated by Andrew Goffey. London: Bloomsbury.

——. 2011. *The Machinic Unconscious: Essays in Schizoanalysis*. Translated by Taylor Adkins. Los Angeles: Semiotext(e).

——. 2009a. "Not so mad." In *Chaosophy: Texts and Interviews 1972–1977*, edited by Sylvère Lotringer, 268–71. Translated by David L. Sweet, Jarred Becker, and Taylor Adkins. Los Angeles: Semiotext(e).

——. 2009b. "The Poor Man's Couch." In *Chaosophy: Texts and Interviews 1972–1977*, edited by Sylvère Lotringer, 257–67. Translated by David L. Sweet, Jarred Becker, and Taylor Adkins. Los Angeles: Semiotext(e).

——. 2009c. "Cinema of Desire." In *Chaosophy: Texts and Interviews 1972–1977*, edited by Sylvère Lotringer, 235–46. Translated by by David L. Sweet, Jarred Becker, and Taylor Adkins. Los Angeles: Semiotext(e).

——. 1995. "Le cinéma, la grand-mère et la giraffe." *Chimères* 9 (26): 141–51.

——. 1966. "D'un signe à l'autre." *Recherches* 1 (2): 33-63.

Hofmann, Wolfgang. *Die "psychothérapie institutionelle": Theorie und Praxis einer psychiatrischen Bewegung in Frankreich*. Frankfurt am Main: Campus, 1985.

Illich, Ivan. 1973. *Tools for Conviviality*. New York: Harper & Row.

James, David E. 2005. *The Most Typical Avant-Garde: History and Geography of Minor Cinemas*. Los Angeles and Berkeley: University of California Press.

Keller, Craig. 2012. "The schizophrenic cinema of René Laloux (2006)." In *La planète sauvage aka Fantastic Planet*. Accompanying Booklet for DVD/Blue-ray Disc, 8–39. The Masters of Cinema Series.

Laloux, René. 1996. *Ces dessins qui bougent: 1892-1992, cent ans de cinéma d'animation*. Paris: Dreamlan.

Lévi-Strauss, Claude. 1966. *The Savage Mind*. Translated by George Weidenfeld. London: Weidenfeld & Nicolson.

Leyssen, Sigrid, and Pirrko Rathgeber, eds. 2013. *Bilder animierter Bewegung/Images of Animate Movement*. Munich: Fink.

Metz, Christian. 1974. *Language and Cinema*. Translated by Donna Jean Umiker-Sebeok. The Hague: Mouto.

Olesko, Kathryn M. 1993. "Tacit Knowledge and School Formation." *Osiris* 8: 16–29.

Polack, Jean-Claude, and Danielle Sivadon-Sabourin. 1976. *La Borde ou Le droit à la folie*. Paris: Calmann-Lévy.

Polanyi, Michael. 1966. *The Tacit Dimension*. London: Routledge and Paul.

Prince, Bernard, and Emmanuel Videcoq. 2015. "Félix Guattari et les agencements post-média: L'expérience de *radio Tomate* et du *minitel Alter*." *Multitudes* 21 (2): 23–30.

Robcis, Camille. 2021. *Disalienation. Politics, Philosophy, and Radical Psychiatry in Postwar France*. Chicago and London: The University of Chicago Press.

Robert, Martial. 1999–2002. *Communication et musique en France entre 1936 et 1986, 3 vols*. Paris: L'Harmattan.

Rodowick, David N. 1997. *Gilles Deleuze's Time Machine*. Durham and London: Duke University Press.

Schmidgen, Henning. 2019. "Jean Oury et la conation esthétique: Un parcours entre Sartre, Goldstein et Lacan." In *Histoire et philosophie de la psychiatrie au XXe siècle: Regards croisés franco-allemands*, edited by Elisabetta Basso and Emmanuelle Delille, 87–98. Paris: CNRS éditions.

———. 2018. *Horn oder Die Gegenseite der Medien*. Berlin: Matthes und Seitz.

———. 2011. "1900—The Spectatorium: On Biology's Audio-Visual Archive." *Grey Room* 43: 42–65.

Simondon, Gilbert. 2017. *On the Mode of Existence of Technical Objects*. Translated by Cécile Malaspina and John Rogove. Minneapolis: Univocal.

Stiglegger, Marcus. 2018. "Der psychedelische Planet: Gedanken zu René Laloux's und Roland Topors Animationsfilm *La planète sauvage/Der wilde Planet*." In Accompanying Booklet for DVD *Der wilde Planet*, n. p. Camera Obscur.

Szymanski, Adam. 2020. *Cinemas of Therapeutic Activism: Depression and the Politics of Existence*. Amsterdam: Amsterdam University Press.

Tosquelles, François. 1991. "Une politique de la folie." *Chimères* 3 (13): 66-81.

Turquety, Benoît. 2019. *Inventing Cinema: Machines, Gestures and Media History*. Amsterdam: Amsterdam University Press.

Vogman, Elena. 2022. "Madness, Media, Milieus. Reconfiguring the Humanities in Postwar Europe." *Bauhaus-Universität Weimar*. Accessed August 8, 2022. https://www.uni-weimar.de/de/medien/professuren/medienwissenschaft/madness-media-milieus/.

———. 2018. *Sinnliches Denken: Eisensteins exzentrische Methode*. Zurich: Diaphanes.

Watson, Janell. 2009. *Guattari's Diagrammatic Thought: Writing Between Lacan and Deleuze*. London and New York: Continuum.

(Audio)Visual Material

Bruckman, Clyde, and Buster Keaton. 1926. *The General*. Feature-length film, 67 min., United States of America.

Crisp, Donald, and Buster Keaton. 1924. *The Navigator*. Feature-length film, 59 min., United States of America.

Dauman, Florence. 2003. *Laloux sauvage*. Documentary, color, 26 min., France.

Keaton, Buster. 1924. *Sherlock, Jr.* Feature-length film, 45 min., United States of America.

Laloux, René. 1982. *Les maîtres du temps* (eng. *Time Masters*). Animation, color, 78 min., France; Switzerland; Germany; Hungary.

———. 1973. *La planète sauvage* (eng. *Fantastic Planet*). Animation, color, 72 min., France/ Czechoslovakia.

———. 1965. *Les escargots* (eng. *The Snails*). Animation, color, 10 min., France.

———. 1960. *Les dents du singe* (eng. *The Teeth of the Monkey*). Documentary and Animation, monochrome and color, 11 min., France.

———. 1958. *Les Achalunés*. Experimental film, monochrome, 5 min., France.

———. 1957. *Tic tac*. Silhouette animation, monochrome, 7 min., France.

Man Ray. 1928. *L'Étoile de mer*. Short film, 17 min., France.

70 Marker, Chris. 1962. *La Jetée*. Featurette, 28 min., France.

Truffaut, François. 1960. *Shoot the Piano Player*. Feature-length film, 81 min., France.

ANIMAL

BIO-LOGGING

SLOW TV

TACIT KNOWING

[3]

Bio-Logs and Non-Humans

Veena Hariharan

In this article, I discuss the Slow TV show *The Great Elk Trek* (Erhag and Edlund 2019–23), an eclectic combination of popular nature cams and bio-logs. The show offers the pleasures of knowing and experiencing wild nature even as it allows us to reflect on human endeavors via the cinematic—to make explicit, in this case, the tacit animal knowledge embodied in the migratory movements of the Swedish moose. The affordances of Slow TV, its felicity to draw the viewer into its enchanted circle that leads them from pleasure to contem-plation, challenges the ways our knowledge of non-human worlds is conditioned by years

of cinematic representation and nature programming.

As the pandemic forced most of the world into government ordered lockdowns in March 2020, following the pandemic, images of wildlife spotting flooded the internet. From dolphins swimming in the canals of Venice to a Malabar civet spotted at a normally busy intersection in Meyappur, Kozhikode; from strolling wild sika deer in Nara, Japan, to migrant pink fla-mingos arriving by the thousands in Navi Mumbai's wetlands, social media was abuzz with images of wildlife reclaiming our cities. While many conservationists dismissed this infodemic of WhatsApp forwards as fake news, others saw this rewilding of cities as a renewed opportunity for bio-logging—tracking wildlife behavior, habitat, and movement via prosthetic animal imaging technologies—even as the ambivalent ethics of these imaging practices are being debated.

What the reactions described above reveal are the increasingly segregated habitats of humans and wild fauna that have made these sightings a rare and even ecstatic spectacle; the prevalence of highly evolved animal tagging and tracking technologies to watch animals; and the all too human desire to make explicit the tacit dimension of non-human knowledge.

Scientist-turned-philosopher Michael Polanyi differentiates between two kinds of knowing—the tacit and articulate—in his deceptively simple formulation: "[w]e can know more than we can tell" (2009, 4). One of his examples is the human capacity to know an individual face, recognizing it among millions of others, yet we cannot explain exactly how we recognize a face we know. Polanyi refers to this inability to articulate the "how" of knowing as the tacit, ineffable dimension of knowledge. In the same vein, we can think of examples from the animal world—how did Siberian cranes know to migrate all the way from the arctic tundra to winter in India's tropical sanctuaries, or the Swedish moose to walk across the melting ice to reach their summer pastures in the foothills? This is knowledge that is passed on from generation to generation of the species ineffably—tacitly.

Humans constantly endeavor to devise ways of making implicit knowledge explicit, whether simply for knowledge's sake, or with more sinister implications, for data mining and the development of lucrative commercial applications. Take the above examples: millions of dollars have been invested in the development of facial recognition software to aggregate data sets that could enable machines to recognize faces like humans do. These efforts have been extended to the animal world, too: from high-definition images of birds in flight to sophisticated telemetric and bio-logging technologies that have been developed over years for mapping moose migratory patterns.

As wildlife habitats have receded farther and farther from human worlds in the modern industrial era, they are increasingly captured as images or sensory data. John Berger and Akira Mizuta Lippit argue that when animals disappeared from the phenomenological world, they appeared as salvage animals in the world of shadows and light (Berger 1980; Lippit 2000). Indeed, this has been the way in which most of us, save a few wildlife experts and forest dwellers, have access to the ways of the wild. Our knowledge of wildlife is always-already mediated by such images and data.

The history of the moving image is itself intimately entangled with animals, Jonathan Burt (2002) goes so far as to claim that the desire to see and know the intricacies of the moving animal body proved to be both challenge and driving force for early cinema technologies. Starting with Eadweard Muybridge's "Galloping Horse Series" (1878)—in which he used a zoopraxiscope to investigate if and when all four hooves of the horse left the ground during its motion (knowledge that was in turn used to ace horses for the racing track),[1] individuals have attempted to capture, in moving images, the elusive and enticing animal, thus contributing to the evolution of cinematic technology. Other examples include Étienne-Jules Marey's attempts to capture the motion of pigeons in flight with his chronophotographic rifle (1883-7), experiments in animatronics and animal modelling, CGI and VFX technologies to reconstruct *Jurassic Park*'s Tyrannosaurus Rex (Spielberg 1993), or the numerous experiments seeking to get as close to the animal as possible with thermal cameras in the "blue chip" documentaries on Discovery Channel or Animal Planet.[2] Indeed, the "fantasy of looking" through the superior mechanical eye of the camera, what Dziga Vertov called the *kino-eye* (1984), "as if through the eye of an animal, to further reveal those realms of nature invisible to the human eye" (Burt 2002, 53), can be said to constitute an epistemic environment encapsulating what the editors of this current volume have termed "tacit cinematic knowledge."

The cinematic experiments of Muybridge and his successors may seem archaic today, even if the guiding principle remains the desire to know the animal world ever more intimately. However, from 1966, when the first grizzly bears in Yellowstone National Park were tagged with high frequency VHF radio collars that pinged approximate locations to receivers, modern devices have been used to map and know animal movement, behavior, and habitats, and now include a range of sophisticated imaging technologies (Gunther, Manen, and White 2017). While nature cams and camera traps are deployed in citizen-science projects, using nothing but simple smart phone technology to log and deliver wildlife information,[3] satellite tracking and remote sensing

---

1 See Burt (2002), Brsown (2012), and Solnit (2004) for studies of these early experiments.

2 Blue chip refers to the classic wildlife documentaries of high production values, closely observed animals and didactic voice overs.

3 See *ZLS Instant Wild* (Zoological Society of London 2023) or *explore.org* (Explore Annenberg LLC 2023) etc. for examples of such webcam-generated citizen-science projects.

devices allow for retrieval of accurate geo-positioned locations and environmental data. Modern biotelemetry tags, also called "bio-logs," fitted around the animal's neck, ear or other body parts, can store or transmit vast packets of vital datasets through electromagnetic waves that are picked up by nearby receivers or communications satellites and decoded using advanced algorithms and AI software.[4]

The Great Elk Trek

Den stora älgvandringen (eng. *The Great Elk Trek*, Erhag and Edlund, 2019–23)[5] first featured on Sweden's public service television network, Sveriges Television (SVT) in 2019, and it has been an annual televisual event every spring. Global audiences have been able to tune in to SVT Play to watch this 24/7 livestream of the annual migration of the moose[6] herd of Jamtland, North Sweden, crossing the Ångermanälven river to get to their summer pastures at the foot of the mountains—a total of nearly 520 hours of footage over three weeks (see fig. 1). "Follow the walk live from Kullberg in the north of Sweden," the tagline announced. The show was viewed over 11.5 million times and clocked nearly 4.6 million viewing hours on SVT Play, making it one of Sweden's most-watched TV shows and resulted in a "national moose fever" in the spring of 2020 (Swedish Radio Västerbotten and Prix Europa 2020).

It was also closely followed by more than 200,000 visitors to the DUO-app, who communicated directly with the production via unique handles. Users could find information such as which camera is active at any given moment, and at what angle, a

---

4   See Hooten (2017) for details of these technologies.

5   Produced by Stefan Edlund, Johan Erhag for Swedish TV and co-produced by Yleisradio, Finland, on a budget of 238.000 Euros according to the Prix Europa Catalogue, 2020.

6   The species *alces alces*—known as a "moose" in America and an "elk" in Britain (not to be confused with the American elk or Wapiti) is known as an *"älg"* in Swedish.

counter showed the number of moose who successfully crossed the river onto the mainland, and there were options to watch the day's highlights and even share a link to a timestamp in the episode. Interactive maps, GPS-tracking, and weather-related information provided environmental data to visitors on the app. The show itself proceeded wordlessly and without commentary. Once in a rare while, a text sign flashed across the screen identifying a species, providing brief information about moose migration or location. The show was also available offline on SVT Natur and Twitch. Selected short clips and highlights of the footage of the day and the year with commentary, are available as edited one-hour programs.

Slow, Snowy, Spectacular

The past years have witnessed the cultivation of slowness as a virtue to counter the fast-paced chaos of technological modernity—slow food, slow travel, slow burn, slow movies, and now slow television. When Andy Warhol first made his five-hour long film on the sleeping poet, John Giorno, calling it simply *Sleep* (1964), it was hailed as an avant-garde film par excellence, spawning similar concept experiments across genres and media. The slow movies of auteurs such as Lav Diaz, Apichatpong Weeraseethakul, Béla Tarr, Nuri Bilge Ceylan, to name a few, have received scholarly and cinephilic attention for countering Hollywood's commercial time-space models based on thrills and quick payoffs. Usually characterized by stillness, emptiness, and silence, the minimalist styles of these classic auteurial films include long shots, slow takes and slower edits, immersing the willing viewer in a world where time flows slowly, laboriously, lyrically. Nature—by turns inert, harsh, hostile, supple or fertile— and the weary protagonists who journey through it are a staple feed of slow cinema.[7]

7   See Jaffe (2014) and Tiago de Luca (2015) for detailed studies of slow cinema auteurs.

[Figure 1] Moose begin the crossing in *The Great Elk Trek* (Source: Erhag and Edlund)

Slow Television is of more recent vintage and was popularized, most notably, by Nordic Television's *Sakte-tv* (eng. *Slow-TV*), Norway even voted it as "word of the year" in 2013 (Ulven 2017). Unlike slow cinema's allure among avant-garde and festival audiences, slow TV was a community event and appealed to a broad demographic from the elderly to children. Slow cinema's melancholy-tinged air is replaced in slow TV by an affect-neutral, even breezy everydayness. Plodding, ponderous protagonists are substituted with anonymous commuters, cats, birds or elk, while nature is restored from its tragic timelessness to an unhurried, yet dynamic interactive environment.[8] Thus, slow TV alludes to the non-extraordinary and typical processing of quotidian knowledge, reflecting the implicit (tacit) qualities of mediatization.

Nordic slow TV's first sensational hit was *Bergensbanen—minutt for minutt* (eng. *Bergen Line minute by minute*, Hellum and Norsk rikskringkasting 2009) and, as the title suggests, was a minute-by-minute rendering of the 7-hour 4-minute train ride of the train

---

8   Something similar can be observed regarding the "drift away" qualities of ambient music from the 1960s and 70s and later in what Gernot Böhme calls the "ecological aesthetics" (Böhme 1989), drawing on the aesthetics of nature.

[Figure 2] Still landscapes in *The Great Elk Trek* (Source: Erhag and Edlund)

from Bergen to Oslo.[9] It was an attempt to mirror in real time the path of the train's journey that had remained unchanged over its 120-year old history. The record of the train's scenic journey was interspersed with interviews of drivers, passengers, engineers, and archival footage of the journey.[10] The show was a sensational hit, with nearly 20% of Norwegians tuning in. Producer Thomas Hellum in his TED talk explains how the live broadcast of long events as they unfold in real time—such as the 7 hours of the Bergen train journey, 10 hours of salmon fishing or 8 hours of knitting made for "the world's most boring... yet hilariously addictive" television (2014). Other Scandinavian countries followed suit and from popular demand, created their own versions of slow TV.

The Great Elk Trek was Swedish television's answer to this call. Emma Beddington, writing for *The Guardian*, exclaims, "[f]orget *Line of Duty*, my must-watch show is the riveting spring moose migration, a natural drama full of atavistic pleasures" (2021), echoing the sentiment of millions of viewers who tuned in. If the slow trainspotting of *Bergensbanen* mapped the

9   See Puijk (2020) for a detailed analysis of Nordic slow TV.

10   In relation to similar strategies in the overnight program of German history of television, Rembert Hüser calls such ritual media approaches "cinema of everyday attractions" (2020, 114).

Norwegian landscape, then the moose's slow migration offered a cartography of Sweden's forest and mountain-scapes (see fig. 2). The show fulfilled all the parameters of slow TV spelt out by the producers: real-time unedited footage, live broadcast on prime time tv to maximize community participation, and content rooted in national culture and focused on something that people could identify with.[11]

The moose is the beloved animal of Sweden, and the moose silhouette is highly visible as a national symbol. Besides being the country's top tourist attraction, it is also its premier sport. About 100.000 moose are shot every year in the hunting season in an activity that is both controlled and legitimized by the Swedish Hunting Association and Environmental Protection Agency. It is also a communal activity, rather than a solitary or stealthy game hunt that we see in many other countries (Heberlein 2000). So, when Swedish National Television decided to film the moose migration, it seemed to be a natural choice. The slow TV format was particularly suited to the ruminating ungulate's annual marathon that was epic, spectacular, and yes, slow.

They are in no hurry. This is slow TV, after all, and the moose will not cross until the last ice on the shore has melted. This means the livestream often offers up an hour or two of a single moose chewing meditatively, the steam of its warm breath dissipating gradually in the forest chill, or just standing looking at the river (Beddington 2021).

Nothing happens, but something *might happen*. Thus, if commercial tv shows have their cliffhangers, then this is the hook of slow TV—the fear of missing out when something just might happen keeps viewers glued to their television sets. The show's presenter, Anders Lundin, points to the human traps not far from the cameras, revealing to us that just as hunters wait patiently,

11   See the Facebook fan community for the show at "Vi som följer den stora älgvandringen!" (Nilsson and Olsson 2023).

[Figure 3] *Moment of Drama* (Source: Christensen 2021)

sometimes for days, for the moose to fall along its journey, these camera traps, too, were waiting to capture images of moose. If dead moose were the trophies of the hunter then these moose images, these grainy silhouettes, were the rewards of the show.

Even if the biggest draw of the show is the illusion of watching nature live, without the heavy human hand of classic wildlife programming, the entangled presence of humans and technology alongside the animals casts a shadow every once in a while. Thus, a moose may stumble into a mic or stare at a night vision camera where the fleeting glimpse of a paved road cuts through the forest, which has itself been rewilded or commodified for hunting, tourism, and television. The program also provides the interested spectator with an overview of the intricate infrastructure that went into the making of the show. Twenty-three PTZ cameras (enabled with pan, tilt and zoom functions) concealed with cam-nets, two night-vision cameras, and multiple drones were placed at strategic locations along the trail of the moose walk. Specially designated mics were set up to isolate the sound of ice thawing and rippling. These devices were operated remotely from the control room in Kullberg, where a team worked round the clock to manipulate the camera every time there was a sighting of a moose or any other wild animal. Sometimes they had to reangle the cameras when the moose strayed from its anticipated path. 17.000 meters of crisscrossed cables (along with embedders for audio) that originated in Kullberg and branched at the mainland were neatly divided into hubs, camouflaged, and placed at several points along the 400-mile path of the moose walk. These fiber-optic cables picked up the video feed and transmitted it back to the control room.

The camera-cable set up tried to follow the well-worn path of the moose as accurately as possible. Usually, the moose would enter through Naset, reach the Passage, then cross the island, before disappearing out of view somewhere beyond the camera. Close ups of the moose are captured as they wade across the waters to cross the island—this is where the main action takes place, and the main hub is placed here. "These moose don't choose Kullberg, but at least we get to see them"[12] says the presenter gesturing to the audience.

What we see, then, are not only moose, but also occasional appearances of other wild animals that roam the forests, including wolves, brown bears, lynx, deer, wolverines, reindeer, and black grouse—most of the time, however, there are no animals in sight in this still landscape. Once in a while, the camera drones travel sinuously over beautiful aerial views of miles and miles of limpid silvery snow and majestic green pines as they sway in the wind. Sometimes, the camera disappears behind a stump, or rustles through the spring forest as we listen in to a birdsong, a ripple in the river on the ridge, or hear ice crack and melt. But even these are minor events in the show, since most of the time, we are just staring into an empty expanse of dark blue waters or a white stretch of nothingness. But then suddenly,

12   All translations by author.

84 something happens: "7-8 moose went through the ice. The moose try to cross here. And when the ice weakens there are still a few who are willing to risk it. When they go through the ice your heart starts to rush" (Erhag and Edlund 2019). Indeed, the drama of the show is a sheer moment of serendipity when a moose falls through the ice, and then heroically rises from it, hesitates before a night vision camera or decides to change its track (see fig. 3).

The gradual revelation of the show, in which every infinitesimal change and each minute detail is apprehended through our slow perception, combines the slow pleasures of watching, knowing, and contemplating moose and other wildlife as they move through snow, forests, and water, or as our gaze is riveted by a still, wild landscape. Linda Williams calls our deliriously voyeuristic pleasures of watching moving subjects on screen the "frenzy of the visible" (1989) while Michael Renov describes our pleasures of documentary viewing as epistephilia—the pleasure of knowing (1993). Rather than transporting us to the wild as classic nature programs do, the wild is brought home through unhurried, unedited real-time footage, sans commentary or music. Indeed, directors Stefan Edlund and Johan Erhag describe the show as "the moving painting in the living room" (Redvall 2020) that enveloped viewers 24 hours a day for three whole weeks in an immersive sensory environment. These enchanted forests, these techno-wilds make us at once remember and forget our culpability in destroying our wildlife and ethical responsibilities toward conserving it.

I thank Shambhavi Prakash, Tobias Toll, and Dhivya Janarthanan for pointing me to the show and listening enthusiastically to a first draft of this article.

Literature

Beddington, Emma. 2021. "Forget Line of Duty: Sweden's Great Elk Trek is giving me hours of joy." *The Guardian*, May 4. Accessed April 4, 2023. https://www.theguardian.com/commentisfree/2021/may/04/forget-line-of-duty-i-have-found-a-show-that-brings-me-hours-of-primal-joy.

Berger, John. 1980. "Why Look at Animals?" In *About Looking*, edited by John Berger, 1–26. London: Bloomsbury.

Böhme, Gernot. 1989. *Für eine ökologische Naturästhetik*. Frankfurt am Main: Suhrkamp Verlag.

Brown, S. Lewis, ed. 2012. *Animals in Motion: Eadweard Muybridge*. New York: Dover Publications.

Burt, Jonathan. 2002. *Animals in Film*. London: Reaktion Books.

Gunther, Kerry A., Frank T. van Manen, and P.J. White. 2017. *Yellowstone Grizzly Bears: Ecology and Conservation of an Icon of Wildness*. Yellowstone National Park: Yellowstone Forever.

Heberlein, Thomas A. 2000. "The Gun, the Dog, and the Thermos: Culture and Hunting in Sweden and the United States." *Swedish Council of America* 13: 24–9.

Hellum, Thomas. 2014. "The World's Most Boring Television and Why Its' Hilariously Addictive." *TED: Ideas Worth Spreading*. Accessed March 1, 2022. https://www.ted.com/talks/thomas_hellum_the_world_s_most_boring_television_and_why_it_s_hilariously_addictive.

Hooten, Mevin B., Devin S. Johnson, Brett Z. McClintock, and Juan M. Morales. 2017. *Animal Movement: Statistical Models for Telemetry Data*. Boca Raton (FL): CRC Press.

Hüser, Rembert. 2020. "Die schönsten Bahnstrecken Deutschlands." In *Die Attraktion des Appartiven*, edited by Stefanie Diekmann and Volker Wortmann, 113–32. Paderborn: Brill | Fink.

Jaffe, Ira. 2014. *Slow Movies: Countering the Cinema of Action*. New York: Wallflower Press.

Lippit, Akira Mizuta. 2000. *Electric Animal: Toward a Rhetoric of Wildlife*. Minneapolis: University of Minnesota Press.

Nilsson, Arne, and Sven Olsson. 2023. "Vi som följer den stora älgvandringen!" *Facebook*. Accessed April 4, 2023. https://www.facebook.com/groups/330650520975928/?locale=sv_SE.

Polanyi, Michael. 2009. *The Tacit Dimension*. Chicago: University of Chicago Press.

Prix Europa. 2020. *Prix Europa 2020 Catalogue*. Accessed April 15, 2023. https://www.prixeuropa.eu/news/2020/10/05catalogueonline.

Puijk, Roel. 2020. *Slow TV: An Analysis of Minute-by-Minute Television in Norway*. Bristol: Intellect Press.

Redvall, Eva N. 2020. "Scandinavian Slow TV is Moving Strongly into the 2020s." *CST Online*. Accessed April 15, 2023. https://cstonline.net/scandinavian-slow-tv-is-moving-strongly-into-the-2020s-and-is-now-also-for-children/.

Renov, Michael. 1993. *Theorizing Documentary*. New York: Routledge.

Solnit, Rebecca. 2004. *River of Shadows: Eadweard Muybridge and The Technological Wild West*. New York: Penguin Books.

de Luca, Tiago, and Nuno Barradas Jorge, eds. 2015. *Slow Cinema*. Edinburgh: Edinburgh University Press.

Ulven, Elisabeth. 2017. "The Ultimate Slow TV: A 168-hour Show on Reindeer Migration." *The Guardian*, April 26. Accessed April 4, 2023. https://www.theguardian.com/tv-and-radio/2017/apr/26/slow-tv-reindeer-migration-norway-nrk-reinflytting-minutt-for-minutt.

86 Vertov, Dziga. 1984 (1896–1954). *Kino Eye: The Writings of Dziga Vertov*. Edited by Annette Michelson and translated by Kevin O'Brien. Berkeley: University of California Press.

White, P.J., Kerry A Gunther, and Frank T. van Manen. 2017. *Yellowstone Grizzly Bears: Ecology and Conservation of an Icon of Wildness*. Yellowstone National Park: Yellowstone Forever.

Williams, Linda. 1989. *Hard Core: Power, Pleasure, and the "Frenzy of the Visible."* Berkeley: University of California Press.

(Audio)Visual Material

Christensen, Christian. 2021. "High Drama on Swedish Television's 'The Great Moose Migration…'." *Twitter*. April 26. Accessed April 4, 2023. https://mobile.twitter.com/chrchristensen/status/1386695874890305538?lang=bg.

Erhag, Johan, and Stefan Edlund. 2019–23. *Den stora älgvandringen*. Slow TV, Sweden.

Explore Annenberg LLC. *explore: Livecams / Currently Live*. Accessed April 4, 2023. https://explore.org/livecams.

Hellum, Thomas, and Norsk rikskringkasting. 2009. *Bergensbanen—minutt for minutt*. Slow TV, 432 min., Norway.

Marey, Étienne-Jules. 1883-7. *Analysis of the Flight of a Pigeon by the Chronophotographic Method*. Two chromophotographic albumen silver prints.

Muybridge, Eadward. 1878. *Galloping Horse Series (plate 628 from Animal Locomotion)*. B/w photograph.

Spielberg, Steven. 1993. *Jurassic Park*. Feature-length film, 127 min., United States of America.

Warhol, Andy. 1964. *Sleep*. Experimental film, 20 min., United States of America.

Zoological Society of London. 2023. *ZSL Instant Wild*. Accessed April 4, 2023. https://instantwild.zsl.org/intro.

[4]

Old Modes, New Moods, or How Soundtracks Can Experiment

Felipe Soares

When dealing with musical modes, instead of exploring a fascinating, millenary history, with millions of possibilities for experimentation, some soundtrack composers and teachers prefer to obey a sort of utilitarian normativity stemming from the industrial logic of film production. Ancient mode-mood associations tend to become norms, and this ends up inhibiting new ones from developing. Here, I put forward Sergei Prokofiev as a privileged example of the opposite trend: working with old modes, particularly on the music for Sergei Eisenstein's *Ivan the Terrible* (1944), Prokofiev demonstrates that soundtrack scoring is a field of experimentation *par excellence*.

As a gigantic dinosaur strolls through the park, we hear the orchestra go from a Bb major chord straight to a C major—instead of the expected C minor (Spielberg 1993). We can hear the same progression—now from C major to D major (not minor)—in the opening to *The Simpsons (Elfman 1989)*, which starts with voices singing a sharp fourth interval (c-#f). This interval defines the Lydian mode. The list of examples of this mode in the film industry is extensive. It is usually linked to stimulating moods described as heavenly, heroic, hopeful, etc. (Beato 2020). Other musical modes bring out similar lists of moods.

For millennia, in several contexts of musical production (not only in Europe), mode-mood associations have been copious and usually taken for granted.[1] Some authors look for explanations, predictable systems of cause and effect. But, after so many horrors have called into question the validity of human progress—and after so many alerts by minorities, in the context of colonial catastrophe, that the supposed universal

1   This is somewhat surprising, because modes are, ultimately, groups of notes, just elements in a set to be used in a composition—like modern scales. Originally, each mode had a strong association with a kind of musical instrument, which could produce only some determined pitches in a sequence, so that the pitches and intervals were physically determined. Music produced in a mode would sound different from that produced in another one. After some training, it would become easy to recognize modes only by listening to the tunes (analogously, it is easy to tell, nowadays, if a song is in minor or major mode.) As with architectural styles, modes were soon associated to Greek tribal names, like Ionian, Lydian, Phrygian, Dorian etc., and this very association, though perhaps groundless, presupposes a vague quality, character or humour (a mood) for each mode. Thus, a poorly defined notion of cultural identity was, in turn, linked to instruments somehow "typical" of that identity. As I will show below, in Plato's *Republic*, for instance, one can already find these associations in use (1897 iii, 398e).

human subject lies at the root of such horrors—, physiological
or cognitive explanations for the production of moods through
music seem unconvincing. Speaking from my place, in Southern
Brazil, sensitive to the day-by-day effects of colonial arbi-
trariness, I always prefer to consider attributions of moods as
movements of historical references, within more or less defined
historic-geographical contexts, based on vague assumptions—
with no *explanation* at all. Similar to word usage in Linguistics:
each proposition is contingent, hypothetical. For any individual,
each mood supposedly stimulated by a mode can be seen as a
memory move.

Thus, mode-mood associations may well be examples of tacit
cinematic knowledge. Michael Polanyi characterizes tacit
knowledge as a movement between two vaguely known terms:
"we know the first term only by relying on our awareness of it for
attending to the second" (2009, 10)—a movement from impre-
cise signifiers to vague but identifiable sensations. It is plausible
to imagine a spectator relying on a vague awareness of the
Lydian mode, from which they derive (by memory) a sensation
of grandeur when seeing a dinosaur on screen. They have seen
dinosaurs before, and they have heard that chord progression
many times, so their memories become accustomed to this tacit
knowledge.

Thought of in this way, tacit knowledge recalls Proustian invol-
untary memory: "let a sound, a scent already heard and breathed
in the past be heard and breathed anew, simultaneously in the
present and in the past, real without being actual, ideal without
being abstract" (Proust 2016, 2535). As old sensations awaken, we
can see things liberated from the order of time—and ourselves
along with them. This possibility becomes clear when we think of
Henri Bergson's *la dureé*: all images accumulate in the past (which
does not pass) (1911). Each new perception makes us actualize
certain memories, concentrated in a certain level of conscious-
ness. "[t]o complete a recollection by more personal details does
not at all consist in mechanically juxtaposing other recollections

92   to this, but in transporting ourselves to a wider plane of con-
sciousness, in going away from action in the direction of dream"
(Bergson 1911, 322). The Proustian narrator is Bergsonian, except
in his attitude towards the past: for Bergson, the past is kept in
itself, and we can only learn how to cope with it, while the Proustian narrator is eager to recover past the way it was (Deleuze
2003, 55).

Links between modes and moods may not recover the past,
but they approximate sensations from different times, allowing
us escape from chronological order. Curiously, if we take one
element away from a film, another may also become part of it: a
camera shot, a related sensation, the afternoon you watched a
movie or the someone you watched it with, a popcorn flavour. In
sum, even if one knows nothing about musical modes, listening to
a modal progression while watching a movie may bring up things
that are "real without being actual, ideal without being abstract"
(Proust 2016, 2535), along with vague but identifiable sensations.

One of the most effective (if regrettable) consequences of
this is the extensive reuse of modes in the film industry. This
indicates that producers seem satisfied with decisions made by
composers, notably when modes *work out fine*, and help sell the
films. The problem is that, through industrial logic, the use of
musical modes for the work with images has become a *method*,
accepted and developed by cinema and music teachers. Rather
than pushing for new research and experimentation with this
rich millenary history, many teach *how to use* modes, seeking
effects (and usually achieving them) by using conventional sound
material that supposedly *works out fine* in Hollywood.

In video published by the Berklee College of Music, Instructor
Tim Huling, "discusses how modes of the major scale can be
used to create different moods and spirits throughout a scene"
(Huling 2020). He argues that John Williams, Hans Zimmer, Danny
Elfman and Randy Newman, despite all differences, have the use
of modes in common. He tries to demonstrate these moods and

spirits, in association with samples of modes. He starts by giving
the spectator/student a schematic example of the Aeolian mode,
only juxtaposing C minor and F minor chords, but not explaining
the difference between this and the usual progression from i
to iv in the tonality of C minor, and not adding that the Aeolian
mode can be found in the other 11 tonalities. He treats other
modes similarly, before concluding by reiterating that modes are
"quite useful when scoring a scene" (Huling 2020). If the student
achieves the desired effects by playing the correct notes, the
class is successful, and the industry may count on new promising
workers.[2]

In this example, history is erased in the name of utility. The
word "modes," as cultural reference, carries with it at least two
hugely different cultural universes, "Greek" and "Medieval,"
both of which involve millions of different lives and centuries of
associations with sounds, silences, sensations, revolutionary
gestures, desires, victories, massacres, etc. Even the reduction
of all this complexity to only two universes is arbitrary, revealing
the violence of such utilitarianism itself. The adjective "Greek"
is as useful for musical modes as it is for yogurt, while the word
"Medieval" is most violent historiographic reductions of all times,
collapsing 15 centuries into an imaginary era of darkness and
blind mysticism.

Even within each of these universes, "modes" are a complex
subject. In the "Greek" variety, each kind of scale depends on
instruments' timbres and pitch ranges, though one must think of
how many different instruments the "Greeks" may have developed over their long history, whose sounds we have never heard.
All we have are references to modes in Greek texts, usually
associating them to different Greek peoples, named, among
others, by the words we use today: Ionian, Dorian, Phrygian,

2 I do not assume this video is a general representation of Berklee's method; it
  is only an example of the usual pragmatism, which appears even on a college
  level.

  Lydian, Mixolydian, Aeolian, Locrian. The simple scheme by which modern musicians define these seven modal scales by associating them with the white keys on a piano (in that order, starting from C) is also an oversimplification of many layers of history.

By contrast, some of the ancient Greek texts seem to take tacit knowledge into account. Aristoxenus, for instance, a student of Aristotle, insisted on the importance of sensibility to music theory. Writing two centuries after Pythagoras, he opposed Pythagorean views, which according to him, overlooked the basic experience of hearing. His method is based upon "an appeal to the two faculties of hearing and intellect. By the former we judge the magnitudes of the intervals; by the latter we contemplate the functions of the notes. … [F]or the student of musical science, accuracy of sense-perception is a fundamental requirement" (Aristoxenus 1902, 189). A (vague but identifiable) knowledge based on "sense-perception" is at the heart of Aristoxenus's investigation, beyond any mathematical schema. This knowledge may be tacit, since it involves a play across time, through memory: "the apprehension of music depends on these two faculties, sense-perception and memory; for we must perceive the sound that is present, and remember that which is past. In no other way can we follow the phenomena of music" (Aristoxenus 1902, 193–94).

Aristoxenus's musical theory relies on *relations*, on (tacit) movements between elements. There must always be an *interval*, and there are fundamental intervals, like those of fourths, fifths and octaves, creating *concords*. Different divisions of a con-cord make tetrachords, which form scales, allowing for infinite possibilities. Scales are classified in three genres, according to intervals between adjacent notes: enharmonic (including quartertones), chromatic, and diatonic. Notes are also nomi-nated according to their relations. In the heptachord scale, we have: *hypate* (the highest), *parahypate* (next to highest), *lichanus* (made with the forefinger), *mese* (the middle), *trite* (the third), *paranete*, and *nete* (the lowest). In the octachord scale, we also see *paramese*. Here the lowest note coincides with the highest, being a permanent tonic, while in the heptachord the *mese* was more important.

The octachord scale becomes a plausible historical foundation for the establishment of modes. Greek instruments were limited in scope, and each had different tunings, so different instruments or tunings were necessary to play different tunes (Macran 1906, 224). Each mode would also be more adequate to this or that singer, and gradually, each mode grew to be associated with a kind of instrument—and perhaps with a particular community. Let's highlight here that "[t]he early Greek *Harmoniai* [modes] or groupings of notes and tetrachords *were experimental in character*" (Rockstro 1907, 222; italics added) since way before Aristoxenus! But also before Aristoxenus, modes were already associated with moods. In Plato's *Republic* (1897, iii, 398e), Socrates argues that modes imitate and stimulate moods and gestures, and that there should only be modes that imitate good things, i.e. only useful or utilitarian modes (Plato 2003, 88). In his *Politics*, Aristotle peremptorily says that pieces of music "contain in themselves imitations of character; and this is manifest" (1959, VIII, 1340a/39–1340b/8, 658-9). He associates Mixolydian, for instance, with a "mournful and restrained state" (1959, 658–59). Curiously, Plato's and Aristotle's historical authorities lead them to be quoted much more frequently than Aristoxenus, who, by contrast, studied modes in depth.

After Aristoxenus, Greek schemes gained complexity over time: some extra tetrachords were added to the seven modal scales, expanding and multiplying them to 15, which functioned similarly to modern Western keys (Macran 1906, 225). Meanwhile, naming problems only increased. Greek names (like Dorian, Phrygian, Lydian etc) appear in several Medieval (and modern) schemes as well, but in association with different scales. Aristotle's Mixolidian mode refers to a scale similar to our Locrian. There is also a crucial difference between two concepts of modes. In the "Greek" concept, the groups of notes "were distinguished from one another by pitch," while in the "Medieval" the difference between groups "depends on differences of tonality, and is comparatively indifferent to pitch. The history of the mediaeval modes is therefore, to a considerable extent, the history of the evolution of tonality" (Rockstro 1907, 222). Such evolution depended on the relation between sounds and two increasingly fixed points of each scale: the Dominant and the Final.

In the 2nd century A.D., contradicting both Pythagorians and Aristoxenians, Ptolemy simplified the complex Greek system, establishing "seven practical working Modes" (Rockstro 1907, 224) with scales built in a very regular way: all of them had a well-defined dominant (the *mese*): one fifth above the lowest note. Even so, the history of "Medieval" modes may be even more confusing than that of the "Greek" ones. After Ptolemy there is, according to Rockstro, a 700-year silence from theoreticians. This gap demands a certain creativity from historians in the search for documents of musical production. "[h]appily at this date when the theorists fail, there becomes available for the western history a large collection of actual musical compositions in which the further evolution of the modal system may be traced" (Rockstro 1907, 224).

Important changes can be seen in this compositional archive, such as the growing importance of the Final note over the Dominant as musical elaboration developed, notably from the 5th to the 8th century. The plagal relation, too, started to prevail, which brought about another scheme, with eight modes divided in four pairs—of plagal and authentic. It might have been difficult for singers, arrangers, and choir directors in the 9th century to reconcile their sophisticated practices with available theoretical works. As Guido d'Arezzo may have said, "the book of Boethius is of no use to singers, but only to philosophers" (Rockstro 1907, 227). This disconnection between practice and theory, though, contributed to the stabilization of tonality, with the Final assuming its place as a main reference. Even the distinction between authentic and plagal modes started diminishing. From

the 12th century on, composers grew open to new forms of
harmonisation, and to elements coming from folk songs. Old
modes soon began inducing nostalgia: "[a] good deal of richness
in melodic beauty was sacrificed in the process, and modern
melody, even with all its chromatic freedom, has not such a wide
range of variety as the old modal system afforded" (Rockstro
1907, 228).

It is obviously much more appealing to explore a universe full of
possibilities and experiments with modes than to search for a
how-to manual. Some composers have indeed explored modes
extensively when working on images, pushing against industrial
logic. I take Sergei Prokofiev as a privileged example of this drive
toward experimentation in soundtracks, due to (1) his profuse and
heterodox work for screen and stage, (2) his curious collaboration
with Sergei Eisenstein (another great example of resistance to
industrial logic in art), and (3) his research into Russian musical
traditions.

A huge amount of Russian popular culture lies on the rich,
manifold Byzantine heritage. The impressive devotion of the
people (as I could see in Moscow) and the huge investment in
churches and monuments all over the country are nowadays just
a hint of how exuberant this heritage is. It has been protected,
for centuries, by a strong conservatism, as demonstrated, for
instance, by the Old Believers, religious dissenters who preserve
elements of Greek ritual, resisting changes proposed in the 16th
century by the Roman Catholic Church, via Polish Jesuits. Beyond
the reach of European regulations, and keeping its own deter-
minations close to its Greek origins, Russian Liturgical music
has, however, been open to domestic alterations—which were
plentiful.

Old Believers refused harmonisation and the five-line stave along
with certain "corrections" of grammar and spelling in liturgical
texts. As the flow of chants depends chiefly on the way words are
spoken, divisions and pitches of melodies follow vernacular rules.

[Figure 1] A Belarusian harvest song (Source: Prokhorov 2002, 8).

Temporal division depends on prosody, and one of the affinities between liturgical and folk music is an irregular meter, as we can see in this Belarusian harvest song (see fig. 1).

Furthermore, a good part of Russian liturgical music was not written in European neumas, but in a system that was much more complicated and open to singers' choices (Birkbeck 1890, 143–57). These conditions made composers open to integrating folk culture.

Great Russian composers of the 19th and 20th centuries, Prokofiev among them, edited collections of Russian folk songs and drew from them often in their own work. In Russia, this relation is characterized by a large use of diatonic modes, which defined some features of a distinctly Russian harmonic language and even helped define Soviet music during its realist (Stalinist) turn (Дубовский et al. 1965, 169).[3] The use of modes here has some specificities. The natural minor mode (Aeolian) abounds in Russian music. In contrast to Western music, the juxtaposition of minor dominant and tonic is quite usual, as are plagal leaps in melody, chordal progressions of third and second, incomplete chords (lacking a 3rd), among other features. Other diatonic modes are common, notably Dorian and Phrygian (minors), and Ionic and Mixolydian (majors) (Дубовский et al. 1965, 169–89). As a teenage student at St. Petersburg Conservatory, Prokofiev had

3   All translations of Dubovsky by author.

already incorporated this amalgam well enough to mock it, as he would do many times afterwards, having already mixed liturgical harmonies with dissonant chords (Guillaumier 2010, 56).

Prokofiev made numerous experiments with modes, notably in his music for film, dance, and theatre—distancing himself not only from *how-to* norms, but even from established schemes of modal scale construction. His music for Eisenstein's *Ivan the Terrible*, has plenty of modal elements that draw from Russian liturgical or folk music, notably chants. Indeed, there are so many chants, sung diegetically by the characters, that I would not hesitate to consider the film a musical. The whole film is highly theatrical (Oliveira 2008)—echoing Ivan IV himself. Prokofiev uses modes so freely that it becomes impossible to systematize them. Sometimes there are notes, or intervals, or chordal relations characteristic of a well-defined mode. At other times, the very modalisation proves ambiguous.

In the opening credits, the song "Туча чёрная" (eng. "Black rain") is written on the 2-flat signature, but each one of its short, repeated phrases (one for each bar) ends in an e natural, directly following an e flat, creating what sounds like an appoggiatura (see fig. 2).

[Figure 2] *Ivan the Terrible's* Opening Chant (Source: Prokofiev 1997, 38).

Using current nomenclature, one can read this melody in Bb Lydian, or in E Locrian. In order to solve this dilemma, we must decide which note would sound like the Final. The bass does not help us: the choral section has 10 bars; in the first 4, there is no bass at all, while in the following 3 bars, the cellos and double basses do exactly the same as baritone voice. All this time, the woodwinds or strings reinforce a Bb chord. In the 8th bar, cellos and basses make a chromatic movement, then the choral ends in the ambiguous final chord of bars 9 and 10, perhaps a Bb(6/#4). In sum, defining the mode is not only impossible, but also useless.

Prokofiev also incorporates old tunes from different sources. When Euphrosyne and young Vladimir watch a Biblical mystery play in which three young men are saved from fire by an angel (based on Daniel 3:1–98), we cannot see the singers of the chorus that opens the play (right after the bells toll), but all people present at the church are listening, and the play's characters move clearly in time to it as they enter. It is impossible to define this choir's diegetic level. For this choral piece, Prokofiev borrows the theme "Дивен Бог во святых своих, Бог Израилев" (eng. "God is wonderful in his saints, the God of Israel"), from the final part of Dmitry Bortnyansky's Concert 34 (1882). This sounds like a traditional choral piece, with chords going from I (Gb) to V (Db), passing through a major VI (Eb) that resolves into a (minor) ii (Abm). Strangely, though, the score is written not in the key signature of Gb, but in that of Db, only with a flat c, which sounds like a b natural.[4] Rigorously speaking, the song goes from IV to I, a plagal move, with the help of a lower seventh (cb)—which in turn brings us to the idea of a Db Mixolydian.

This difference between what we hear and what we read in the score, visible only at an analytical level, is one of several tacit, theatrical undecidabilities—adding to the ambiguous diegetic levels. We can see Prokofiev enacting Bortnyansky, telling a well-known story attributed to Daniel, the three boys performing the role of believers, who sing in the fire without a singe, the three respective actors playing these characters, who in turn perform the boys, and the clowns who escort them, tacitly reminding us a vague theatrical tradition of vaudeville or *commedia dell'arte* etc.

This overflowing chain of enactments reaches a climax in the famous coloured scene, when Vladimir, impersonating Ivan, is

---

4   Шумилина (2011, 96–99) analyses this scene, but does not mention this difference in key signature.

truly murdered—which echoes a dreadful play actually executed
by the historical Ivan IV.[5] This scene cements the brutality and
theatricality of Ivan and his guards, the *Opritchnik*, who dance and
sing in this moment. The lip-synching fails in some shots, which
intensifies the distance among levels of representation. The main
theme is sung by Fiodor (Mikhail Kusnetzov), and the *Opritchnik*
respond. This inevitably alludes to folksongs of the 16th century,
praising the way the real Ivan and *Opritchnina* "boiled 'traitor-
boyars' alive in cauldrons …, impaled them on stakes, and sewed
them into bearskins and threw them into rivers" (Pavlov and
Perrie 2003, 160).

The theme is very simple, sung in a rather mordant way. There
is no tonic, and the note we can consider as Final is the c of a
C Phrygian (in a 4-flat signature), but without its characteristic
halftone. The first response characterizes, once again, a plagal
movement (from f to c below), highlighted by a charming one-
octave *glissando*. After a funny whistle, Fiodor repeats the line,
changing only the lyrics, and the choir sings a new repetition,
now in the same octave as him, adding a natural b, and ending
on f (which makes identifying this mode even more complicated). Then we have the signature of C major, now with the same
natural b as the leading tone, but soon the bass voices come and
repeat a phrase ending in eb (still with a natural b): still a modal
appeal, but with no hint of a specific mode.

Here the choir encourages the singer to talk ("говори!"). Then
a soloist, almost speaking (as is suggested in the score), insists
on the use of axes against traitors. After another whistle, the

---

5   Ivan Petrovich Fedorov-Chelyadnin, leader of a Boyar Council, allegedly
wanted Ivan's throne. He was taken to the palace, ordered to dress Ivan's
royal attire and sit on the throne, holding the sceptre. "Ivan then bowed and
knelt before him, saying: 'Now you have what you sought and aspired to …
Just as it is in my power to place you on this throne, so it is also in my power
to remove you.' After that the Tsar plunged a dagger into the boyar's chest,
and the *oprichniki* who were present followed with knife blows of their own"
(Pavlov and Perrie 2003, 138, quotation from Шлихтинг 1935, 21).

[Figure 3] *Ivan the Terrible*, Song of the Opritchniki (Source: Prokofiev 1997, 191–92).

choir repeats the same natural B many times, saying "жги" (eng. *"burn!"*), along with the Tsar himself. All this is repeated entirely twice. Fiodor's lyrics evoke images of festive and violent attacks on boyars with axes and fire (see fig. 3).

"Sarcastic" might be a good word to refer to this composition by Prokofiev and Eisenstein. The recipient of this sarcasm is sarcastically multiple: the old boyars (why not?), Ivan IV himself, his ridiculous Opritchnik, his ridiculous pupil Joseph Stalin, the absurdity of socialist realism—and of course, for me, Brazil's ridiculous fascist former president (2019-2022), and his ridiculous entourage. No wonder Stalin censored the film (which would be seen in theatres only in 1958, 5 years after Stalin's and Prokofiev's deaths, 10 years after Eisenstein's).

A very different mood appears when Euphrosyne (Serafima Birman), *acappella*, sings "The beaver song" over her dead son, Vladimir (Pavel Kadochnikov). She is one of the ghastliest characters of the film—the one who poisoned Anastasia. Yet, her final singing is quite doleful. Prokofiev writes a beautiful line, simple on its face, but difficult to sing, and Birman shows absolute freedom when singing it. The lyrics talk about the dead beaver, an animal affectionately associated with Vladimir. The first part moves apparently in a G# Locrian, the second, we may say, starts in B Aeolian, but ends in a surprising E Dorian, after a diatonic semi-scale from b to e and a one-octave *glissando* to the lower e. Beautiful! Any other mode identifiable here would obviously recall grief, but the piece is all about Euphrosyne's madness, in which nothing is predictable. There is no use for *how to* manuals; modes are vaguely written, and a criminal woman's body beautifully sings her grief—that is all.

Literature

Aristotle. 1959 (ca. 322 B.C.). *Politics* [bilingual]. Translated by Harris Rackham. London: William Heinemann / Cambridge: Harvard University Press.

Aristoxenus. 1902 (ca. 335 B.C.). *Αριστοξενου Αρμονικα Στοιξεια / The Harmonics of Aristoxenus*. Edited and translated by Henry S. Macran. Oxford: Clarendon.

Bergson, Henri. 1911 (1896). *Matter and Memory*. Translated by Nancy Margaret Paul and W. Scott Palmer. London: George Allen and Unwin / New York: Macmillan.

Birkbeck, W. J. 1890–1. "Some Notes on Russian Ecclesiastical Music, Ancient and Modern." In *Proceedings of the Musical Association*, 17th sess., 143–57.

Deleuze, Gilles. 2003 (1976). *Proust e os signos*. Translated by Antonio Piquet and Roberto Machado. Rio de Janeiro: Forense Universitária.

Дубовский, Н., Евсеев, С., Способин, И, Соколов, В.. 1965. Учебник гармонии. Москва: Издательство Музыка.

Guillaumier, Christina. 2010. *From Piano to Stage*. Doctoral dissertation. St Andrews: University of St Andrews.

Macran, Henry Stewart. 1906. "Greek Music." In *Grove's Dictionary of Music and Musicians*, Vol. 2, 223–231. New York and London: MacMillan-

Oliveira, Vanessa T. 2008. *Eisenstein ultrateatral*. Sao Paulo: Perspectiva.

Pavlov, Andrei, and Maureen Perrie. 2003. *Ivan, the Terrible*. London: Pearson.

Plato. 2003 (ca. 375 B.C.). *The Republic*. Edited by G. R. F. Ferrari and translated by Tom Griffith. Cambridge: Cambridge University Press.

———.1897 (ca. 375 B.C.). *The Republic of Plato* [in Greek]. Edited by James Adam. Cambridge: Cambridge University Press.

104 Polanyi, Michael. 2009 (1966). *The Tacit Dimension*. Chicago and London: The University of Chicago Press.

Prokhorov, Vadim. 2002. *Russian Folk Songs: Musical Genres and History*. London: The Scarecrow Press.

Prokofiev, Sergei.1997 (1944-6). *Iwan der Schreckliche*. Hamburg: Hans Sikorski.

Proust, Marcel. 2016 (1927). *Time regained* (*In search of lost time*, v. 7). Translated by Sidney Schiff. Guimaraes: Centaur Editions.

Rimbaud, Arthur. 1996 (1886). "Ville." In *Iluminuras*, translated by Rodrigo G. Lopes. Sao Paulo: Iluminuras, 44.

Rockstro, William Smyth. 1907. "Modes, The Ecclesiastical." In *Grove's Dictionary of Music and Musicians*, Vol. 3, 222–232. New York and London: MacMillan.

Шлихтинг, А. 1935. *Новое известие о россии времени Ивана Грозного*. Ленинград: Акадкмии Наук.

Шумилина. 2011. "О тематических связях музыки С. Прокофьева к кинофильму "Иван Грозный": *Музичне Мистецтво*. Випуск 11. Донецьк-Львів: Юго-Восток.

(Audio)Visual Material

Beato, Rick. 2020. "The Lydian Mode | Why Film Composers and Rock Guitarists Love This Sound." *YouTube*, January 5. Accessed August 6, 2022. https://www.youtube.com/watch?v=O4lJnSTS84A&ab_channel=RickBeat.

Berklee Online, and Tim Huling. 2020. "How to Use Musical Modes to Change Moods in Film Scoring | Tim Huling." *YouTube*, February 11. Accessed August 6, 2022. https://www.youtube.com/watch?v=ZsSLJzEPiak&ab_channel=BerkleeOnline.

Bortniansky, Dmitry. 2011 (1882). "Concerto 34: Let God Arise, Let his Enemies Be Scattered." *YouTube*, May 20. Accessed April 28, 2023. https://youtu.be/aqFyBaqFUn4.

Eisenstein, Sergei. 1944. *Ivan the Terrible*. Feature-length film, 187 min., Soviet Union.

Elfman, Danny. 1989. The Simpsons Theme. Theme song, 1 min. 23 sec., United States of America.

Prokhorov, Vadim. 2002. "A Belarusian Harvest Song." In *Russian Folk Songs: Musical Genres and History*. London: The Scarecrow Press, 8.

Prokofiev, Sergei. 2022 (1946). "*Ivan the Terrible*'s The Beaver Song" [01:20:00–01:21:14]. *YouTube*. May 27. Accessed April 28, 2023. https://youtu.be/vnNgoS8VsoQ.

———. 2022 (1944). "*Ivan the Terrible*'s Black Rain (Opening Chant)" [00:05–02:12]. *YouTube*. May 27. Accessed April 28, 2023.. https://youtu.be/ZYOxxp_EVxc

———. 2022 (1946). "*Ivan the Terrible's*, Song of the Opritchniki" [01:00:02–01:03:50]. *YouTube*, May 27. Accessed April 28, 2023. https://youtu.be/vnNgoS8VsoQ.

Prokofiev, Sergei, and Sergei Eisenstein. 2022 (1946). "*Ivan the Terrible's 'God is wonderful in his saints' (from the final part of Dmitry Bortnyansky's Concert 34)*" [35:03–37:13]. *YouTube*, May 27. Accessed April 28, 2023. https://youtu.be/vnNgoS8VsoQ.

Spielberg, Steven. 1993. *Jurassic Park*. Feature-length film, 127 min., *United States of America*.

MONTAGE
____

SCIENTIFIC MODELS
____

INFRASTRUCTURE STUDIES
____

WATERY ASSEMBLAGES
____

[5]

From the Construction Site via the Highway to the Guided Tour

Rebecca Boguska

This is a report of my research trip to the Large Wave Flume in Hanover, an indoor water channel used by coastal researchers and engineers to explore the effects of water movements on coastal areas. In three "stations," from the construction site, via the highway, to the guided tour, this essay offers a film studies perspective on the infrastructural assemblages of coastal research. Guided through these stations by the notion of montage—understood as a filmic technique, a filmic principle of perception, and a film studies method—I show how difficult it can be to tell where cinematic perception begins and where it ends.

 "Maybe you should go for a walk on our homepage, if you haven't done so already" (Kudella 2021).[1] This was the reply I received from Matthias Kudella, the deputy site manager of the FZK Coastal Research Centre in Hanover, to my e-mail request for a guided tour through the Large Wave Flume—an indoor water channel in which a steel plate generates waves that crash against a simulated coastline. To his invitation, Kudella added the following remark: "There's also a link to the construction site camera" (ibid.).

The following essay is a report of my research trip to the Hanoverian Coastal Research Center and the guided tours I took through its experimental milieus. However, this essay takes as its starting point not the guided tour itself, but Kudella's suggestion to take a glimpse at the Large Wave Flume via the construction-site camera. Progressing through three stations—from the construction site, via the highway, to the guided tour—this essay offers a film studies perspective on the socio-material assemblages of coastal research. In order to apply the disciplinary perspective of film studies to think through the research practices and media configurations employed by coastal engineers who explore the movements of water and their effects on coastlines, I must pose the following question: where does cinematic perception take place?

I argue that objects that are apparently non-filmic—that is, objects that do not necessarily consist of moving images—can nevertheless suggest a cinematic mode of perception to the spectator or visitor. To support this argument, I will introduce my thoughts on the coastal research center in Hanover with a brief foreword on montage and sequence.

---

1   All translations by author.

Montage and Sequence

Reading about an "[o]bsession with this search for cinematography outside cinema" (Bois 1989, 112) one might be led to speculate that as early as in 1989, the art historian Ive-Alain Bois was already predicting the developments within the field of film studies that would take place over the next 30 years. However, he is referring here to the obsession of Sergei Eisenstein, which later came to be an obsession shared by many scholars within the field of film studies in their writings on post-cinema (Hagener, Hediger, and Strohmaier 2016; Denson and Leyda 2016; de Rosa and Hediger 2016; Shaviro 2010), expanded cinema (Balsom 2013; Beckmann 2021; Youngblood 1970), useful cinema (Acland and Wasson 2011; Hediger and Vonderau 2009; Masson 2012), amateur (Zimmermann 2011; Schneider 2004; Slide 1992; Mattl et al. 2015; Norris Nicholson 2012) and scientific film (Curtis 2015; Curtis and Lue 2015; Feiersinger 2018; Gaycken 2015; Turquety 2019; Wellmann 2011). Bois' remark appears in the introduction to the English translation of "Montage and Architecture," an essay written by the Soviet filmmaker between 1937 and 1940 (Eisenstein 1989). In this posthumously translated and published text, Eisenstein not only connects the principle of montage to a filmic technique—the practice of cutting and gluing analogue film at the editing table—but also positions montage as a principle of cinematic perception.

A particularly broad understanding of the notion of montage forms the basis for Eisenstein's observation that the architectural assemblage of the Acropolis constitutes a "perfect example of one of the most ancient films" (1989, 117). Based on a deliberate and clearly provocative anachronism, for Eisenstein the immobile arrangement and architecture of the Acropolis is transformed into a film through the bodily technique of walking (Schüttpelz 2010) or the simultaneous activities of walking and watching. Eisenstein writes: "It is hard to imagine a montage sequence for an architectural ensemble more subtly composed, shot by shot, than the one that our legs create by walking among the buildings of the Acropolis" (1989, 117). The moving legs of the mobile spectator or traveler become part of the montage apparatus. The mental arrangement of the images and the accumulated impressions of the architectural sequence crystalize that which is already anchored within the architectural ensemble itself. As the art and architecture historian Martino Stierli observes, Eisenstein proposes a model of an embodied spectatorship that is based on the "sequencing of visual impressions" (Stierli 2020, 65), and it is the juxtaposition of these "visual impressions" recorded by our sensory apparatus that, according to Eisenstein, is central to the principle of montage. Only the comparison of images or impressions sets the architecture in motion; the mobile viewer or visitor thus transforms the Acropolis into a film, and their perception figures as a filmic recording and projection apparatus at the same time.

From the Construction Site...

The Acropolis is one of the oldest films, and as those who have visited it might know, a permanent construction site as well. At the time of my visit, in September 2021, the Hanoverian Large Wave Flume was a filmic construction site too. Despite being more than 200 kilometers away from the German coastline, it is also a milieu for coastal experimentation. Echoing Bruno Latour's reflection on the research practices of Professor Bijker and his team at the hydraulic laboratory in Delft, the researchers in Hanover also "find new ways to make the port mobile" (Latour 2009, 135). At 300 meters in length, 7 meters in depth, and 5 meters in width, the Large Wave Flume is one of the largest freely accessible wave flumes in Europe, and the visiting researchers can generate water waves up to 3 meters high there. The peculiarity of large wave flumes is that they enable the investigation of coastal phenomena at a 1-to-1 scale. As Stefan Helmreich rightly points out in "Domesticating Waves in the Netherlands," such "[p]hysical models have not vanished in the age of computers"

(2019, 156), a fact that becomes especially pertinent when looking at the role of wave flumes in the field of coastal research and engineering.

"The meeting of human and wave scale," as Helmreich writes, "signals a readiness to meet waves on their own terms" (ibid.). It also alerts us to the ways in which wave flumes in coastal research centers figure as places in which knowledge production and embodied knowledge appear in non-human entities, carried by and within the waves and by a wide range of "bodies of water" (Neimanis 2017). Throughout several experiments conducted in the Large Wave Flume, the researchers and technical staff expect to produce an almost identical arrangement of coastal phenomena in a stable and consistent indoor climate in order to conduct research on such mechanically generated waves. As the researchers have emphasized in our conversations, in the Large Wave Flume one encounters hardly any model and scale effects, which means that the modelling and scaling practices are assumed not to strongly affect the examined phenomena.[2]

When I visited the Large Wave Flume back in 2021, however, the wave sequences usually generated there were interrupted—since 2020, the facility had been a construction site. Nevertheless, the mobility that is fundamental to the coastal research project—the translation of a coastline into a full-scale laboratory model—was not halted. Rather, it had been temporarily replaced by the mobility of the construction site, enabled by an on-site time-lapse camera produced by the French company *enlaps*, which recorded the construction progress until the end of 2022, and was then disassembled (see fig. 1). According to the coastal researchers,

2   When it comes to the modeling and scaling practices of coastal phenomena, not all properties of water can be scaled down. Two examples that the researchers mentioned in the interviews were surface tension and the air bubbles which appear in the water when a wave breaks. Furthermore, one also has to consider the so-called "laboratory effects," which include "[b]oundary conditions," "[w]ave generation with a paddle," "[n]eglection of processes" (Schimmels 2020, 4).

[Figure 1] View from the Construction Site Camera at the FZK Coastal Research Center in Hanover (Source: my.tikee.io Platform 2021).

the main purpose of this camera was to document, record, and surveil the construction progress. At hourly intervals, from 6 AM to 6 PM, the camera photographed the view from the exterior of the hangar of the Large Wave Flume.

If it had not been raining and the lenses were not covered by rainwater, the visitors saw the changing positions of the cranes, excavators, the sun, cars, clouds, and less often, the changing

positions of human actors involved in the construction process.
The side-by-side view of two images from the two wide-angle
lenses of the *Tikee*-camera enabled a panoramic look at the
facade from left to right and from right to left.

Visitors to the online platform *my.tikee.io* showing the construction site were able to choose between three modes:
"Panoramic," "Before / After," and "Immersive." The "Before /
After" perspective allowed a comparison between the first and
the last recorded image, but the visitors were also free to choose
among the different images themselves. In this mode, the displayed images divided the screen into two sides: what the visitor
saw was a split screen.[3] The proportions of the split screen, which
are normally fixed in the cinema, were set in motion by the visitors of the platform. By clicking on the small circle visible in the
middle of the composite image, the border dividing the images
changed its position. Images and times were superimposed, and
time and space expanded through the movement of the visitor's
mouse.

"Space" as Doreen Massey writes in her essay "Traveling
Thoughts" is a "configuration ... of a multiplicity of trajectories.
The coexisting multiplicities and the necessary but incomplete (potential) interrelatedness which that entails give rise to
time and space together" (2000, 225).[4] She rightly argues that
it is not the histories or past events which continue to live on
in "the spatial surface of today;" rather, one has to reflect on
simultaneity *as* "'the spatial surface of today'" (Massey 2000, 228).

3   In the context of the coronavirus pandemic, it is no surprise that discourse
     on the mobilization and multiplication of split screens has acquired even
     more social relevance. As Malte Hagener argues, "Whereas before it was
     either the spectators that moved (as tourists, passengers, attraction vis-
     itors) or the images that showed movement ..., now both have been put into
     motion" (2020, 37).
4   I was directed to Massey's thoughts on time and space by Christina Lutter's
     essay "Baustellen in Wien: Ein kulturwissenschaftlicher Werkstattbericht"
     (2002).

This form of simultaneity crystalizing in everyday surfaces points us again to the principle of montage, and, at the same time, emphasizes the processual nature not only of construction sites, but of cinematic perception as well.

The processual nature of the virtual walks through the construction site that one could have taken thanks to the *Tikee*-camera shows that both the images themselves and the *my.tikee.io* platform belong to a much wider field of cultural representation: the "process genre" (Aguilera Skvirsky 2020). As Salomé Aguilera Skvirsky writes, the "process genre" runs through different histories, media, platforms, and includes a breadth of works spanning from Étienne-Jules Marey's chronophotographic images to industrial and educational films. The construction-site camera at the Large Wave Flume and the *my.tikee.io* platform showed a "sequentially ordered representation of someone doing something" (ibid. 2020, 2): they showed one workday in 13 images, one piece of infrastructure, multiple juxtapositions, and one attempt at montage.

The idea of process is also central to the coastal research practices carried out in Hanover. Stefan Schimmels, the site manager of the FZK Coastal Research Center, provided me with the following answer, when I asked him about the advantage of physical 1-to-1 models in wave flumes over numerical models:

> Numerical models are no more than the solution of mathematical equations and belong to the field of physics. The equations can only be as good as our understanding of the process. Here, we try to bring nature into the laboratory, the waves into the laboratory, the sand into the laboratory. But it doesn't mirror nature since in nature everything is three-dimensional. (Schimmels 2021)

Schimmels' statement echoes John Durham Peters' observation that "media are infrastructures that regulate traffic between nature and culture. They play logistical roles in providing order and containing chaos" (2015, 32). Conceiving of the wave channel

as infrastructure foregrounds the coastal researchers' idea that
their facility plays an important role in regulating the conceptual
traffic between the laboratory (as a site of cultural production)
and moving water (as a distinct, natural phenomenon), while
optimizing the protection of coasts from water movements.

Furthermore, the Large Wave Flume as an "enabling environment
… provide[s] the habitats" (Peters 2015, 46) for a wide range of
different measurement techniques and sensing technologies.
Nevertheless, in both the discussions with the researchers and
on the homepage of the FZK Coastal Research Center, the complex video system was highlighted as particularly relevant to
the improvement of the scientific understanding of processual
changes:

> Four of these cameras record 30 images per second …,
> another camera 300 images per second … With an appro-
> priate positioning of the cameras, the system also enables
> the photogrammetric recording of morphological changes
> and other processes that are subject to temporal and spatial
> development. (FZK 2021)

Interestingly, the construction-site camera also recorded the
morphological changes of the architecture as a simultaneously
temporal and spatial phenomenon; it rendered the trajectories
and movements visible, and, at the same time, it also altered
the mobility of the body of the spectator or visitor. For example,
the third mode of this construction site camera, "Immersive,"
automatically set the composite image into motion, so that the
visitors took a "walk" with their eyes from left to right over the
surfaces of the image in one illusory single camera pan. In all
three modes, the spectators or visitors took on the perspective of
a bird on a branch, and, floating in the air, came closer to the construction site through the techniques of zooming in and zooming
out. By clicking, moving, scrolling, zooming, by taking a walk with
the index finger and moving the eyes on the screen, the already
mobile body of the visitor became even more mobile.

... via the Highway...

The construction-site camera allowed one to visit the FZK Coastal Research Center without having to leave their living room or office. But how does one physically get to the research center in Hanover? If one has a car, one could choose the highway; if one does not own one, one can travel by train—two means of transportation that have permanently transformed the landscape of filmic images. The video artist and film theorist Harun Farocki visited the Large Wave Flume twice, and in the course of his second visit he filmed the opening sequence for *Images of the World, Inscription of War* (1988). The first time Farocki took the train, the second time he drove by car via the highway, the A2, which stretches itself from Berlin to Hanover. In his recently published essay "Irregularly, not haphazardly," Farocki reports on his journey as follows: "On June 18, 1987, we left Berlin in the very early morning to take the A2 to reach Hanover. Our goal there was the so-called wave flume, a test facility for researching water movements. ... It is my aim here to relate the wave flume and the highway, two words that came to me in one sentence" (2021a, 205).

One sentence, two types of infrastructure; one juxtaposition, and one attempt at montage.[5]

5   In response to the presentation of my postdoctoral project, entitled "Watery Assemblages," at the University of Zurich in November 2022, Volker Pantenburg pointed out that only a few weeks before his death, Farocki questioned the concept of montage in the context of computer-animated images by relating it to the notion of "navigation" (Farocki 2014). As the editors of the forthcoming e-flux journal issue "Navigation Beyond Vision" write: "Farocki briefly referred to navigation as a contemporary challenge to montage—editing distinct sections of film into a continuous sequence—as the dominant paradigm of techno-political visuality. For Farocki, the computer-animated, navigable images that constitute the twenty-first century's 'ruling class of images' call for new tools of analysis" (Aranda et al. 2024). The notion of navigation thus offers an interesting perspective on the construction site, the highway, and the guided tour as well.

If, as suggested by Eisenstein (1989), the notion of montage signifies not only a medium-specific technique, but a broad principle of thinking and meaning-making as well as a principle of perception, an embodied and mobile vision, then Farocki's writing (and printing) in combination with my reading experience are also examples of the practice of montage. Furthermore, according to Farocki, the highway that connects point A with point B has developed in such a way that it became "a piece of entertainment, and it was built in such a way that it offers a change to the driver's eye, as a series of images" (Farocki 2021a, 206). Thus, thanks to our moving perception, the highway also becomes a sequence of images of passing cities, landscapes, and signs.

Even if one decides to take the train to get to the Large Wave Flume in Hanover, the A2 cannot pass by the visitor unnoticed. The A2, which was the route for Farocki's second visit to Hanover with his camera team, sweeps past the coastal research center, and the cars and the constant traffic are acoustically present on site. The comparison of the experience of the highway with that of film thus does not end with the juxtaposition of images; listening is also central to Farocki's attempt at montage[6] and at relating these two infrastructure projects to each other. Farocki writes:

> When I came to Hanover in January, it was so cold that the water in the car's cooling systems froze, and the engines overheated and detonated. … When I was shown the video recordings of the flume in operation, the noise of the detonations came from the highway, as a result of the overheating engines due to the extreme cold. (Farocki 2021a, 207)

In January, due to low temperatures, no experiments were taking place at the Large Wave Flume. The scientific, administrative, and technical team, however, remained busy planning the

---

6   I would like to thank Fabienne Liptay for the suggestion that Farocki is conducting an acoustic montage.

  next projects. Nowadays, however, the car engines only rarely detonate.

In 1987, the frozen water, through its materiality and its physical properties, which caused the detonations, also functions as a link between coastal research and the highway. It is therefore not only the geographical coexistence of A2 and the Large Wave Flume, but also water, which at its freezing point became part of an acoustic montage. Water—which is also an environment in which mammals and fish live in oceans, lakes, and rivers—surrounds components of the engine, and usually flows from the top to the bottom: if the freezing point is reached, the engine overheats and detonates. It is precisely water in Farocki's storytelling that makes it so difficult to decide "where nature begins and artifice ends" (Peters 2015, 33). The research into the movements of water, the mobile coasts in the Large Wave Flume, and Farocki's fascination with frozen water seem to inscribe themselves into a movement of thought that makes precisely such things as water, construction sites, and highways so exciting. I share with Farocki and the coastal researchers this fascination with water and movement, and beyond that, I am interested in the translation efforts that encourage us to think of the traffic connecting one action (water freezing) to another (the disruption of motors or the pausing of research) as a mediated phenomenon—efforts that make this traffic graspable to us.

If we think further about the modeling practices that are of central importance to coastal research and engineering, it is interesting that not only "nature," as Schimmels has put it, is brought into the laboratory, but also that the modeling traffic runs in both directions. According to Farocki in his film *Wie man sieht* (1986) and his essay with the same title, highways built by the Federal Republic of Germany have been modelled after the shape of rivers. In the posthumously published essay, two images of different highways are accompanied by the following descriptions:

Figure 1 (Nazi Germany) shows a highway that runs towards
the horizon without a curve. Military roads are straight; the
Nazis built the highways for war.
Figure 2 (Federal Republic) shows a highway that compares
itself with a river, rivers take a natural course ... The Federal
Republic used the motorways for non-war. (Farocki 2021b, 41)

Two images, two descriptions, one comparison.

What the readers experience here is the montage effect, the
sequential juxtaposition of two images, of different times and
of politics of war and non-war, which in *Wie man sieht* (1986) is
part of a critique of surveying as a tool of colonialism. Seen in
this way, not only are the Large Wave Flume or the coast itself
naturecultures, where the demarcation between nature and
culture implodes (Haraway 2006, 110), the highway in the Federal
Republic of Germany is a natureculture *par excellence,* too. When
one recognizes the river and the streams of water in the winding
highway, in the flow of its traffic as well as the rustling of the
engines and air, then one sees it as one of the many "reinventions
of nature" (Haraway 1990, 140).

... to the Guided Tour

The way from *Fahren* (eng. *driving*) to *Führen* (eng. *guiding*) is short,
the latter derives itself from the former and thus resumes the
idea of movement and mobility. The guided tour evokes walking,
hiking, and being in motion, as well as the path which the water
might take. My body is also watery, as Astrid Neimanis states
in her book *Bodies of Water: Posthuman Feminist Phenomenology*
(2017, 7). Consisting of somewhere between 45% and 60% water
(Water Science School 2019), I also count it among what I call the
watery assemblages of coastal research. It is my watery body in
motion that becomes a filmic projection and recording device;
it too belongs among the phenomena I observe in my efforts to
understand coastal research practices. Here water figures as
a link as well. It is therefore not only important to consider the

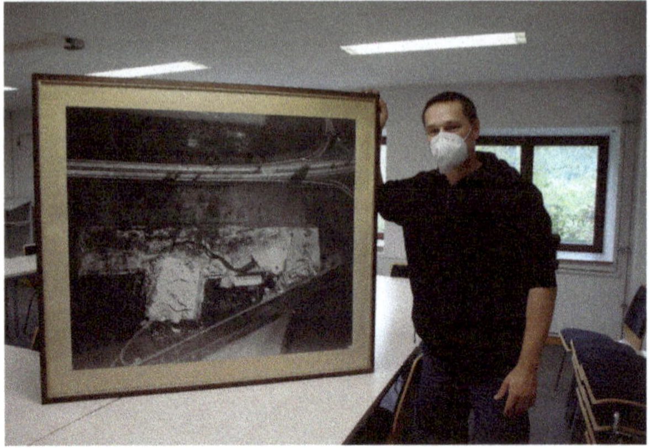

[Figure 2] A photograph showing Nils Kerpen holding a picture frame with an aerial view (ca. 1970) of the model of the Elbe (Source: Rebecca Boguska).

bodies of water researched in the centers and the media and narrative devices employed by the coastal scientists, but it is also crucial to reflect upon one's own relation to these research environments. As a watery body among other watery bodies, I will include a few thoughts on the co-documented self.

It was early in the morning of September 16, 2021, when I took the Intercity Express from Frankfurt am Main to Hanover and then took the subway to the Marienwerder district, where one can find the research facilities of the Ludwig Franzius Institute of Hydraulic, Estuarine and Coastal Engineering (LuFi) as well as the Large Wave Flume of the FZK Coastal Research Center. On the premises I was greeted by Nils Kerpen, LuFi's operations manager, and briefed on what I am allowed to photograph as well as on the timeline—namely that we had exactly one and a half hours for the tour. The dramaturgy of Kerpen's narration and tour began in a seated position, in a seminar room, and debuted with a photograph from the 1970s hanging in a picture frame on the wall (see fig. 2).

The photograph shows an aerial perspective of what used to be
on the same location: a hydraulic model of the Elbe, which is a
river that stretches itself across Germany at a length of over 1000
kilometers, and which in this picture frame is also accompanied
by the A2. When I was about to take a photograph of the aerial
view, Kerpen took the frame off the wall, put it down on a table,
and stood next to it. At this point, it became clear to me that not
only would the dramaturgy of the walk through the experimental
facilities be carefully considered and the movements precisely
choreographed, but also that the staging of the talking points
would be as important as the information communicated during
the tour about the research conducted at the center.

I hoped that on this day I would see wave flumes in operation
and would be given the opportunity to think about how the
movements of the scientists adapt to the movements of the
waves; how human, machine, and wave choreographies meet
or imitate each other, but this hope remained unfulfilled. When
you visit a coastal research center briefly, the research usually
pauses. Instead, I was led into various empty wave pools covered
with puddles and sand in order to receive an approximation of
the coastal research carried out here. Nevertheless, in connection with Kerpen's storytelling, the traces of water and sand
allowed me to experience the coastal research through a mental
montage. The physical walk through the empty experimental
facilities of coastal research was thus accompanied by this mental
montage of the movements of the machines, people, and other
watery bodies.

Two-Way-Traffic[7]

The traffic of thoughts from film to the construction site, to the
highway, and to the laboratory is accompanied by oncoming

7   I would like to thank Rebecca Schneider for our exchanges, which have
     inspired me to think about this traffic of thoughts as a two-way-traffic.

 traffic: film is also a construction site, a highway, and a laboratory. Here it is also difficult to decide where cinematic perception begins and where it ends. The traffic of thoughts that connects A to B, puts B in relation to A, configures A, B, C in an assemblage, and, to come back to Eisenstein's notion of montage, shows us that film studies can forge a path "across a multiplicity of phenomena, far apart in time and, gathered in a certain sequence into a single meaningful concept" (Eisenstein 1989, 116). Montage, as this essay tried to show, is thus simultaneously a filmic technique, a filmic principle of perception, and a film studies method of relational and network-based reflections on objects, infrastructures, and practices across time and space.

This article was written during a Postdoc.Mobility fellowship from the Swiss National Science Foundation (Grant Number: 206586).

Literature

Acland, Charles, and Haidee Wasson, eds. 2011. *Useful Cinema*. Durham: Duke University Press.

Aguilera Skvirsky, Salomé. 2020. *The Process Genre: Cinema and the Aesthetic of Labor*. Durham: Duke University Press.

Aranda, Julieta, Kaye Cain-Nielsen, Anton Vidokle, and Brian Kuan Wood, eds. 2024 (forthcoming). *E-Flux Journal: Navigation Beyond Vision*. London: Sternberg Press.

Balsom, Erika. 2013. *Exhibiting Cinema in Contemporary Art*. Amsterdam: Amsterdam University Press.

Beckmann, Marie Sophie. 2021. *Spilling: Undoing the Cinema of Transgression*. Dissertation Thesis. Unpublished.

Bois, Ive-Alain. 1989. "Introduction to Sergei M. Eisenstein: Montage and Architecture." *Assemblage* (10): 111–5.

Curtis, Scott. 2015. *The Shape of Spectatorship: Art, Science, and Early Cinema in Germany*. New York: Columbia University Press.

Curtis, Scott, and Robert Lue. 2015. "Bridging Science, Art, and the History of Visualization: A Dialogue between Scott Curtis and Robert Lue." *Discourse: Journal for Theoretical Studies in Media and Culture* 37 (3): 193–206.

De Rosa, Miriam, and Vinzenz Hediger, eds. 2016. Post-What? Post-When? Thinking Moving Images Beyond the Post-Medium/Post-Cinema Condition. *Cinéma & Cie* 16 (26/27).

Denson, Shane, and Julia Leyda, eds. 2016. *Post-Cinema: Theorizing 21st-Century Film*. Falmer: REFRAME Books.

Eisenstein, Sergei. 1989 (1937–40). "Montage and Architecture." Translated by Michael Glenny. *Assemblage* (10): 116–31.

Farocki, Harun. 2021a (1992). "Unregelmäßig, nicht regellos." In *Harun Farocki: Unregelmäßig, nicht regellos. Texte 1986–2000*, edited by Tom Holert, 205–12. Berlin and Köln: n. b. k. Diskurs.

———. 2021b (1986). "Wie man sieht." In *Harun Farocki: Unregelmäßig, nicht regellos. Texte 1986–2000*, edited by Tom Holert, 31–44. Berlin and Köln: n. b. k. Diskurs.

———. 2014. "Talk: Computer Animation Rules." *IKKM Weimar—IKKM Lectures*. Accessed August 9, 2023. https://www.ikkm-weimar.de/publikationen/video-audio/ikkm-lectures/computer-animation-rules/.

Feiersinger, Luisa, ed. 2018. *Scientific Fiction: Inszenierungen der Wissenschaft zwischen Film, Fakt und Fiktion*. Berlin: de Gruyter.

FZK. 2021. "Synchronisiertes Videosystem." *fzk-uni-hannover.de*. Accessed October 16, 2021. https://www.fzk.uni-hannover.de/de/das-fzk/ausstattung/gwk/messtechnik/videosystem/.

Gaycken, Oliver. 2015. *Devices of Curiosity: Early Cinema and Popular Science*. New York: Oxford University Press.

Hagener, Malte. 2020. "Divided, Together, Apart: How Split Screen Became Our Everyday Reality." In *Pandemic Media: Notes Toward an Inventory*, edited by Laliv Melamed, Philipp Dominik Keidl, Vinzenz Hediger, and Antonio Somaini, 33–40. Lüneburg: meson press.

Hagener, Malte, Vinzenz Hediger, and Alena Strohmaier, eds. 2016. *The State of Post-Cinema: Tracing the Moving Image in the Age of Digital Dissemination*. London: Palgrave Macmillan.

Haraway, Donna. 2006. "Encounters with Companion Species: Entangling Dogs, Baboons, Philosophers, and Biologists." *Configurations* 14 (1–2): 97–114.

———. 1990. "Investment Strategies for the Evolving Portfolio of Primate Females." In *Body Politics: Women, Literature, and the Discourse of Science*, edited by Fox Evelyn Keller and Mary Jacobus, 139–61. London: Routledge.

Hediger, Vinzenz, and Patrick Vonderau, eds. 2009. *Films That Work: Industrial Film and the Productivity of Media*. Amsterdam: Amsterdam University Press.

Helmreich, Stefan. 2019. "Domesticating Waves in the Netherlands." *Bomb* (146): 153–9.

Latour, Bruno. 2009. "Die Logistik der *immutable mobiles*." In *Mediengeographie. Theorie—Analyse—Diskussion*, edited by Jörg Göring and Tristan Thielmann, 111–44. Bielefeld: Transcript Verlag.

Lutter, Christina. 2002. "Baustellen in Wien: Ein kulturwissenschaftlicher Werkstattbericht." In *Die Werkzeugkiste der Cultural Studies: Perspektiven, Anschlüsse und Interventionen*, edited by Rainer Winter, Lothar Mikos, and Udo Göttlich, 63–84. Bielefeld: Transcript Verlag.

Massey, Doreen. 2000. "Travelling Thoughts." In *Without Guarantees: In Honor of Stuart Hall*, edited by Paul Gilroy, Lawrence Grossberg, and Angela McRobbie, 225–32. London and New York: Verso.

Masson, Eef. 2012. *Watch and Learn: Rhetorical Devices in Classroom Teaching Films after 1940*. Amsterdam: Amsterdam University Press.

124   Mattl, Siegfried, Carina Lesky, Vrääth Öhner, and Ingo Zechner, eds. 2015. *Abenteuer Alltag: Zur Archäologie des Amateurfilms*. Vienna: Synema.

Neimanis, Astrida. 2017. *Bodies of Water: Posthuman Feminist Phenomenology*. London: Bloomsbury Academic.

Norris Nicholson, Heather. 2012. *Amateur Film: Meaning and Practice, 1927–77*. Manchester: Manchester University Press.

Peters, John Durham. 2015. "Infrastructuralism: Media as Traffic between Nature and Culture." In *Traffic: Media as Infrastructures and Cultural Practices*, edited by Marion Näser-Lather and Christoph Neubert, 29–49. Leiden: Brill.

Schimmels, Stefan. 2020. "Large Scale Experiments in Coastal and Ocean Engineering: A Short Introduction to the Large Wave Flume (Großer Wellenkanal, GWK)." Unpublished PowerPoint Presentation. Forschungszentrum Küste (FZK).

Schneider, Alexandra. 2004. *"Die Stars sind wir": Heimkino als filmische Praxis*. Marburg: Schüren Verlag.

Schüttpelz, Erhard. 2010. "Körpertechniken." *Zeitschrift für Medien- und Kulturforschung* 1 (1): 1–20.

Shaviro, Steven. 2010. *Post Cinematic Affect*. Hants: O-Books.

Slide, Anthony. 1992. *Before Video: A History of the Non-Theatrical Film*. New York: Greenwood Press.

Stierli, Martino. 2020. "Verkörperte Zuschauerschaft: Zu Sergej Eisensteins Theorie architektonischer Montage." In *Film | Architektur: Perspektiven des Kinos auf den Raum*, edited by Johannes Binotto, 60–74. Berlin: Birkhäuser.

Turquety, Benoit. 2019. *Inventing Cinema: Machines, Gestures, and Media History*. Amsterdam: Amsterdam University Press.

Water Science School. 2019. "The Water in You: Water and the Human Body." *USGS: Science for a Changing World*. Accessed August 9, 2023. https://www.usgs.gov/special-topics/water-science-school/science/water-you-water-and-human-body.

Wellmann, Janina. 2011. "Science and Cinema." *Science Context* 24 (3): 311–28.

Youngblood, Gene. 1970. *Expanded Cinema*. New York: P. Dutton & Co.

Zimmermann, Yvonne, ed. 2011. *Schaufenster Schweiz: Dokumentarische Gebrauchsfilme 1896–1964*. Zurich: Limmat Verlag.

(Audio)Visual Material

Boguska, Rebecca. 2021. A photograph showing Nils Kerpen holding a picture frame with an aerial view (ca. 1970) of the model of the Elbe. September 16. Hanover.

Farocki, Harun. 1988. *Images of the World, Inscription of War*. 16 mm., 75 min., Germany.

———. 1986. *Wie man sieht*. 16 mm., 75 min., Germany.

my.tikee.io Platform. 2021. "Baustellenkamera: Großer Wellenkanal (GWK)." *my.tikee.io*. Accessed January 7, 2022. https://my.tikee.io/time_lapses/13926/photo_gallery/8640d20e-6312-4b12-ae76-7bd9b7609c50.

Other References

Kudella, Matthias. 2021. E-Mail Conversation. September 7.
Schimmels, Stefan. 2021. On-Site Conversation. September 16.

LABOR

EPISTEMIC TEMPLATES

CINEMATIC MEDIATION

DISCIPLINARY SYSTEMS

EDUCATION AND TRAINING

POST-INDUSTRIAL DISCIPLIN

6

Scripting Organizations: How Labor Is Becoming Cinematic

Guilherme Machado

As cinematic techniques become common mediators of labor-related knowledge in contemporary corporations, scripting practices assume a prominent role in the development of social, material, and cognitive interactions at work. This article addresses the epistemological implications of current organizational uses of cinematic techniques, particularly in professional training. After a brief overview of existing organizational cinematic practices in France, it provides examples of how cinematic-epistemic templates are produced to regulate the self-realization of efficient performance in the era of post-industrial labor.

Organizational Cinematic Practices

In 2016, the third edition of the video game *Défi ingénieur* (*The Engineer Challenge*) was launched by SNCF, the French national railway company. The game featured a series of engineering problems that the company was facing at the time. It was pitched as a near-impossible game in an attempt to grab the attention of engineering students and overcome the "notoriety problem"[1] of a wide range of intellectually challenging activities in the company. On their mobile screens, players plunged into a futuristic universe and followed storylines that engaged them in engineering issues related to renewable energy, big data, and 3D printing. 180 French *écoles* participated in the game, which was credited with a major increase of applications for positions in the company's Innovation Research & Development Department.

In the early 2000s, the French wine-producing region of Burgundy funded research to develop software to teach the pruning of vines. In view of the aging population of vineyard pruners, the program was commissioned to train a new generation of rural workers, not through the representation of prescribed behaviors, but through the training of "pruning reasoning." It offered a "didactic staging of work situations" (Caens-Martin 2005) and a series of visual scenarios that engage students with different stages of plant development, so that trainees could build relevant patterns of action on their own. The software was used in several farming regions of the country and inspired versions adapted to other agricultural sectors in Europe.

In 2013, in association with the Institute for an Industrial Safety Culture, a group of large French companies launched the Safety Academy, a shared platform of ready-to-use multimedia resources to support corporate "safety cultures" (Safety Academy 2023). The platform offers a rich collection of audiovisual

1   Personal interview with Marc Fraissinet, director of the advertising agency TBWA/Paris, on January 2, 2022. All translations by author.

material, from didactic animations to recorded conferences,
designed to facilitate educational meetings, analyze work situations, raise awareness to risk, foster preventive safety methods at the organizational level and cautious behavior at work. Currently, this platform is open to any company or manager wishing to make use of its resources for the management of local organizational cultures.

These examples of the use of moving-image apparatuses for recruitment, training, and knowledge-management in various companies, regions, and industrial clusters are clearly not isolated. In France alone, one could add a whole series of audiovisual tools used on a daily basis by companies such as Accor (hospitality), Air France (airline), AXA (insurance), BNP Paribas (banking), Bouygues (construction, real estate and telecommunication), Carrefour (retail), Danone (food), EDF (energy), L'Oréal (personal care), Michelin (manufacturing), Renault (automobiles), Sanofi (healthcare), TotalEnergies (oil and gas), and Veolia (water and waste treatment)—just to name just a few. In all these companies, moving-image apparatuses perform knowledge-mediation functions in the areas of sales, marketing, production, logistics, purchasing, finance, and/or related services.

Car salesmen in Renault stores receive part of their training through video games, as do financial advisors in BNP Paribas bank branches, while job seekers practice their job interviews with a free game offered by the French government agency Pôle Emploi. High school students, new hires in multinational companies, and trainee surgeons all enjoy access to increasingly sophisticated video databases to guide them and familiarize them with actual forms of labor.[2] A 2014 report revealed that the 40 companies represented on France's main stock market index, the

2   Meanwhile, in the United States of America, Walmart announced a project in 2018 to train one million employees with Virtual Reality. In association with the firm Strivr, the retail company designed scenarios to train cashiers to engage with customers, shelf fillers to recognize under-stocked aisles, store associates to manage peak hours, and so on (Pearson 2019). Immersive

 CAC40, routinely use up to nine video-based games of different sorts for recruiting, training, or managing internal knowledge (Allal-Chérif et al. 2014). It goes without mentioning that screen-based data visualization and communication tools have become crucial to labor organization across industries.

Along with these image apparatuses, a whole range of cinematic narrative *techniques* play a role in labor mobilization, increasing job performance, and organization. For those who still think that the practical knowledge of labor has little to do with the imaginary worlds of cinema, a simple look into contemporary organizations would help persuade them of how corporate "information networks" are densely populated by stories and emotional rhetoric worthy of Hollywood. When developing his theory of "sensemaking" in companies, the organizational psychologist Karl E. Weick (1995) argued for the use of narrative rhetorical models to complement the usual argumentative style of managerial discourse. For him, narratives have the capacity to improve organizational communication because "people think narratively rather than argumentatively" (Weick 1995, 127). For the organizational theorists Ian I. Mitroff and Ralph H. Kilmann, who pioneered this narrative organizational perspective, stories are "the spirit of organizations" (1976, 19). When engaging corporate stories have made their way through the networks of a company, they tacitly become part of its decision making and work planning processes.

Managers were quick to learn this lesson, and when audiovisual tools became widespread, they joined this narrative organizational perspective to cinematic practices in a more systematic way than had ever been done. In 1998, knowledge management experts Thomas Davenport and Lawrence Prusak reported on a series of organizational daily practices of cinematic storytelling:

> audiovisual technologies are currently highly valued by large corporations for mass training.

Many firms already do something like this when they send 131 videos to branch offices to be shown over lunch. In the past, they were likely to contain a speech or exhortation by a senior executive. Increasingly, though, firms distribute tapes that tell the story of an important business event, such as how a key sale was made. Knowledge is more likely to be absorbed if it adheres to the listeners' sense of ground truth, is delivered with feeling, and is placed in a context or frame that is at least partly shared by its audience. One well-known securities firm sends out a message every morning on its 'hoot and holler' network to all its brokerage agents, giving them what is called 'useful information' about a particular sale, an upcoming event, or some valuable piece of customer feedback. These messages almost always take the form of a story. At Verifone (a recently acquired subsidiary of Hewlett-Packard), where workers are widely dispersed around the world, stories of desirable business behavior are circulated electronically under the banner of 'Excellence in Action.' (Davenport and Prusak 1998, 82)

Besides the use of cinematic narrative techniques, a series of motifs from cinematic genres inform the modes of interaction at work and labor education. In its recruitment campaigns, the French National Gendarmerie draws on a body of narratological mechanisms to produce effects typical of comedy, action and documentary movies (narrative focalization and humorous breaks of expectation, heroic characters, thrilling car chases, empathetic testimonies, etc.), as well as on visual and editing techniques (unusual camera angles, tracking and aerial shots, slow motion, image/sound combinations, professional acting, fast cuts, etc.) to "inform" viewers about the organization's duties and activities.[3]

All these uses of cinematic techniques are certainly not new (Hediger and Vonderau 2009; Vignaux 2007), however, they are

3   See the YouTube channel of the Gendarmerie Nationale (2022).

 now becoming more frequent and more generalized than ever. They are also one of the allegedly innovative organizational methods that advocates proudly distinguish from old-fashioned forms of prescriptive education and hierarchical structures of power. All signs point to the fact that the future of labor requires cinematic techniques as a regular mode of knowledge mediation. To share a glimpse of a wider project of elucidating how cinematic techniques transform labor by making new regimes of discipline possible, let me take a few examples of professional training *dispositifs* that reveal some of the ways labor has become increasingly informed by cinema.

Scripting Educational Situations

One reason cinematic techniques now appear to be such relevant tools for the transmission of labor-related knowledge is that they can provide carefully designed images of *educational situations*. The circulation of standardized forms of productive behavior—as exemplified in the early 20th century by Frank Gilbreth's image-based management of efficiency (Curtis 2009; Hoof 2020; Price 1989)—is no longer the main organizational task assigned to images. Instead, managers and trainers today seek to provide aesthetic conditions under which operators can develop their own operational knowledge.

Ergonomic psychology, which developed in the last decades of the 20th century, has been both a driving theoretical force of this new framework for the organizational use of image technologies, and an indispensable practice of labor analysis for designing non-prescriptive didactic scenarios. Indeed, labor psychologists have promoted a reappraisal of the value of analyzing idiosyncratic conditions of labor in singular environments, which is opposed to the former conventional methods of analyzing labor as a manifes-tation of universal physiological laws (Rabinbach 1990). Largely influenced by Soviet theories of activity (Lev Vygotski and others), Western labor psychologists have stressed the importance of

taking specific social and material interactions into account **133**
in order to evaluate the *conditions of emergence* of effective
behavior.

Additionally, in contrast to the behaviorist tradition, which was
uninterested in the mental processes behind human action,
ergonomic psychologists investigate the mind at work by
analyzing the multiple, localized interactions among which the
cognition of workers is distributed (Bedny and Meister 1997;
Clot 1999; Rasmussen, Brehmer, and Leplat 1991). Such perspectives have brought forth new pedagogical trends that draw
on psychological analyses of labor environments to develop
customized professional-education *dispositifs*. As stated by one
labor psychologist, "How to build *the model of the situation that
will generate the relevant behavior*, what are the attributes of
this model, how to promote its development and maintenance:
these are questions that arise in [professional] training and that
cognitive psychology can help to answer" (Leplat 2002, 25; italics
added).

Psychological analyses of actual labor situations are now
commonly used by educators to design training scenarios. They
reveal specific settings and interactions that make real work
behaviors possible. "Professional didactics is based on labor and
its analysis as the starting point of training design. ... Learning
from situations and through situations is thus the first organizing
principle of professional didactic engineering" (Mayen, Olry, and
Pastré 2017, 470).

But these didactic engineers do not merely reproduce actual
labor situations by means of simulation (such *mimesis* would be
of little pedagogical interest). Instead, they break down actual
situations in order to create a progressive method of adapting
human performance to the needs of specific labor settings.
Their educational *dispositifs* are intended to stage "an organized
sequence of situations designed to support learning" (Pastré
2011, 257). To promote transitions from operational incapacity

134 to legitimate operational knowledge, they offer scripts of paths through *problematic situations*,[4] at the end of which trainees will have autonomously developed the conceptual resources for action and decision-making necessary to manage ordinary labor situations.

This is where the articulation[5] of educational and psychological practices with moving-image apparatuses becomes so useful. There are at least three fundamental contributions that digital moving images make to professional training as it is formulated by educators trained in the school of ergonomic psychology. First, moving-image apparatuses offer the possibility of a sensory (sometimes sensorimotor) activity within a figurative space of a "great plasticity" (Mellet-d'Huart and Michel 2005, 342). This means that visual, acoustic, linguistic, and even gestural interactions between trainees and their environment can take place within a *scripted space*, where aesthetic affordances are minutely programmable.

Secondly, and consequently, cinematic techniques of staging and composition allow educators to design a *pedagogical progression* based on a *mimetic progress* of representations in relation to reference situations. That is, cinematic images offer the possibility of recontextualizing a set of scattered, simultaneous, or contingent events that characterize actual labor situations within the deliberately arranged space-time of representation.[6] This means that cinematic techniques enable the fictional arrangement of interactional situations into steps of progressive

4   As explained by Pierre Pastré: "[W]e seek in work situations the spots where a problem arises. A problem exists when the procedures available to the operator are insufficient to control the situation" (2016, 23).

5   Here and throughout this article, I use a vocabulary borrowed from Bruno Latour's (2001; 2006) actor-network theory.

6   For René Amalberti, this cinematic asset raises important problems of scripting: "[t]his constriction of time and events, this acceleration of reality to make it express a range of pedagogical situations imposed in the time of the training exercise, is undoubtedly the main distortion of reality and poses a series of daunting difficulties in the construction of scenarios" (2011, 3).

complexity, gradually linking trainees to the signifying entities that make up their future work environments.

Finally, cinematic records allow for situational data collection. As an epistemic archive of a company's activities, this data can be mobilized anywhere and anytime to enact transformations of the company's human workforce.

The moving-image apparatuses I have addressed throughout this essay are digital and somehow "interactive." Physical interaction with these virtual spaces often appears to educators as a way out of "passive learning." Active learners are expected to engage in select environments to understand the wide range of *effects* their choices and actions have. Hence, the importance of algorithms for delivering simulated environmental responses to actions carried out by trainees. The "cinematic realism" sought by designers of training *dispositifs* is usually not primarily linked to the audiovisual support or content quality (i.e., to high-definition interfaces, richness of scenic details, etc.). Rather, this realism depends on the quality of *feedback scenarios* (Barot et al. 2013; Pastré 2016; Soler and Marescaux 2011). It is necessary for the environmental reactions experienced in the simulated environment to reproduce an interactive dynamic with the user that is as faithful as possible to the dynamics of their reference work situations, for *learning progress* is assumed to depend directly on the trainees' capacity to assess the environmental feedback generated by their actions.

Therefore, training *dispositifs* generally embody one of the fundamental cybernetic principles for building systems of efficient behavior *self-production*, as formulated in 1950 by Norbert Wiener: "effective behavior must be informed by some sort of feedback process, telling it whether it has equaled its goal or fallen short" (1989, 58). Accordingly, an *autopoietic* system of behavioral efficiency emerges from circuits linking workers to environments in which "positive" and "negative" reactions are made readable by the workers. Digital figures offer a *logistics* of information feedback and a precise *legibility* of the environmental metamorphoses that follow from user actions—since digital environments must always first be *cinematically scripted*.

Cinematic-Epistemic Templates for Situated Actions

In this context, cinematic knowledge stands for a capacity to read and assess the impacts of one's actions on a given environment. This capacity is cinematically informed insofar as it is enhanced by digital feedback scenarios.

In the aforementioned software designed to train vineyard pruners, the users' ability to visualize the consequences of their pruning decisions is configured by the software. Its *sequences of images* reduce the actual growth time of plants—which can last several years—to a few clicks. An algorithm simulates the development of the vines following the users' pruning choices, but also factors in the probability of various outcomes related to the growth characteristics of the vines, climatic and biological incidents affecting the plants, and the aging of the wood. Trainees quickly realize what constitutes "incorrect" pruning-reasoning, as the software simulates their interaction with a multiplicity of agents involved in the dynamic process of plant development over time. "The construction of probable growth and development scenarios is thus organised according to different temporalities," as the researcher who developed the scenarios explains (Caens-Martin 2005, 88). The pedagogical interest of the software is that it "compresses the response time of the plants" (Caens-Martin 2005, 101). Trainees can thus adjust their pruning strategies based on the developmental fictions produced by the software. These fictions eventually build up the users' "own" ability for self-assessment.

Feedback loops generating self-regulatory performance processes are conceived according to the capacity of cinematic and image techniques (scripting and coding) to encompass the dynamic interactions that define a given labor environment. To get an idea of the complexity of carrying out cinematic translations of vague and minute interactions into visible (and often quantifiable) data, it is worth looking at another example, this one related to the education of surgeons.

Surgery is currently a leading area for the development of professional training technology, since like piloting aircraft and other high-risk activities, it involves a multitude of actions that need to be performed efficiently. Today, there are several companies offering screen-based surgical simulators with a view to standardizing operating procedures and performance.[7] In laparoscopic surgery training,[8] simulators apply algorithmic geometry models for the representation of anatomical surfaces. Their visual interfaces are connected to haptic force-feedback systems, thus ensuring accurate calculation of surgical performance and objective assessments of the trainees' compliance with official safety thresholds.

A simulator such as ULIS [Unlimited Laparoscopic Immersive Simulator], developed by the German company Karl Storz, allows the use of identical replicas of laparoscopic instruments for simulation. Its software provides a series of clinical scenarios arranged in an orderly and didactic series of training modules (Soler and Marescaux 2011). For a delicate exercise such as the introduction of the instruments into the patient's body, for example, once the gestures have been performed, the simulator indicates whether the instruments have crossed a blood vessel or organs that they should not have crossed, and whether or not they have achieved their objectives. It features the exact percentage of pathological

7   For example, Surgical Science in Sweden, Simbionix in Israel, Karl Storz in Germany, or the Simsurgery in the USA.
8   Laparoscopy is a type of telesurgery that involves the introduction of an optical cable into the body of a patient, which requires extensive training. The patient's internal cavity and the surgeon's actions can be observed on a screen.

 cells collected (in the case of biopsy training), or the percentage of pathological tissue destroyed (in the case of thermal ablation training). Unlike previous training methods on living animals that did not provide clear visual feedback on the trainee's accomplishments, the digital simulator gives the trainees accurate feedback on the multiple effects of their actions: "[the simulator] incorporates an automatic assessment mode providing the student with a quick and clear view of the progress they are making as they learn" (Soler and Marescaux 2011, 109).

However, cinematic training *dispositifs* do not simply display data that remains concealed in traditional training methods. They do not just make explicit what was implicit in the progress of apprentices before the arrival of digitally designed figures and finely calculable simulated gestures. Cinematic techniques *stage* interactive situations, i.e., they compose, build, arrange, and code the responses of fictional environments. In so doing, they *select* the items that generate feedback information and *frame* the meaningful domain within which individual performance assessments can happen.

This selective staging practice can be evidenced by controversies among educational scriptwriters. There is not always consensus on what interactive elements should be featured in learning scenarios. Dr. Bin Zheng from the Department of Surgery of the University of British Columbia stated that an important interactive component in an operating room and an essential aspect of a surgeon's expertise, *vigilance*, was not featured or assessed in training simulators: "[w]hen observing surgical performance, it is noticeable that the senior surgeon usually keenly detects signs that may concern patient safety" (Tien et al. 2011, 658). To overcome this flaw in training scenarios, Zheng and his colleagues experimented with a scenic and technical complement that added an interactive item to the training sets—a screen where the patient's vital information was displayed, and a mobile gaze tracker to detect the frequency and duration of glances the trainees took towards this screen. This addition, he argued, allows for a calculation of *how vigilant the trainees are.*

If Zheng's proposal is to be incorporated into training *dispositifs*, we would obviously have a slightly different cinematic template[9] for trainees to assess their performance compared to simulators that do not provide any means to read "vigilance." Or to put it differently, one could say that if apprentice surgeons are to be aware of their patients' safety cues, it is best not to rely on occasional reminders from their instructors: what is more reliable is to reconfigure the cinematic templates they use to train, to assess their own skills, to regulate their performance, and to prove (to others and to themselves) their "vigilance" as an integral part of demonstrating their expertise.

Beyond controversies about what should be included in the cinematic settings for learning particular kinds of labor, other disputes may also be noted regarding the *mise en scène* and the narrative effects of educational fictions. Scriptwriters of cinematic-epistemic templates are also careful directors of their audience's *emotional experiences*. Under the influence of contemporary labor psychology, they strive to "avoid the ruinous dualism of the cognitive and the emotional" (Clot 2008, 4).

This is apparent in the training of surgeons as well as other professionals whose "emotions" are most unquestionably involved in the efficiency of their "reasoning," from firefighters (Clifford et al. 2019) to office workers (Tichon and Mavin 2016). What Wiener once called a "feedback process" (informing a behavior whether or not it has achieved its goal) is also conceived by educational scriptwriters in its figurative details, as these are deemed to determine the trainees' emotional involvement with the outcomes of their activity.

9   The term "template" is used here in the sense of a roughly stable format that can be used by an indeterminate number of users (learners). For an approach to media formats as templates and their epistemic functions, see Jancovic, Volmar, and Schneider (2020).

 Indeed, accidents due to clumsiness are often a source of serious psychological shock for surgical trainees. This is at times inevitable in the case of training on living animals. By contrast, digital simulators risk producing an opposite effect on the emotional economy of apprentice surgeons: in the absence of adverse effects, there is a risk that cinematic training results in recklessness and the "trivialisation of patient death" (Soler and Marescaux 2011, 110).

This problem of balancing shock and indifference requires didactic programming to manage the progress of affective interactions during surgical simulations: "we do not want the student to be immediately confronted in the first exercise with the handling of a hemorrhage, which is introduced in the 5th and 6th exercises" (Soler and Marescaux 2011, 110). Thus, even if the simulator in question does depict a hemorrhage due to an error in the first exercises (since it must faithfully respect the dynamics of actual labor situations), this depiction is not made *in the same way* as it is at the end of the training period. The solution found by the didactic engineers is grounded in the possibilities of cinematic *staging*:

> We therefore believe that the immediate feedback of the gesture's effectiveness and its consequences must be provided in a pedagogical and progressive way. Thus, this feedback can be *textual* in an initial learning phase, indicating for example to the student that their gesture would have led to a hemorrhage, then simulated in a realistic way in an advanced learning phase, by *simulating for example the bleeding* caused by the error. (Soler and Marescaux 2011, 111; italics added)

Here, a program incorporating both cognitive and affective interactions of trainees with their labor environment is designed through cinematic staging techniques. The plan of a media infrastructure lays the ground for the trainee to develop an autonomous capacity for action. Cinematic images, in all their plastic and semiotic variety, in all their combinations and semantic effects, become as essential to reproducing an experience of "efficiency" as to sensing the "seriousness" of a mistake.

The Tacit Regulation of Labor

Cinematic templates for professional education act as effective regulators of how apprentices recognize progress in their own performance. By mediating learners' interaction through standard figurative environments that respond to the trainee's actions according to specific patterns of visibility and legibility, they normalize paths of self-improvement and produce normalized means of performance assessment. The design of cinematic templates can thus provide a basis for self-development of performance capabilities on a massive scale.

In this context, the more cinematic techniques extend the audiovisual legibility of workplace dynamics, the more the self-production of efficiency expands across the zones shaped by cinematic feedback. The practices of scripting, staging, and coding that make cinematic-epistemic templates must then be recognized as disciplinary practices of a new sort, all the more effective because they make the shaping of operational knowledge appear as a result of an autonomous effort of activity regulation, while cinematic inputs remain largely unacknowledged, i.e., a tacit epistemic infrastructure.

Instead of considering the operational knowledge of post-industrial labor as strictly "personal knowledge," as readers of Michael Polanyi in management (Baumard 1999) or economic notions such as "human capital" (Machlup 1984) invite us to do, interactive digital learning tools show that operational knowledge is largely embodied in labor environments, and that cinematic techniques can create epistemic conditions for the docile adaptation of workers. These image apparatuses attest to an organization of labor by virtue of cinema's power to effect a deliberate pre-organization of sensibility. Evidently, cinematic creation has become an integral part of the disciplinary systems of labor.

Literature

Allal-Chérif, Oihab, Mohamed Makhlouf, and Armand Bajard. 2014. "Les Serious Games au service de la gestion des ressources humaines: une cartographie dans les entreprises du CAC40." *Systèmes d'information & Management* 19 (3): 97–126.

Amalberti, René. 2011. "Préface." In *Améliorer la pratique professionnelle par la simulation*, edited by Philippe Fauquet-Alekhine and Nane Pehuet, 1–4. Toulouse: Octarès.

Barot, Camille, Domitile Lourdeaux, Jean-Marie Burkhardt, and Kahina Amokrane. 2013. "V3S: A Virtual Environment for Risk-Management Training Based on Human-Activity Models." *Presence: Teleoperators and Virtual Environments* 22 (1): 1–19.

Baumard, Philippe. 1999. *Tacit Knowledge in Organizations*. London: Sage.

Bedny, Gregory, and David Meister. 1997. *The Russian Theory of Activity: Current Applications to Design and Learning*. New York: Psychology Press.

Caens-Martin, Sylvie. 2005. "Concevoir un simulateur pour apprendre à gérer un système vivant à des fins de production: la taille de la vigne." In *Apprendre par la simulation: De l'analyse du travail aux apprentissages professionnels*, edited by Pierre Pastré, 81–106. Toulouse: Octarès.

Clifford, Rory M.S., Sungchul Jung, Simon Hoermann, Mark Billinghurst, and Robert W. Lindeman. 2019. "Creating a Stressful Decision Making Environment for Aerial Firefighter Training in Virtual Reality." In *Proceedings. 26th IEEE Conference on Virtual Reality and 3D User Interfaces*, 181–9. Piscataway: NJ IEEE.

Clot, Yves. 2008. *Travail et pouvoir d'agir*. Paris: PUF.

———. 1999. *La fonction psychologique du travail*. Paris: PUF.

Curtis, Scott. 2009. "Images of Efficiency: The Films of Frank B. Gilbreth." In *Films that Work: Industrial Film and the Productivity of Media*, edited by Vinzenz Hediger and Patrick Vonderau, 85–99. Amsterdam: Amsterdam University Press.

Davenport, Thomas, and Laurence Prusak. 1998. *Working Knowledge: How Organizations Manage What They Know*. Boston: Harvard Business School Press.

Hediger, Vinzenz, and Patrick Vonderau, eds. 2009. *Films that Work: Industrial Film and the Productivity of Media*. Amsterdam: Amsterdam University Press.

Hoof, Florian. 2020 (2015). *Angels of Efficiency: A Media History of Consulting*. Translated by Daniel Fairfax. Oxford: Oxford University Press.

Jancovic, Marek, Axel Volmar, and Alexandra Schneider. 2020. *Format Matters: Standards, Practices, and Politics in Media Cultures*. Lüneburg: Meson Press.

Latour, Bruno. 2006 (2005). *Changer de société: Refaire de la sociologie*. Translated by Nicolas Guilhot. Paris: La Découverte.

———. 2001 (1999). *L'espoir de Pandore: Pour une version réaliste de l'activité scientifique*. Translated by Didier Gille. Paris: La Découverte.

Leplat, Jacques. 2002 (1992). "Les aspects cognitifs dans la formation." In *Psychologie de la formation: Jalons et perspectives*, edited by Jacques Leplat, 25–52. Toulouse: Octarès.

Machlup, Fitz. 1984. *Knowledge: Its Creation, Distribution and Economic Significance. Volume III: The Economics of Information and Human Capital.* Princeton: Princeton University Press.

Mayen, Patrick, Paul Olry, and Pierre Pastré. 2017. "L'ingénierie didactique professionnelle." In *Traité des sciences et des techniques de la formation*, edited by Philippe Carré and Pierre Caspar, 467–82. Paris: Dunod.

Mellet-d'Huart, Daniel, and Georges Michel. 2005. "Faciliter les apprentissages avec la réalité virtuelle." In *Apprendre par la simulation: De l'analyse du travail aux apprentissages professionnels*, edited by Pierre Pastré, 335–54. Toulouse: Octarès.

Mitroff, Ian I., and Ralph H. Kilmann. 1976. "Stories Managers Tell: A New Tool for Organizational Problem Solving." *Management Review* 64: 18–28.

Pastré, Pierre. 2016 (2005). "Apprendre par la résolution de problèmes: le rôle de la simulation." In *Apprendre par la simulation: De l'analyse du travail aux apprentissages professionnels*, edited by Pierre Pastré, 17–40. Toulouse: Octarès.

———. 2011. *La didactique professionnelle: Approche anthropologique du développement chez les adultes.* Paris: PUF.

Price, Brian. 1989. "Frank and Lillian Gilbreth and the Manufacturing and Marketing of Motion Study, 1908–24." *Business and Economic History* 18: 88–98.

Rabinbach, Anson. 1990. *The Human Motor: Energy, Fatigue, and the Origins of Modernity.* Berkeley: University of California Press.

Rasmussen, Jens, Berndt Brehmer, and Jacques Leplat, eds. 1991. *Distributed Decision Making: Cognitive Models for Cooperative Work.* Chichester: John Wiley.

Soler, Luc, and Jacques Marescaux. 2011. "Simulation chirurgicale virtuelle: les premiers pas d'une nouvelle formation." In *Améliorer la pratique professionnelle par la simulation*, edited by Philippe Fauquet-Alekhine and Nane Pehuet, 91–114. Toulouse: Octarès.

Tichon, Jennifer G., and Timothy Mavin. 2016. "Using the Experience of Evoked Emotion in Virtual Reality to Manage Workplace Stress: Affective Control Theory (ACT)." In *Integrating Technology in Positive Psychology Practice*, edited by Daniela Villani et al. Hershey: PA Information Science Reference.

Tien, Geoffrey, Bin Zheng, and Stella Atkins. 2011. "Quantifying Surgeons' Vigilance during Laparoscopic Operations Using Eyegaze Tracking." In *Medicine Meets Virtual Reality 18*, edited by James D. Westwood, 658–62. Amsterdam: IOS Press.

Vignaux, Valérie. 2007. *Jean Benoît-Levy ou le corps comme utopie: une histoire du cinéma éducateur dans l'entre-deux-guerres en France.* Paris: AFRHC.

Weick, Karl E. 1995. *Sensemaking in Organizations.* Thousand Oaks: Sage.

Wiener, Norbert. 1989 (1950). *The Human Use of Human Beings: Cybernetics and Society.* London: Free Association Books.

(Audio)Visual Material

Gendarmerie Nationale. 2022. *Gendarmerie Nationale* [Official YouTube-Channel]. *YouTube*. Accessed August 6, 2022. https://www.youtube.com/c/Gendarmerienationaleofficiel.

Safety Academy. 2023. *Safety Academy: Safety Culture Resource Centre*. Accessed April 24, 2023. http://safetyacademy.icsi-eu.org/dashboard/guest.aspx.

POLYGRAPH

MATERIALITY

LIE DETECTION

POPULAR CINEMA

VISUAL ITERATION

TACIT KNOWLEDGE

7

Iconic Materiality, or the Ambivalent Fascination of Cinematic Lie Detection Depictions (in Germany)

Bettina Paul and Larissa Fischer

Popular ideas about lie detectors are dominated by the image of the polygraph machine. The iconic old suitcase polygraph is a vital part of North American film history and it still has not lost any of its visual power today. The imagined function of the polygraph as a lie detector is not just part of a vivid visual narrative, but has also influenced actual fields of research and practice, even in Germany. Here, tacit knowledge (Collins 2001) about the supposed, or even imagined, abilities of the polygraph works in reciprocal ways, even though its depiction stands in contrast to the actual knowledge in the field. We argue that the cinematic images of the polygraph test and their implied fictional

 knowledge support the credibility of both scientific and applied lie detection by grounding them in an analog materiality.

Merciless Investigators: American Movies and German Practice[1]

You're more familiar with the procedure from old American feature films: the accused is wired up, a merciless investigator whips out his trick questions, and soon after the polygraph signals its incontrovertible verdict. As a human being, one feels mercilessly exposed to the technology—cruelly. (Berger 2017)

This statement was made by a German judge who uses polygraph testing in court. Judges, researchers, and legal psychologists who engage in lie detection via polygraph examinations are affected by the cinematic portrayal of lie detection, even though they distance themselves from it. Their disciplinary background and their practice differs fundamentally from what they see on the screen, and yet they are still affected by popular American imagery of lie detectors. How is this possible?

The entanglement of the cinematic depiction and the actual practice of lie detection goes way back. Leonard Keeler and William Marston, two key figures in the early development of the polygraph, were heavily entangled with the motion picture industry. Marston repeatedly employed his lie detection test for audience testings and even wrote a manual for screenwriters (Alder 2009, 187ff.). Keeler followed Marston to "[monitor] the viewers' physiological reactions" (Alder 2009, 188) of the

1   The research underlying this paper was conducted as part of the project "From Polygraph to Brain Scan: Continuous Attractivity and Sociotechnical Reconfiguration of Lie Detection" (project code HE6448/5-1) funded by the German Research Foundation. All translations from German into English are by the authors.

[Figure 1] Leonard Keeler playing himself in *Call Northside 777* (Source: Alder 2022).

pre-screenings; Keeler also played himself in the 1948 movie *Call Northside 777* (Hathaway 1948) (see fig. 1).

Portrayals of interrogations that made prominent use of polygraph machines were especially vivid in 1930s genre films featuring newspaper reporters, private investigators, and gangsters, as well as in "jailhouse movies," genres which culminated in the film noir of the 1940s. Such films established Hollywood's position against crime (Denzin 2008, 107–8; Moonkin and West 2001; on the detective genre in general, see Thomas 2003). These classic films consistently portray an interrogation protocol that is also found in contemporary thrillers like *Snowden* (Stone 2016), sci-fi movies like *Blade Runner* (Scott 1982), or dramas like *Blackkklansman* (Lee 2018), even though the genres in which this protocol is featured are more diverse today.

The image of the antiquated suitcase polygraph has become interchangeable with the idea of a lie detector due to its vital role in the North American film history. Even though off-screen the analog polygraph has mostly been replaced by its digital descendants, the image has not lost any of its visual power today.

 The imagined operation of this device, which developed into a vivid visual narrative, can also be found in corresponding fields of actual research and practice, even in Germany.

The use of polygraph in Germany has been a subject of controversy since the first attempt to introduce one in a court case, which occurred with the support of the US Army in 1954. The polygraph had its peak in the 1990s, when many child-abuse cases had to be scrutinized, leading a dozen legal psychologists to undergo training to become polygraph examiners. Following few of restrictive rulings by the Federal Court of Justice (Bundesgerichtshof), very few psychologists still practice polygraph examinations in a legal context, primairly in family law cases. If polygraph examinations are used in penal cases, they are only permitted to facilitate exonerations and are never employed as incriminating evidence. The opposite is true in the US context. There, polygraph examinations are done by police officers, state agents, probation officers, and many others, while psychological expertise is less prevalent. In practice, this means that the polygraph is primarily used for motivating confessions in preliminary proceedings. Thus, German and US practice are applied in opposite contexts and to opposite ends. For this reason, the practice of polygraphy is not very well known in Germany, and the prevalent public knowledge about it comes only from movies, foremost North American movies.

One iconic representation of a polygraph machine in use comes from a comedy. In the motion picture *Meet the Parents* (Roach 2000), Jack Byrnes (Robert De Niro) subjects his future son-in-law, Greg Focker (Ben Stiller), to a lie detector test and asks him embarrassing questions such as whether he has ever watched pornographic films (see fig. 2). Even before the younger man is able to give an answer, the needles of the analog polygraph to which Greg Focker is connected during this interrogation produce frantic lines on the paper that De Niro's character is reading. This interrogation scene underlines various assumptions that can be found in the collective imaginary about what a polygraph test consists of. Some of these assumptions came to the foreground when we talked to polygraph practitioners in Germany.

Cinematic Iterations of Polygraphs as Tacit Knowledge

The iteration of certain images throughout the history of film facilitates their entrance into the collective memory of the viewing public, for whom these images become shared symbols. The reiteration of a practice in a particular context—like consistently showing the use of polygraph machines in interrogations instead of research or medical settings—stabilizes a knowledge-image relationship through its naturalization (Nohr 2014, 305). The highly discursive practice of the on-screen world is naturalized as a seemingly undeceitful, direct, and truthful depiction of the real world. This also fits the way that the sociologist Norman Denzins characterizes early cinema's dependence on the epistemological framework of scientific realism (2008, 92).

The Secret Service Context

One of the reiterated depictions of polygraph use links it to clandestine services. Jack Byrnes turns out to be a former CIA agent who keeps his intelligence equipment, including a polygraph ensemble, in a secret chamber of his house. In this context, the polygraph scene conveys the notion of an unequal balance of power between the characters. The skeptical father turns out to be skeptical by profession. In applying a lie detector test to his future son-in-law, he takes the ultimate position of power to rule on the trustworthiness of his counterpart.

In Germany, lie detection is a subject of experimental research in neuroscience. Scientists in this field prefer to use the terms "deception detection" or "memory detection" instead of "lie detection." They aim to find the most valid testing protocols by using the same strict parameters as are used in polygraph

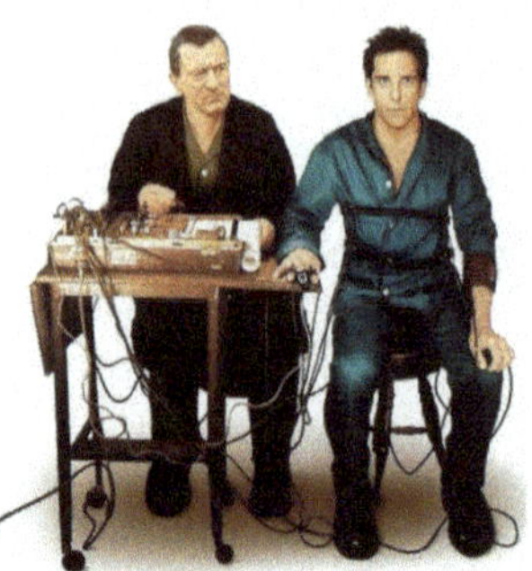

[Figure 2] Excerpt from *Meet the Parents'* movie poster (Source: IMDb 2022).

testing, but the researchers focus on experimenting with various questioning protocols within mock crime scenarios. It is important to note that this basic research has no direct affiliation with the psychological practice that deals with real cases. The scientists critical reflections on the practical field speaks to the power imbalance which is often reiterated on film:

> In the classic application, it's also an instrument of power in the situation that someone has such a machine. And if you look at the situation in the Ben Stiller films, where he is polygraphed by the father-in-law, who sits in his CIA cellar somehow in front of his machine, and of course only he sees the machine and the other person is helplessly turned away somehow and at the mercy of the machine. So, this power situation, I think, also plays a role in the application (Researcher 2).

The judges we talked to who request polygraph examinations also referred to the power imbalance within the court setting. The dim, cramped, bunker full of secret-agent stuff that is the setting for the polygraph interview in *Meet the Parents* is quite similar to the spaces where contemporary polygraph tests take place. The setting and décor is effective in itself, structuring relations and expectations. One judge pointed to the effect that the court

building has on the interviewee, showing us the special hearing
room with "heavy, soundproof doors," (Judge 26) where the
participants can be isolated. That this room is part of the court
house "shouldn't be underestimated. There are men and women
running around in black robes" (Judge 26).

The judges invite psychological experts to conduct the procedure
in the rooms of the court house. For the legal psychologists, the
handling of the test protocol and the psychological experience
of the interview are central aspects of a successful examination,
and judges praise the work of the psychologists as a kind of art.
This tacit knowledge of the experts (Collins 2001) is embodied in
a skillful ritual; the intuition and sensitivity of the psychologist
is key to the process. In one of the most intense descriptions, a
judge compared the examination carried out by the psychologist
to a cathartic experience. He very vividly described how the
interviewees would sweat out everything, making it feel like
a cleansing process to be interviewed in this manner. This
bears some resemblance to the way intelligence operatives
are perceived: as skilled experts in interrogation practices who
provide the opportunity for a cathartic experience through
confession.

The notion of power exists furthermore in the collective
imagination that surrounds the practice, and, specifically, the
device. The lawyers, judges, and psychologists talked with dis-
comfort about the association of the polygraph with CIA interrogation methods, as well as with spy films, and, in both cases,
with the fact that the collective imagination has embedded "lie
detection" within North American practices. One judge estimated
that many were opposed to the polygraph because they had this
image in mind that the device would be used like a torture rack,
where a person would be forced to say something. The image
of being strapped to a polygraph machine bears some resemblance to more coercive images, such as being forcibly restrained
in a chair. This can provoke vivid imagery, like that described by
the historian John Baesler: "[S]uch is the aura of intimidation

 attached to the machine and the rickety curves it produces when hooked up to a body" (2018, ix). Baesler describes the ways in which the polygraph was used as a "spector of totalitarianism" during the cold war, which points to a more forceful and extremely power-laden practice. In *Meet the Parents*, Jack Byrnes represents the state as a former special agent who uses his power as the future father-in-law to scrutinize Greg Focker, who gives in voluntarily. In fact, Greg has no option to refuse, if he wants to be on good terms with his future parents-in-law. It is this unequal situation that underlies the power dynamic between the two characters involved in a polygraph test—between the one who is strapped with a thoracic belt around the chest that measures the frequency and depth of his breathing and the one who controls the situation, directs the procedure, and decides when it ends and whether it was a success. In Germany, however, the procedure is used in court only if it is requested by persons who see it as their last chance to prove their innocence. And even though this reverses the whole situation, the collective imagination in Germany has not been influenced by the very different legal situation. In the public view, it remains laden with power.

The Antique Machine: "This Old, This Polished Thing with the Chrome"

In contemporary portrayals, the polygraph "machine" is merely a notebook or a laptop, but the staging of the test and the performance thereof is still clearly identifiable. In *Meet the Parents*, despite its contemporary setting, the characters use—in Jack Byrnes' words—"an antique polygraph machine." The reason for using the analog device might have something to do with the fact that De Niro plays a retired agent who loves the gadgets from his former job. However, we want to argue that this choice has more to do with cinema's longstanding fascination with the old equipment.

Most polygraph examiners today no longer use analog devices, since handling them distracts from the questioning practice. The analysis of the measurements though is done by hand out of a lack of trust in the precision of the analytic software. Professional polygraph examiners are confronted by film studios who ask them to show their devices, and who expect to see an analog machine. For them, the viewer's ability to identify the device as a lie detector is crucial. A regular notebook will not provide the visual power of the reiterated image of a lie detector scene.

The expectations the film industry has of polygraph examiners are self-sustaining. On many occasions, we were referred to old black-and-white North American movies, "where you are tied to a electric-powered device" (Judge 28), since these films were believed to be responsible for popularizing preconceived notions about polygraph practices. "I know this only from … from American TV-series, this old, this polished thing with the chrome" (Judge 30), stated a judge. In addition, it is believed that other judges, prosecutors, and lawyers acquired their knowledge of polygraph practices only through their exposure to North American black-and-white films, which were part of their social upbringing. For the judges, the connotation of the "old" device as something solid, "accountable," and "down-to-earth" is decisive for the entire procedure. It is often compared to an old watch, of which the mechanical clockwork is the dependable part.

Some legal psychologists were repelled by the reiterated images that they were confronted with. One legal psychologist criticized his laboratory for resembling too closely the US American picture of an intelligence agency and portrayals of the FBI, in particular—even though this is how a regular laboratory looks. It is here that the cinematic depiction of secret agents resembles the experimental psychologist's actual setting—both look similar, but have little in common in terms of what actually takes place. The dominant cinematic image produces "templates in the head," as one legal psychologist phrased it, which prompt ideas of the test that he resents, since they have nothing in common with the German practice. He even thought of changing the interior of his examination room in order to avoid prompting such comparisons

 (Psychologist 12). Others, however, are compelled by the thought of gaining more publicity by corresponding to this image. A private investigator who works with a digital polygraph thought of buying an analog machine just "for the performance, just as a show." (PI 24)

The recognition of a piece of technology as a lie detector is just one aspect of the reiterated imaginary of the *antique machine*; its specific material form is another. Judges are also enchanted by its optical and tactile features and specific manner of functioning. The antique object "signals precision, it signals technology" (Judge 26). It was described as "compelling," "forceful," and especially compared to the digital version, "something, that you can mentally comprehend" (Judge 26). In its analog materiality, it gives the impression that the observer can actually understand what the device does according to the following scheme: "This are all things … I can touch, I can understand" (Judge 26). This seemingly simple, clear cut statement is actually quite complex. Once trust in the device is established, one can ascribe an "expected acting" to the device (Wagner 1994, 151). The expectations of the analog device arise from its material functionality: the visible recording of the transmitted measurements. "The machine works; that's not a question. It is there. It works" (Judge 26). The tactile and seemingly comprehensible quality of the old polygraph machine is emphasized by the fact that the reiterated image always portrays a freestanding device. This view of the polygraph strongly resembles the self-recording systems of 19th-century physiology (De Chadarevian 1993, 272), which embodied the ideal of mechanical objectivity (Daston and Galison 2007). Even the anachronistic analog polygraph which is used today is electrically, not mechanically, operated. Nevertheless, the twitching ink (or thermal) writers seem to render the reactions of the person being tested immediately visible. Moreover, they feed into the idea that there is a direct transfer of the subject's physiological reaction to the paper readout.

The transformations of this signal disappear. The human deter-
minations of cut-off values that influence how the measurements
are taken and even the inevitably necessary adjustments in the
course of operation are obscured by the conviction that the
apparatus produces results without human intervention.[2]

But even with a psychologist's explanation of how various values
are interpreted, it is difficult to understand from the multiple
lines recorded on the printout how the measurement actually
takes place, and on what basis. To actually see a polygram means
not being able to understand what it actually means. Seeing the
measurements in their specific visual dynamic makes compre-
hension impossible (Denzin 2018, 113). To think that seeing is
knowing, and more so—understanding—proves to be an illusion,
an illusion nourished by an "imagined instrument" (Littlefield
2011, 9) that is, as Melissa Littlefield shows, shaped by popular
cultural ideas and desires for an independent truth machine.

Utilizing the "Capacity to Suspend Disbelief"[3]

The iterative cinematic representation is also the basis for familiarity with the polygraph in Germany, where its actual use is
largely unknown. The device's prevalence on the screen not only
promotes recognition of the machine, but also implies a certain
familiarity with how it is used. David Kirby (2010) calls these kind
of devices "diegetic prototypes," by which he means the cinematic
creation of familiarity with a certain technology, wherein one
becomes accustomed to its usage even before it is encountered
in reality. The representation of polygraphs establishes a belief
in the functionality of these machines as lie detectors, which
may be sustained alongside a real skepticism about the depicted
practice. Furthermore, the idea of being able to detect lies and
to find out the truth has a historical fascination that contributes

---

2   For an intensive discussion on the "anachronistic progress" in the field of the
     German polygraph practice see Paul, Fischer, and Voigt (2020).
3   See Alder 2009, 188.

 to belief in the technology despite all the skepticism. This supposedly ambivalent view of the polygraph can be summarized as a parallel trust (belief in) and distrust (skepticism) of a technique.

This skepticism is even taken up by Greg Focker in the polygraph scene of *Meet the Parents*, when he says that "these aren't a hundred percent accurate, right?" His skepticism is immediately dispelled by Jack Byrnes, who replies, "you'd be surprised how accurate they are." This ambivalence is also observed by researchers who work in the field of lie detection, and who struggle with the public images and imaginaries that cinema perpetuates about the polygraph.

Legal psychologists in particular are not fond of the cinematic portrayals, since the dominance of the device and the simplification of the procedure obscures the real importance of the psychologist's expertise and the role of the test protocol. Researchers who study "lying" also push back against the notion of "lie detection."

Despite skepticism about the label "lie detector" and "lie detection", all of those who engage with the field of lie detection make use of the existing ambivalence. Skepticism towards the technology is based on the belief in its autonomous functioning and the fear of the empowerment of technology over humans. This apparent contradiction of trust and skepticism with regard to the device is actually a functional component of the polygraph test procedure. This procedure includes a so-called number test, which is important for generating belief in the device, but which necessitates the concealment of the actual process at work. The test subject connected to the device is asked to select a number in a given range. The subject is then shown individual numbers, and when their number is reached, they are asked to deny that this is the number they have selected. The subject's psychophysiological reaction to this "lie" (the denial of the correct number) is used to demonstrate that an accurate interpretation can be made via the physiological measurements of the device throughout the test procedure. Therefore, it implies that the subsequent, actual questioning procedure will be just as successful.

Confidence in the procedure is established through the persona of the expert as well as the successful demonstration of the number test. The subject undergoing the text can, once convinced, expect the actual test to be effective. From the legal psychologists point of view, this is "the big mistake, everyone thinks the device does it now" (Psychologist 8). But the experts take advantage of this fallacy. In the course of a long preliminary discussion and the number test that follows, the expert tries to reduce any fears in order to "bring [the device] back to the foreground, so to speak, and also instill confidence in the person who operates it" (Psychologist 8).

Neuro- and biopsychological researchers also make use of the polygraph when interacting with the media, during public events, or when advertising their discipline to students. In these contexts, they play with what they anticipate to be the collective image of lie detection, and use the polygraph module to attract students to their specific field of study. The polygraph and the specific number test that legal psychologists use nourish the illusion of simplicity and clarity as well as that of comprehensibility. Herein lies the tacit knowledge instilled by the cinematic portrayal and the fascinating ambivalences that surround the device.

Appropriated Fictional Knowledge

The case of Germany is interesting, since here the polygraph test is traditionally discredited. Neither the procedure for using the instrument, nor the fact being confronted with one are part of common experience. The cinematic image alone offers a certain familiarity in the sense of Kirby's (2010) diegetic technologies, which, however, seems foreign and does not permit to draw any conclusions about the practice in Germany.

[Figure 3] Authors' own image from field research

Those references from the field that draw on the cinematic portrayal—the power imbalance, the material significance, and the ambivalence of belief and skepticism—all refer to a specific fascination with "old technology." This speaks to a traditional cultural appropriation (Hård and Jamison 2005, 163), which values the authenticity of the so-called "antique."

The analog polygraph is an epistemic object, a multi-channel writer that simultaneously measures and records several peripheral physiological parameters, and which psychological researchers have used for various types of experiments (see fig. 3). Yet cinema only depicts these machines in a law enforcement context. The tacit cinematic knowledge that this reiterated image produces contains a specific dialectic, which shows itself in the way that practitioners struggle with the public image of a dominant machine, while, at the same time, making use of exactly this misconception. The cinematic image of the polygraph test helps psychologists to build trust in the capabilities of the device as well as helping neuroscientists to attract students and the wider public to their field of research. In both fields, there is a playful utility to the visual representation of the polygraph that prompts the sociotechnical imaginary of a truth-machine that can produce objective results.

The tacit cinematic knowledge has a valuable impact on the effectiveness of the test procedure but also within the realms of the cinematic depiction. It works here through the reiterated popular representations of the polygraph. The scene is repeated, retold, and has its own status within actual, scientific practice.

The cinematic representation engages predominantly with the antique polygraph machine and has popularized it as an epistemic object. We are living in times of a dematerialization of technology through automation and digitization: everything is defined by function and no longer by matter (Berr 1990). The polygraph's portrayal, however, highlights the relevance of materiality, since the belief in its function is based on its haptic, acoustic, and visual presence.

Where the void of matter begins, the imaginative irreplaceability of materiality takes hold through the persistent image of the analog polygraph as the ultimate lie detector. In its antiquated form, it produces belief in the process. The polygraph owes this belief to the cinema, and even practices that distance themselves from the "false idea" of the polygraph actually employ cinema's imagery. As Alder rightly observes, "The lie detector cannot be killed by science, because it is not born of science. Its habitat is not the laboratory or even the courtroom, but newsprint, film, television, and of course the pulps, comic books, and science fiction" (2009, 251). The example of polygraph portrayals in Germany shows a theoretical tension not just between film and science, but also, furthermore, between how fictional knowledge becomes relevant in an actual practice, especially one that is disputed.

Literature

Alder, Ken. 2022. "The Lie Detectors: The Lie Detector at the Movies." *Kenalder.com*. Accessed August 31, 2021. http://www.kenalder.com/liedetectors/movies.htm.

———. 2009. *The Lie Detectors: The History of an American Obsession*. New York: Free Press.

Baesler, John Philip. 2018. *Clearer Than Truth: The Polygraph and the American Cold War*. Amherst/Boston: University of Massachusetts Press.

Berger, Jens. 2017. "Werden Verbrecher in Sachsen bald mit Lügendetektor überführt?" *TAG24. Accessed March 5, 2019*. https://www.tag24.de/nachrichten/sachsen-gericht-luegendetektor-erlaubt-verboten-verhoer-richter- bautzen-forderung-beweismittel-369179.

Berr, Marie-Ann. 1990. *Technik und Körper*. Berlin: Dietrich Reimer Verlag.

Collins, Harry M. 2001. "Tacit Knowledge, Trust and the Q of Sapphire." *Social Studies of Science* 31 (1): 71–85.

De Chadarevian, Soraya. 1993. "Graphical Method and Siscipline: Self-Recording Instruments in Nineteenth-Century Physiology." *Studies in History and Philosophy of Science* 24 (2): 267–91.

Daston, Lorraine, and Peter Galison. 2007. *Objectivity*. New York: Zone Books.

Denzin, Norman K. 2008. "Die Geburt der Kinogesellschaft." In *Ethnographie, Kino und Interpretation—die performative Wende der Sozialwissenschaften*, edited by Rainer Winter and Elisabeth Niederer, 89-136. Bielefeld: Transcript Verlag.

Hård, Mikael, and Andrew Jamison. 2013. *Hubris and Hybrids: A Cultural History of Technology and Science*. New York: Routledge.

Kirby, David A. 2010. "The Future is Now: Diegetic Prototypes and the Role of Popular Films in Generating Real-World Technological Development." *Social Studies of Science* 40 (1): 41–70.

Littlefield, Melissa. 2011. *The Lying Brain: Lie Detection in Science and Science Fiction*. Ann Arbor: The University of Michigan Press.

Mnookin, Jennifer L., and Nancy West. 2001. "Theaters of Proof: Visual Evidence and the Law in Call Northside 777." *Yale JL & Human* 13: 329–90.

Nohr, Rolf F. 2014. *Nützliche Bilder: Bild, Diskurs, Evidenz*. Münster: Lit Verlag.

Paul, Bettina, Larissa Fischer, and Torsten H. Voigt. 2020. "Anachronistic Progress? User Notions of Lie Detection in the Juridical Field." *Engaging Science, Technology and Society* 6: 328–46.

Thomas, Ronald R. 2003. *Detective Fiction and the Rise of Forensic Science*. Cambridge: Cambridge University Press.

Wagner, Gerald. 1994. "Vertrauen in Technik." *Zeitschrift für Soziologie* 23 (2): 145–57.

(Audio)Visual Material

Hathaway, Henry. 1948. *Call Northside 777*. Feature-length film, 112 min., United States of America.

IMDb. 2022. "Meet the Parents." Movie poster. *IMDb*. Accessed August 8, 2022. https://www.imdb.com/title/tt0212338/mediaviewer/rm1335233536/.

Lee, Spike. 2018. *Blackkklansman*. Feature-length film, 135 min., United States of America.

Roach, Jay. 2000. *Meet the Parents*. Feature-length film, 108 min., United States of America.

Scott, Ridley. 1982. *Blade Runner*. Feature-length film, 117 min., United States of America.

Stone, Oliver. 2016. *Snowden*. Feature-length film, 134 min., United States of America.

REPRODUCTIVE TECHNOLOGIES

VISUALIZATION

FEMINISM

EMBODIED KNOWLEDGE

AGENCY

8

"When Pregnancy Becomes a Moving Picture": Negotiating Tacit Cinematic Knowledge in Fetal Ultrasonography

Claire Salles

Pro-life activists publicly use moving images of fetal ultrasounds to equate fetuses with life, targeting pregnant persons' rights such as the right to abortion, surrogate pregnancy, and adoption at birth. Feminist scholars have highlighted how anti-abortionists capture the cinematic features of moving images of fetal ultrasounds. In this essay, I deepen their insights by arguing that giving meaning to fetal moving images requires cinematic knowledge. But, when facing the "blobs" (Haraway 1997, 26–27) in these images, tacit cinematic knowledge also requires mediation by a trained echographer. Drawing on ethnographic studies, I show the coexistence of multiple and conflicting

 interpretations of moving images of fetal ultrasounds and analyze the ways in which this tacit cinematic knowledge is being negotiated.

The many communities of practice who are held together around the technofetus are by no means necessarily in harmony.
— *Donna Haraway*

June 2022, a landmark decision of the US Supreme Court held that the Constitution of the United States does not protect the right to abortion (Dobbs v. Jackson Women's Health Organization 2022). This ruling overturns Roe v. Wade (1973), which had guaranteed the right to abortion at the federal level since 1973. Each state will now be able to adopt its own legislation and may decide to illegalize the voluntary interruption of pregnancy. Many have already done so. When access to abortion is restricted, racialized persons, the LGBTQ+ community, young people, lower income families, people with disabilities, and people who identify as women are the most strongly affected. The US decision, however, runs counter to recent developments around the world on this issue. Over the past two decades, more than 50 countries have adopted less restrictive abortion laws, sometimes recognizing the essential role abortions play in protecting the lives, health, and rights of persons able to gestate. In this essay, I feel, think, and work on the visual politics of pregnancy from a feminist perspective. Fetal ultrasound imagery is appropriated in many ways—if there is a negotiation, it is because there are power relations and struggles at play. The equation of "moving image of a fetus = life = restriction of abortion rights" is not the only interpretation of moving ultrasound images, nor should it be. Let us multiply the tacit modes of knowledge associated with ultrasound imaging (cinematic, and otherwise) and spread feminist narratives around this technology.

Importantly, the development of 3D and 4D visualization
technologies since the mid-1990s increased the resemblance
between images of fetuses and images of babies, leading to
the rise of private, non-medical ultrasound studios. Before the
advent of these technologies, the association of the fetus' visibility with the juridical status of the fetus as a person had already
been widely discussed, mainly in the context of feminist defenses
of abortion rights (for recent syntheses see Hopkins, Zeedyk, and
Raitt 2005; Taylor 2008; Roberts 2012). In the US, anti-abortionists
use fetus images publicly. For example, the widely distributed
pro-life film, *The Silent Scream* (Dabner 1984), features fetal ultrasound images which are being shown by a doctor to illustrate
that abortion is painful for fetuses. The film's medical biases
have been widely criticized (New York Times 1985), as has the
decontextualized visual knowledge upon which the film depends
(Givner 1994).

Feminist scholars have analyzed how pro-life activists' public
insistence on using fetal images forged the idea of fetuses as
autonomous living subjects that should be endowed with rights
that supersede those of pregnant persons.[1] The art historian
Anne Higonnet writes: "Ultrasound images encourage us to
ignore the bodies of pregnant women, not to mention women's
financial and social circumstances. Under what real conditions
will the woman carrying the fetus conclude her pregnancy, give
birth, and raise a child? The form of ultrasound images convinces
us these issues are irrelevant" (Higonnet 2017, 134). Barbara
Duden (1993), a medical historian and gender-studies scholar,
emphasizes that fetal images had become a projection screen
for the equation "fetus = life." This use of fetal images indeed

---

1   I choose to talk about "pregnant persons." Using "Women" risks invisibilizing pregnant persons who do not identify with this gendered language.
"Mothers" suggests that every pregnancy ends in birthing a living child, and
that all pregnant persons will take care of the child, invisibilizing abortion,
miscarriage, adoption at birth, and surrogate pregnancy. Using "Pregnant
persons" resists the power relationships maintained by patriarchy.

 risks blurring the intelligibility of bioethical debates on rights to abortion, surrogate pregnancy, anonymous childbirth, and abandonment at birth. It also raises questions relating to neo-eugenics, perceptions of functional diversity, and illness.

In Germany, non-medical fetal ultrasound practices are known as *Babyfernsehen* (eng. *baby television*), *Babykino* (eng. *baby cinema*) or Babyviewing. Why suggest that the screen shows a "baby" rather than a fetus? Why refer to cinema and to television (where tele- and fern- mean "remote")? Do we see a baby, as if from afar?

The idea of treating fetal ultrasonography as a cinematic experience is quite common in feminist pro-choice literature, but it has not yet been fully analyzed. Higonnet spots the need for an analysis of prenatal images by image specialists. For her, it is urgent to reaffirm that images are not what they represent (Higonnet 2017, 128). Does the "fetus = life" equation indeed rely on the biased equation, "fetus moving image = baby"? As early as 1987, the political scientist Rosalind Pollack Petchesky wrote: "every image of a fetus we are shown ... is viewed from the standpoint neither of the fetus nor of the pregnant woman but of the camera" (1987, 269–70). Speaking about the point of view of the camera in relation to ultrasonography may seem confusing. There is no camera. The ultrasonic waves are transmitted from the exterior of the belly, pass through bodily substances, and echo back to a receiver, which allows the echographer to measure the fetus and other abdominal masses. This is sound transformed into visual information. Furthermore, a fetal ultrasound screen displays multiple windows. Grids of screenshots frame the central, moving image. The screen also features letters and numbers such as date, name of the pregnant person, name of the medical center, and various measurements.

The idea of tacit cinematic knowledge provides a fruitful lens through which to analyze the assimilation of moving images of fetuses to early manifestations of life (and thus, rights). As the editors of this volume define it, this is "implicit, informal, and uncodified knowledge acquired in, with and through film and cinema that informs cultural and social practice outside the cinematic dispositif" (Boguska et al. 2019, 1).

In this essay, I will first describe the cinematic features of the fetal ultrasonography display. These features may be used by anti-abortion activists in order to naturalize the equation between fetus and life, but they are also acknowledged by pregnant persons outside the pro-life political movement. In the second section, I will show that these cinematic features are not obvious: for an untrained eye, it can be hard to distinguish a coherent and isolated image of the fetus. Giving meaning to the fetal moving image thus requires the mediation of a medically trained person who incorporates tacit cinematic knowledge.

Below, I gather ethnographic studies on the discourses that surround fetal ultrasound images in order to show that the equation "fetus moving image = life" is not the only interpretation pregnant persons have of their ultrasound experiences. Multiple and conflicting understandings of fetal ultrasound moving images are built through human and non-human interactions, which are mediated by discourses about pregnancy, parenthood, and disability. These interactions cannot be understood as univocal; they are situated in power relationships. I assemble these studies in order to highlight that—and how—tacit cinematic knowledge is being negotiated throughout these discourses.

Beyond the domain of fetal imagery, considering how tacit cinematic knowledge is negotiated in the fields of med-ical diagnostics opens up paths of inquiry about the audio-visualization of processes and phenomena usually invisible to the naked eye, and shows more broadly that tacit cinematic knowledge is constructed and politically conflictual.

Tacit Cinematic Features in Fetal Ultrasound Moving Images

How does the equation "fetal moving image = baby = life" work? What can be learnt from considering it through the lens of the cinematic illusion of life?

At first sight, fetal ultrasonography's history does not seem to be related to the history of television or cinema. At the beginning of the 20th century, ultrasound technology was first used to track submerged icebergs, and during World War I, to search for enemy submersibles. As a medical technique, it was introduced into obstetrics in the US in the 1950s (Donald, McVicar, and Brown 1958), and was popularized in the 1970s. Most European and North American states reimburse three obstetric ultrasonograms during pregnancy. Medically speaking, their only purpose should be to determine the anticipated date of delivery, detect illnesses or anomalies, and to anticipate complications during delivery.

It used to be common for doctors to give a tape with the 2D recording to the pregnant persons, in addition to a required number of snapshots printed on paper. This practice decreased as the medical field tried to differentiate medical ultrasounds from entertainment. An anonymized doctor, quoted in a 2005 French report on sonography, stated that "[p]ractices have become healthier, there is no more ultrasound cinema" (Moyse and Diederich 2005, 38). This insight suggests that giving a tape with the recording was considered entertainment ("cinema") for the pregnant person. In Germany, since January 1, 2021, ultrasound examinations that are not medically justified are prohibited. The new regulation is intended to protect embryos from an unnecessary, excessive dose of radiation. The fetus is considered a person who cannot consent to the examination and its possible side effects, and who does not derive any benefit from it (Aerzteblatt 2020).

Duden talks about "the public fetus" when showing how ultrasound images gained cultural meaning beyond their medical use and came to represent life. This equation of fetus images with life has been used by anti-abortion activists to restrict access to abortion. In doing so, they aimed to shift the recognition of the emergence of human life from the moment of birth to the moment of conception (Duden 1993).

But the equation "moving images of fetal ultrasounds = life" is not confined to anti-abortion activism; it also infuses other viewing practices of ultrasound images. What is specific to the anti-abortion deployment of moving images of fetal ultrasounds is the political agenda of rolling back the right to choose what is right for one's own body. The distribution of the tape by doctors and the spread of Babycinema studios support viewing practices of ultrasound images where the moving images of fetal ultrasounds is associated, in anticipation, to the life of a new family member. The medical anthropologist Janelle S. Taylor shows that the distinction between medical and entertainment is not confirmed by the observation of social practices (Taylor 2008, 144–168). Whether old 2D images or recent 3D or 4D ones, these visualization technologies seem to bring the image of the fetus ever closer to that of the first cinematic portrait (Mitchell 2001; Roberts, Griffiths, and Verran 2017). Introducing an anticipated new member of the family through moving images of fetal ultrasounds pushes back the limits of the family film beyond even films of a delivery itself.[2]

The trend of introducing the fetus as a new family member highlights a fundamental misunderstanding. From a medical standpoint, fetal ultrasounds aim to detect anomalies, a practice which can lead to abortion, whereas Babycinema aims to create family bonds (see fig. 1). The ultrasound studios' advertisements are clear: The Pregnancy Studio in the US states that they "bring

2   Roger Odin (1995) showed that family films are used to reinforce family as a
     fundamental social structure.

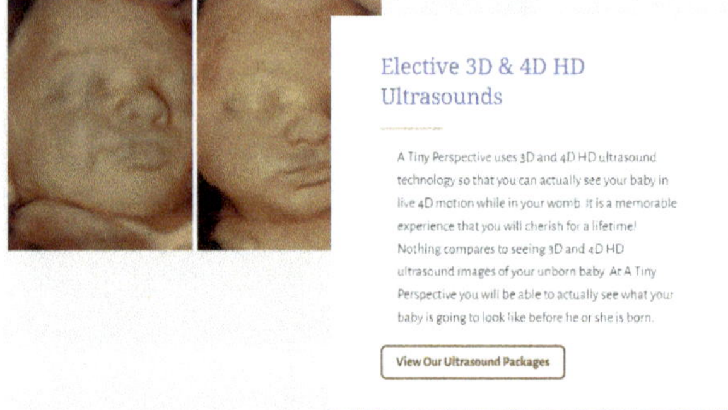

[Figure 1] Advertising for a babycinema studio (Source: A Tiny Perspective 2021).

unbelievable images of your unborn baby to life" (The Pregnancy Studio 2023), and the Baby Skan Studio's motto in the UK reads: "[w]here the miracle of life meets modern technology" (The Baby Skan Studio 2023).

What is it in the ultrasound display that permits the association of these moving images with the life of a new family member (for studios and their clients), or with the life of an already-human being endowed with rights against pregnant persons (for anti-abortionists)? I want to deepen Duden's insight: fetal moving images are not by themselves evocative of life. They need the mediation of cinematic features already *tacitly* associated with life. I argue that five cinematic features are activated during an ultrasound examination:

1. The setting of the room: the echographer and the pregnant person (and eventually relatives) look at the screen of the ultrasound machine; sometimes, a second screen is installed so that the pregnant person and relatives can view the images more comfortably.
2. The contents visible on the screen(s): still images derived from the ultrasonic echoes are shown at a quick pace, giving an illusion of continuity and movement (although the movement is often jerky).

3. The scale: the image is enlarged to accommodate human perception (Higonnet 2017, 130–33).
4. The timing: moving images are seen "live" as the sensor touches the skin.
5. The intermediality: the sight of the moving images is reinforced by the sound of the heartbeat.

Seeing Babies in "Blobs"

Donna Haraway emphasizes how hard it is for untrained eyes to decipher what she calls "the blobs" of a fetal sonogram: "[t]he televised sonogram is more like a biological monster movie, which one still has to learn to view even in the late twentieth century" (Haraway 1997, 25). It seems that we cannot see much in a fetal ultrasound image, unless we are told what we are supposed to see. It is therefore paradoxical that the association "fetus = life" relies on the illusion of reality, even though untrained people cannot decipher it without additional help. Even in 4D, one has to differentiate between the colors in order to form a coherent, isolated image of the fetus. This is why anti-abortion activists tend to prefer using easily readable free-floating digital representations of fetuses when suggesting the presence of life. This mirrors what they have done with the work of the Swedish photographer Lennart Nilsson. In 1965, Nilsson published a series of photographs in *Life* magazine, which have been considered the first photographs of fetuses (Nilsson 1965). The purpose was to show the invisible processes of embryonic life, but what he actually photographed were aborted embryos. The artificial setting required to create the illusion of life was not indicated in the article. These images were immediately used by anti-abortion activists because they did not require a trained medical expert to be deciphered.

According to Duden, pregnant persons of the late 20th and early 21st century are accustomed to seeing what they are told to see rather than bringing their own images and experiences to the table. Michelle Stanworth (1987) and Jana Sawicki (1991) develop the idea that reproductive technologies are means for the medical and scientific communities, dominated by men, to appropriate reproductive capacities. In "The Mind's Eye," Evelyn Fox Keller and Christine R. Grontkowski (1983) trace the privilege of sight in Western scientific and philosophical culture, showing that knowledge production through visualization and objectification has long served as a basis for gender binarism and hierarchy. Correspondingly, sensory, bodily experiences were denigrated as modes of knowledge. Duden fears that as a result of these historically entrenched practices, pregnant persons lose their ability to communicate experiences of pregnancy beyond the visual form.

We might now better understand why Petchesky calls for seeing fetal images from the point of view of pregnant persons, and not from the supposedly neutral point of view of the camera, which is an aspect of male visual power (Mulvey 1975). Analyzing reproductive freedom from the point of view of the affected groups is necessary, and we need situated knowledge in science studies to do so (Haraway 1988).

Conflicting Interpretations

Fetal ultrasound images are not deciphered univocally. What happens when we see fetal images from the perspective of pregnant persons? Ethnographic studies have demonstrated the "ambiguity" (Stephenson 2016) of interpretations of fetal images, equating them not only to "life," but also to death, seeing the fetus in some cases as a monster and a threat to the pregnant person, related to the fear of disability. Interpretations go from "just a fetus" to "my baby" (Petchesky 1987), and include a wide range of metaphors: person, future, family, choice, origins, nation (Haraway 1997).

On the one hand, Marcel O'Gorman, a media theorist who accompanied his pregnant wife to an exam, describes the fetus as an alien: "[t]he silent, wispy, slow-moving image of this semi-human shape had the aura of a cryptic message from an alien world, or perhaps from the afterworld" (2003, 155–56). On the other hand, Tsipy Ivry (2009) shows that in the Israeli context, the predominant idea surrounding pregnancy is risk and pregnancy is seen as something temporary. Multiple ultrasound exams and a battery of tests accompany the possibility of late-stage abortions. Pregnant persons and relatives build strategies to not get attached to the fetus: not giving it a name during pregnancy, ignoring movements, not preparing the bedroom, providing for delivery of nursery purchases only after birth. She quotes a participant in her study: "[i]f I felt a movement I ignored it, I felt nothing. … if they told me that the fetus has a terrible disease and that I have to abort it, what then?" (Ivry 2009, 204). In Japan (Ivry 2006) and Vietnam (Gammeltoft and Nguyen 2007), fetal sonography is not so much about the fetus, but about the pregnant person. Checking on the fetus is a way for pregnant persons to adjust their diet or resting time if needed, suggesting that pregnant persons play an active role in their pregnancy.

Scholars also show that the appreciation of fetal ultrasound images depends on the appreciation of the pregnancy (wanted/unwanted) and on other factors such as age, class, race (Bridges 2011), and, above all, the fertility history of the pregnant person (Firth 2009). For instance, ethnographic studies show that middle- and upper-class individuals value the deliberate scheduling of babies and control over the pregnancy, allowing a better acceptance of reproductive technologies (Rapp 2000).

Ann Rudinow Saetnan, Nelly E.J. Oudshoorn, and Marta Kirejczyk (2000) showed that ultrasound exams do not affect pregnant persons' confidence in their own bodily senses. They identify them as a supplement rather than replacement. Sensations take precedence, except for first pregnancies, in which the ultrasound is often more important than somatic feelings. Rayna Rapp (2000), whose research deals with amniocentesis, found that even when a fetal malformation is diagnosed, pregnant persons retain their interpretive flexibility. They can refuse further testing or abortion.

All of these studies highlight the agency of pregnant persons. Visual reproductive technologies are appropriated by them (Metselaar 2022; Müller-Rockstroh 2012), showing that they may not merely be the victims of the patriarchal system that appropriates pregnancy through visualization technologies. But in order to translate between their somatic feelings and images on the screen, it remains necessary to negotiate with medical authority that embodies specific discourses about pregnancy, abortion, and parenthood.

Negotiation

Tacit cinematic knowledge is plural and "ambiguous" (Stephenson, McLeod, and Mills 2016). It is negotiated in multiple and conflicting ways. In the following section, I want to broaden a concept from cultural studies, proposed by Stuart Hall in 1973. In "Encoding, Decoding" (1973), Hall distinguishes three viewing positions. In the dominant-hegemonic position, the viewer decodes the message in terms of the codes legitimated by the encoding process and the dominant cultural order. In the negotiated position, the viewer has the potential to adopt and oppose the dominant codes. In the oppositional position, the viewer recognizes the dominant codes and opposes them. Applying the concept of negotiation to our understanding of tacit cinematic knowledge regarding fetal ultrasound moving images enhances our ability to see the agency that pregnant persons exercise.

To acknowledge negotiation is to understand that the wide spectrum of tacit cinematic knowledge, partly fostered by cinematic illusion, does not operate on its own. It is reliant on external discourses and situated actors.

The ethnographic studies I synthetized previously show how important the discourses surrounding fetal images are. Scholars

underline the importance of what the echographer says to help
decipher the images, even for 4D ultrasounds: "look how cute
he is," "she's tired," and so on (gender performance often starts
with the ultrasound). In public contexts, the experience of fetal
images is mediated through their use by anti-abortion activists
who played a big part in the association of the fetus with early life
(and who encourage hospitals to purchase more "lifelike" 3D and
4D devices).

Beyond the human interactions, Haraway draws our attention to
the interconnections among machines, babies, fetuses, clinical
equipment, various professionals, parents, and the circulation
of discourses (1997, 37). Taylor also explores "the public life of
the fetal sonogram" from a perspective that sees technology
as an inextricable economic and social network, dependent on
society (2008, 7–8). She calls for thinking not only in in terms of
how technology impacts a society, but also how conflicting actors
and discourses are part of technologies. Negotiation therefore
points to the political dimension of tacit cinematic knowledge in
scientific visualization technologies.

A good example of this political dimension can be found in digital
videos of fetal development. Their accelerated narration always
goes from fertilization to birth, and even *The Silent Scream* used
analog acceleration to give the impression of convulsions caused
by the pain supposedly experienced by the fetus. According to the
media theorist Friedrich Kittler (1993), visualization technologies
indeed enable the manipulation of time: this is what defines
them. In her study on Kittler's "time axis manipulation," Marie
Rebecchi ties together different time-lapses of slow phenomena
such as crystallization, plant growth, and fetal growth (Rebecchi
2020). I suggest that considering how tacit cinematic knowledge
is negotiated shapes the time axis manipulation politically and
works against the depoliticization of the cinematic medium. A
hypothesis for further research is that fetal time-lapse videos
implicitly relate embryos and fetuses to babies that have
been born. By doing so, they do not acknowledge abortion or

   miscarriage and invisibilize *in vitro* fertilization, although they do allow for multiple ways of parenthood, beyond the hetero-normative coitus (Preciado 2013).

Conclusion

Through her counter-intuitive statement—"when pregnancy becomes a moving picture" (Petchesky 1987, 265)—Petchesky encourages us not to see fetal ultrasound moving images from the supposedly neutral point of view of the camera. This avoids the equation "fetus = life" and helps us to understand how anti-abortionists make political use of the tacit cinematic features of fetal ultrasound moving images with the aim of restricting pregnant persons' rights. However, images do not create knowledge by themselves: they are used to mobilize political groups. Ethnographical studies about fetal ultrasound moving images show the diversity of responses to these images. These images are constantly negotiated. Their cinematic features are constructed by the discourses and the human/non-human interactions that surround them.

Emphasizing negotiation allows us to go beyond the mere repetition of the dominant discourse about the patriarchal use of visualization technologies to contravene pregnant persons' rights. The agency of pregnant persons is yet to be investigated, and we need to continuously underline the political dimension of supposedly neutral visualization practices. Tacit cinematic knowledge should be examined through ethnographic tools, which can show multiple standpoints, rather than only the most visible or dominant ones.

Literature

Aerzteblatt. 2020. "Ultraschall als 'Babyfernsehen' wird ab 2021 verboten." *Aerzteblatt*, December 17. Accessed March 31, 2023. https://www.aerzteblatt.de/nachrichten/119505/Ultraschall-als-Babyfernsehen-wird-ab-2021-verboten.

Boguska, Rebecca, Guilherme Machado, Rebecca Puchta, Marin Reljic, and Philipp Röding. 2019. "Histories of Tacit Cinematic Knowledge." *Konfigurationen des Films.* Accessed March 31, 2023. https://konfigurationen-des-films.de/wp-content/uploads/2019/10/191114_Histories-of-Tacit-Cinematic-Knowledge_V2-VH_RB.pdf.

Bridges, Khiara M. 2011. *Reproducing Race: An Ethnography of Pregnancy as a Site of Racialization.* Berkeley: University of California Press.

Dobbs v. Jackson Women's Health Organization. 2022. 597 US.

Donald, Ian, John McVicar, and Tom Brown. 1958. "Investigation of Abdominal Masses by Pulsed Ultrasound." *Lancet* 1: 1188–95.

Duden, Barbara. 1993. *Disembodying Women: Perspectives on Pregnancy and the Unborn.* Cambridge/London: Harvard University Press.

Firth, Georgina. 2009. "Re-Negociating Reproductive Technologies." *Feminist Review* 92: 54–71.

Fox Keller, Evelyn, and Christine R. Grontkowski. 1983. "The Mind's Eye." In *Reality: Feminist Perspectives on Epistemology, Metaphysics, Methodology, and Philosophy of Science*, edited by Sandra Harding and Merrill B. Hintikka, 207–24. Dordrecht: D. Reidel.

Gammeltoft, Tine, and Hanh Thi Thuý Nguyen. 2007. "The Commodification of Obstetric Ultrasound Scanning in Hanoi, Viet Nam." *Reprod Health Matters* 15 (29): 163–71.

Givner, Jessie. 1994. "Reproducing Reproductive Discourse: Optical Technologies in *The Silent Scream* and *Eclipse of Reason*." *Journal of Popular Culture* 28 (3): 229–41.

Hall, Stuart. 1993 [1973]. "Encoding, Decoding." In *The Cultural Studies Reader*, edited by Simon During, 507-17. London, New York: Routledge.

Haraway, Donna. 1997. "The Virtual Speculum in the New World Order." *Feminist Review* 55: 22–72.

———.1988. "Situated Knowledges: The Science Question in Feminism and the Privilege of Partial Perspective." *Feminist Studies* 14 (3): 575–99.

Higonnet, Anne. 2017. "The Motherless Fetus: Ultrasound Pictures and Their Magic Disappearing Trick." In *Reassembling Motherhood. Procreation and Care in a Globalized World*, edited by Yasmine Ergas, Jane Jenson, and Sonya Michel, 125–43. New York: Columbia University Press.

Hopkins, Nick, Suzanne Zeedyk, and Fiona Raitt. 2005. "Visualising Abortion: Emotion Discourse and Fetal Imagery in a Contemporary Abortion Debate." *Social Science and Medicine* 61 (2): 393–403.

Ivry, Tsipy. 2009. "The Ultrasonic Picture Show and the Politics of Threatened Life." *Medical Anthropology Quaterly* 23 (3): 189–211.

———. 2006. "At the Back Stage of Prenatal Care: Japanese Ob-Gyns Negotiating Prenatal Diagnosis." *Medical Anthropology Quarterly* 20 (4): 441–68.

Kittler, Friedrich. 1993. *Draculas Vermächtnis: Technische Schriften.* Leipzig: Reclam.

Metselaar, Ross. 2022. "'A Wonderful Movie!': The Appropriation of Entertainment Ultrasound Technology in The Netherlands." *Journal for Undergraduate Ethnography* 12 (1): 21–35.

Mitchell, Lisa Meryn. 2001. *Baby's First Picture: Ultrasound and the Politics of Fetal Subjects.* Toronto: University of Toronto Press.

180   Moyse Danielle, and Nicole Diederich. 2005. "L'impact de l'"arrêt Perruche' sur les échographistes et les gynécologues obstétriciens." Paris: Ehess.

Müller-Rockstroh, Babette. 2012. "Appropriate and Appropriated Technology: Lessons Learned from Ultrasound in Tanzania." *Medical Anthropology* 31 (3): 196–212.

Mulvey, Laura. 1975. "Visual Pleasure and Narrative Cinema." *Screen* 16 (3): 6–18.

New York Times. 1985. "A False 'Scream.'" *The New York Times*, March 11. Accessed March 31, 2023. URL: https://www.nytimes.com/1985/03/11/opinion/a-false-scream.html.

Nilsson, Lennart. 1965. "Drama of Life Before Birth." *Life*, April 30, 1965.

Odin, Roger. 1995. *Le film de famille: usage privé, usage public*. Paris: Méridiens/Klincksieck.

O'Gorman, Marcel. 2003. "What is Necromedia?" *Intermédialités* 1: 155–64.

Petchesky, Rosalind P. 1987. "Fetal Images: The Power of Visual Culture in the Politics of Reproduction." *Feminist Review* 13 (2): 263–92.

Preciado, Paul B. 2013. "Procréation politiquement assistée." *Libération*, September 27. Accessed March 31, 2023. https://www.liberation.fr/societe/2013/09/27/procreation-politiquement-assistee_935256.

Rapp, Rayna. 2000. *Testing Women, Testing the Fetus: The Social Impact of Amniocentesis in America*. London: Routledge.

Rebecchi, Marie. 2020. "Time-Lapse Machine. Plants, Crystals and Clouds: The Kaleidoscope of Time." In *Time Machine: Cinematic Temporalities*, edited by Antonio Somaini, Éline Grignard, and Marie Rebecchi, 197–210. Milan: Skira.

Roe v. Wade. 1973. 410 US 113.

Roberts, Julie. 2012. *The Visualised Foetus: A Cultural and Political Analysis of Ultrasound Imagery*. Farnham: Ashgate.

Roberts, Julie, Frances Griffiths, and Alice Verran. 2017. "Seeing the Baby, Doing Family: Commercial Ultrasound as Family Practice?" *Sociology* 51 (3): 527–42.

Saetnan, Ann Rudinow, Nelly E.J. Oudshoorn, and Marta Kirejczyk, eds. 2000. *Bodies of Technology: Women's Involvement with Reproductive Medicine*. Columbus: Ohio State University Press.

Sawicki, Jana. 1991. *Disciplining Foucault: Feminism, Power, and the Body*. New York: Routledge.

Stanworth, Michelle, ed. 1987. *Reproductive Technologies: Gender, Motherhood, and Medicine*. Minneapolis: University of Minnesota Press.

Stephenson, Niamh, Kim McLeod and Catherine Mills. 2016. "Ambiguous Encounters, Uncertain Fetuses: Women's Experiences of Obstetric Ultrasound." *Feminist Review* 113: 17–33.

Taylor, Janelle S. 2008. *The Public Life of the Fetal Sonogram: Technology, Consumption, and the Politics of Reproduction*. New Brunswick: Rutgers University Press.

The Baby Skan Studio. 2023. *The Baby Skan Studio: Where the Miracle of Life Meets Modern Technology*. Accessed March 31, 2023. https://www.thebabyskanstudio.com.

The Pregnancy Studio. 2023. *The Pregnancy Studio: Boutique PreNatal Imagining*. Accessed March 31, 2023. http://www.thepregnancystudio.com.

(Audio)Visual Material

A Tiny Perspective. 2021. "Elective 3D & 4D HD Ultrasounds." *A Tiny Perspective.*
    Accessed March 31, 2023. https://www.atinyperspective.com.
Dabner, Jack Duane. 1984. *The Silent Scream.* Short film, 28 min., United States of
    America.

CINEMA

ASTRONOMY

AESTHETICS

PHOTOGRAPHY

TIME LAPSE

SUN

9

Phantasms of the Sun and Venus: Tacit Cinematic Knowledge in Astronomy

Jelena Rakin

This article examines aesthetics as a form of cinematic episteme in moving images produced from contemporary astronomical observations. This analysis is followed by a closer examination of significant historical image *dispositifs*, such as drawing, photography, and film in respect to how they create visual renditions of time-based astronomical phenomena. Consequently, the article draws connections between media ontologies and aesthetics in an interdisciplinary context, from cinema to contemporary astrophysics. This examination demonstrates the role of aestheticizing principles in natural sciences by focusing on the techniques of time-lapse, editing, and superimposition.

Mesmerizing Color Spheres: Solar Images from the US National Aeronautics and Space Administration (NASA)

On June 5 and 6, 2012 Venus transited across the Sun. The event was captured by NASA's Solar Dynamics Observatory satellite (SDO), launched in 2010 to gather information about the Sun. The transit of Venus is a rare astronomical event and its last occurrence in 1874 led to the development of a novel, proto-cinematographic device—the photographic revolver that the French astronomer Jules Janssen constructed to capture the planet's transit, frame by frame.

As part of NASA's outreach to the general public, the SDO's recordings of the 2012 transit are available for viewing on the observatory's website. The visitors can watch "Venus Transit Movies" under the category "Outreach" in mp4 format (NASA 2021a). The multiple available transit movies differ as to what portion of the Sun is visible in the frame, as well as in the data they use. They show either a detail of ingress (the planet's intitial "entrance" over the sun), a detail of egress (the end of the transit), or a view of the entire sun. The data comes from two of the SDO's three instruments: the Helioseismic and Magnetic Imager (HMI) and the Atmospheric Imaging Assembly (AIA).[1] Data from the AIA includes images of the Sun in ten wavelengths every ten seconds, whereas some of the Venus transit movies are also composites of several AIA wavelength recordings and of HMI data (NASA 2021b). The website's video player specifies that the movies are being played at 16 frames per second.

The choice of the word "movies" and the reference to the standard projection measurement of 16 frames per second suggests a paratextual reference to the cinematographic *dispositif* as a general strategy of outreach from the scientific astronomy

---

1   SDO also carries the Extreme Ultraviolet Variability Experiment (EVE).

community to the public. One finds similar references on the website of the Solar and Heliospheric Observatory (SOHO), where under the site heading "SOHO Movie Theater," the viewers can generate videos of Venus' transit and many other movies of the Sun by entering two dates (NASA 2021c). In an additional paratextual reference to cinema, the design of the SOHO website's gallery shows the image icons of the movies framed by digital imitations of the perforations on an analog film strip. This is an obvious reference to a media imaginary since the technology at work in both the SDO and the SOHO is digital. But it is, however, not too far-fetched to allude to such technological "antecedents"[2] in this case, since many of the epistemic questions that these moving images raise pertained to earlier, analog models of image generation as well. Therefore, in this essay, I go beyond mere paratextual references to the cinematic *dispositif* to examine the ontological and epistemological connections between cinema and the production of moving images in astronomy. Specifically, I analyze the visual renditions of time-based, processual, astronomical phenomena as a form of film-photographic knowledge. Significant for my study are the heterogenous manifestations of temporal synthesis in film and photography, and the aesthetic role ascribed to the perceiving subject. What I call the heterogeneity in the visual rendering of temporal phenomena in astronomy encompasses such aspects as the choice of varied time intervals and the different manifestations of time as a phenomenon on the surface of the image.

The SDO website offers several different forms of time-lapse movies. The viewers learn that the observatory captures an image of the Sun every second, a frequency that supersedes the two other spacecraft also recording the images of the *Sun: Solar and Heliospheric Observatory* (SOHO) and *Solar TErrestrial RElations Observatory* (STEREO): "SDO takes 1 image every second.

---

2   Antecedents here does not refer to a strict technological genealogy but to a shared image practice in a functional sense.

 At best STEREO takes 1 image every 3 minutes and SOHO takes 1 image every 12 minutes" (NASA 2021b). Given the extent of the data collected in one-second intervals, it is interesting that the SDO website provides—perhaps even showcases—various formats of time lapse movies. These movies opt for sequences with much longer time intervals than the available data allows for. Significantly, the longer intervals are of central importance to the visual rendering of motion. In a sense, they create motion that would otherwise not be perceivable as such—just as looking directly at the Sun would not reveal most of the information collected by the observatory. Thus, the time-lapse effect becomes a form of producing visibility. Furthermore, "The Sun Now" webpage offers "48hr videos" that play in twenty-second time-lapse loops (NASA 2021e). The "Browse Data" category allows visitors to generate a movie from historical data. They can choose two dates in the calendar as well as different AIA or HMI data channels (or their composites) as the basis for the movies. Visitors can also choose their own image cadence: for instance, choosing a "5," means that "the application will return one in every fifth image to the user" out of a total limit of 500 per query (NASA 2021d). The generated movies show the sun positioned centrally in the image, rotating as the video loops. Different colors are used for different wavelengths: gold, bronze, red, teal, blue, green, yellow/green, pink, gray etc. (see fig. 1). Numerous variations of the same sphere that represent the Sun exemplify both a literal as well as a metaphorical plurality of views. The movies are aesthetically mesmerizing, hypnotic loops of rotating, colored spheres.

These fascinating spheres in "false colors" (chromatic renderings commonly used to visualize the information on the non-visible parts of the electromagnetic spectrum) point to epistemic models other than the scientific ones—particularly, models that could be identified as cinematic. On a most basic level, these movies are examples of a conventionalized visualization, i.e. the representation of a process enabled by moving images.

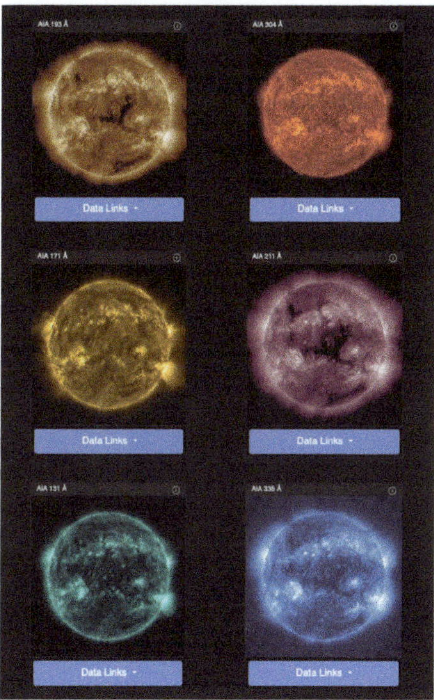

[Figure 1] Detail of the Solar Dynamics Observatory website with various videos of the Sun (Source: NASA 2021e, courtesy of NASA/SDO and the AIA, EVE, and HMI science teams.)

Underlying the evidentiary status of a physical reality translated in familiar codes, however, are mechanisms of aesthetic crafting that capitalize on the malleability of the moving cinematic image and its ability to produce a distinctly wonderous reality.[3] This crafted sense of wonder is significant, since as I will show later, the word "magic" is often used in relation to today's science, notably in regard to its speculative nature and the covert or overt

---

3   Lynda Nead identifies aesthetics of wonder as one of the key qualities of the astronomical images (2007, 201–206).

 role of aesthetic choices informing theories and the presentation of experimental results.

Several approaches to visual representations of the passage of time which were developed in the 19th century and are still used today—including the techniques of long-exposure photography, instantaneous photography, and moving images—exemplify the specific relationship between aesthetics and epistemes, or rather they exemplify *aesthetics as an episteme*. They underline the contingencies involved in rendering the passage of time as an image surface phenomenon and bring to fore the significant role that aesthetic and subjective choices play in shaping such renderings. Therefore, the next section of this essay looks at historical ways aesthetic concerns have shaped the production of astronomical images and their unique relation to the perceiving human subject.

Aesthetic Time in Drawing, Photography, and Cinema

Images of the cosmos are a particularly instructive corpus for examining the temporal dimensions of film and photography, since celestial phenomena generally exceed human sensory capacities (in terms of their limited vison, human life span, etc.). Throughout the history of astronomy, the human body and its limited scale posed specific challenges for the observation of astronomical phenomena, such as the strain of observing over long time periods and the necessity for optical devices like a telescope to aid the naked eye.[4] Thus, the phenomenological unavailability of the cosmos underlines the constructed nature, mediality, and the influence of cultural imaginaries (both

4   With regard to the strain of a long observation of the nights sky, Dava Sobel (2016) studied how the Harvard Observatory employed women because they were practical, cheap labor, and, at the same time, executed the strenuous work with the necessary precision.

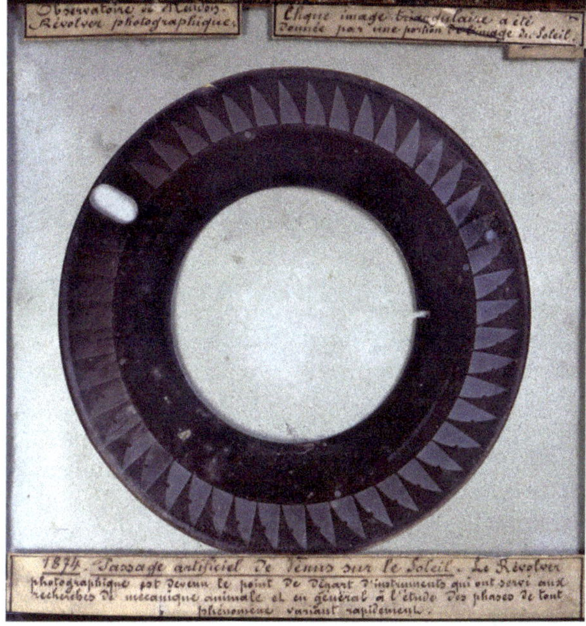

[Figure 2] Disk-plate recording of the 1874 Venus transit (Source: Library of the Paris Observatory 2021).

aesthetic and scientific) that characterize those images that represent it.

The non-immediacy of the experience of the cosmos was greatly influenced in the 19th century through the introduction of an intermediary, the photographic apparatus, that propelled astronomy to become a highly visual science at the end of that same century. Jimena Canales identifies the introduction of photography into astronomy as a "cinematographic turn," pointing out the fact that the cinematographic apparatus itself emerged from the field of astronomy—namely, from Janssen's photographic revolver, which he had constructed in 1874 to photograph the Venus' transit across the sun at intervals of about one second (see fig. 2). The apparatus that Janssen developed was further modified and adapted in Etienne Jules Marey's physiological laboratory and then in the studio of the Lumière brothers, where it served as a basis for the development of the cinematographic camera (Canales 2002, 588). The recordings of Venus' transit were captured on a disk that resembles 19th-century optical devices such as the *phenakistiscope*, which came into use around the 1830s and which provided an illusion of motion through the rotation of the disk, producing a looping repetition of the motif.

The discourses surrounding the introduction of photography in place of astronomical drawings show the degree to which the generation of images involved intervention of an aesthetic nature, not solely in the service of verisimilitude. Whereas photography was associated with "verisimilitude" and empirical exactness, it was not necessarily associated with "truth" (Canales 2006, 281), and in the second half of the 19th century many discourses questioned the supremacy of the mechanical reproduction of the stars offered by photography (Soojung-Kim Pang 2016). Drawings, especially, were preferred over the photography for their predisposition to separate the "important" from the "irrelevant." In his manual on astronomical drawing from 1882, the French Astronomer Étienne Léopold Trouvelot pointed out the supremacy of a well-trained eye over a photographic camera (1882, VIf.). The remarks he made about his drawing of "November Meteorites" are informative about the importance of making subjective choices in the visual synthesis of time. Trouvelot recorded an impression from 3000 observed meteorites, where an ideal view implies that "the shooting stars delineated, were not observed at the same moment of time, but during the same night" (1882, VI–VII). The period of transition from astronomical drawing to astrophotography in the late 19th century thus brings to the fore a fluctuation in the location of meaning and perceived truth, vacillating somewhere between the perceptual and cognitive faculties of the subject and the physical world, and, as a

consequence, demonstrating the interrelation of aesthetics and
science in representations of the cosmos.

A very cautious attitude towards the assumption that a film-photographic image provides unambiguous evidence also informs some classical texts on film and photography of the early 20th century. For example, both, Walter Benjamin and Jean Epstein, point out film and photography's ability to record phenomena beyond what is perceptible with the mere human eye: Benjamin does this with his notion of the *"optical uncon-scious"* and Jean Epstein by musing about the ramifications of the invisible spectrum of ultra-violet light in the cinematographic image (Benjamin 1979, 202; Epstein 2008, 33). Both thus suggest that the evidentiary status of film-photographic images extends the limited scope of anthropocentric vision.

For Benjamin, there is also a significant difference between long exposure and instantaneous photography. He compares the result of long exposure to that of a painted portrait, where, owing to the time passing during the photo-chemical inscription, the history of the photographed person is inscribed into the image. However, according to Benjamin, this does not apply to instantaneous photography (Benjamin 1979, 204). The idea of a single truth that cannot be captured in photography also informs Siegfried Kracauer's (1997) thinking. Similarly to Benjamin, he compares portraiture in painting and photography, concluding that photography captures the coherence of the surface but not the meaning.

These different observations point to the belief that the semantic (or epistemic) locus of temporal synthesis and the selection of information is the human subject executing the painting or a drawing. In contrast to a mechanical apparatus, a painter filters visual information, separating the relevant from the irrelevant. The time and subject represented in painting and drawing are thus, principally, an inner image of the human subject.

192 In photography this synthesis is done by the apparatus: stars draw themselves, as the vocabulary of the 19th-century discourses implies. However, as Benjamin was right to point out, time does not simply equal time in photography. Photography opens a range of techniques for translating time onto a two-dimensional surface. When contrasted, interval photography, long exposure, and instantaneous photography of celestial skies show different manifestations of time as an image surface phenomenon, with varying graphic qualities. It becomes evident that the reference to time here relates not only to the astral phenomenon under observation, but also—and importantly—to the apparatus itself as the producer of the visibility of time.

As opposed to the synthesis of time on a still, two-dimensional surface in drawing and photography, moving images also make time perceptible through motion. Cinematographic time-effect techniques such as slow motion and time lapse draw attention to the character of time as well as the process of its construction and visualization. Still the lifelikeness of cinematic representation has repeatedly been disputed, starting with turn-of-the-19th-century discourses on the synthesis and analysis of movement. Informative in this case are two opposing philosophies predominant in 19th-century France: one ascribed to the notion that "synthesis is composed through the summation of discrete moments of analysis" and the other being an "alternative philosophy of form and movement where 'sentiment' and 'spirit' played essential roles" (Canales 2006, 289). The proponents of the latter argued that "movement was not composed of discrete moment summations" (Canales 2006, 278), but was instead "life, volition and, therefore, divinity. Representations of movement were ultimately representations of 'grace'—the quality which brought all of these elements together" (Canales 2006, 279). By stressing the sentiment and the spirit, they warned that meaning and knowledge cannot be grasped by mathematical principles or by logic alone—even if, by contrast, in the same century, the promise of "photographically mathematized nature" propelled the French astronomer François Arago to find in the photographic medium the "universal language" (Fisher 2016, 211).[5]

Vital Movement in Cinema and Magic Bodies

The notion of "vital" movement in cinema is also taken up in contemporary film scholarship (Albera 2002). François Albera contrasts the notion of "vital" movement with (merely) sequential movement in cinema editing. Importantly, he also recognizes the act of editing in the photographic long-exposure process and makes a point to distinguish it from the kind of editing that produces the sequential nature of cinematic photograms. Instead, for Albera, editing also encompasses superimpositions on the same photogram, and, moreover, is not merely a technical operation.

There is an unlikely comparison that can be drawn between the video loops of the Sun on the SDO website described earlier and the observations Albera makes in relation to the *zoetrope* and *phenakistiscope* (see fig. 3). In the circular movements of these 19th-century optical devices, Albera identifies non-narrative, vital movement as well as epistemic questions raised by the process of editing to create this repetitive motion:

> The alternation of the phases in a zoetrope or some other optical toy does not have as its goal so much to narrate, to unfold a temporal sequence (he jumps, he runs) as to incite the dynamics of a jump or a run. There is a notion of a 'vital' movement: one that differs from succession. ... On certain phenakistiscope disks one can observe a multiplicity of movements generated by a rotational motion ... it is a

5 The notion of film being a universal language ensued a couple of decades later, in the early 20th century, but it took the physiognomy of a gesture (cf. Balázs 2001) as its point of departure, which, in turn, is related to the vitality-of-the-movement line of thinking.

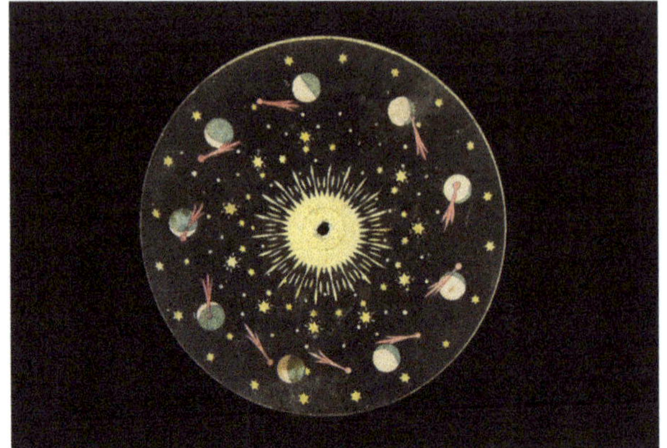

[Figure 3] Phenakistiscope disk showing a shooting star, 1833 (Source: Australian Centre for the Moving Image 2021, photographed by Egmont Contreras, ACMI).

movement 'in place,' every different shape being super-imposed over the preceding one. (Albera 2002, 16)[6]

And, furthermore: "[t]he recognition of the process of montage in the mere passage from one state to another, as minimal as it can be, represents at the same time an artistic as well as an epistemological question" (Albera 2002, 21).

It is precisely the vitality of movement-as-passage that the SDO's Sun recordings offer their viewers. Even though the movies make an ostentatious case for the existence of a linear interval through the use of time-lapse composition, the sense of vital passage is prominent in the contrast between the circular movement of the Sun disk and its static framing in the center of the image. Not only are the viewers presented with the rotational movement "in the same place" ("mouvement 'sur place' ") (Albera 2002, 16), but in the movies that layer several data channels within a single image, the viewers are also presented with *editing through*

6   All translations by author.

superimposition. The Sun becomes a malleable body, first dis-aggregated into different wavelengths and then re-constituted through superimpositions and the time-lapse effect. The loop option also undermines the notion of linear succession. Instead, what is captivating is the flux of perpetual transformations, comparable to observing a water surface ruffled by the wind. The exact meaning of the consistent motion seems to be less certain. What is established as the dominant perceptual principle, however, is the anticipation of enchained transformations.

In the case of Georges Méliès' films, Albera identifies a similar focus on composable and decomposable bodies instead of linear action: "[i]n the case of Méliès, the editing does not strive for the linearization of the filmic signifier; instead, it plays with the reference to the mechanical body, disassemblable, super-imposable. … Méliès brings us unequivocally into the area of the aforementioned superimposition" (Albera 2002, 27). The tendency of disaggregating and compositing physical bodies bears witness to the desire to link mechanics with magic, an impulse Albera recognizes in the Méliès's films when he points out that editing belongs to the genealogy of magic techniques that precede cinema. This, in turn, raises questions about the place of astronomical images in that same genealogy. Indeed, the earliest records of superimposition techniques are found in trick photography and film manuals instructing the reader in how to create magic illusions (Hopkins 1897; Seeber 1979).

Aesthetics and Science

Recently, the physicist Sabine Hossenfelder (2018) has written at length about how aesthetic judgement drives contemporary scientific research. In addition to arguing that most new theories are speculative and "practically untestable," while still others are "untestable even theoretically," she points to the significant role played by subjective judgement. "When asked to judge the promise of a newly invented but untested theory, physicists draw upon the concepts of naturalness, simplicity or elegance, and beauty. These hidden rules are ubiquitous in the foundations of physics. They are invaluable. And in utter conflict with the scientific mandate of objectivity" (2018, 2). Though Hossenfelder is invested in propagating a dialogue between the natural sciences and philosophy in their shared search for meaning, she is critical of the aesthetic criteria applied to theories in physics.[7] Significantly, the word "magic" also appears in Hossenfelder's book in the title of her subchapter , "Quantum Mechanics is magic" (2018, 130). Other scientists, however, more openly admit that aesthetic criteria inform their work. For instance, the astrophysicist Trinh Xuan Thuan writes, "In my work, I am often guided by aesthetic considerations that are often attached to those of the rational order" (2011, 134).[8] Large portions of his book read like translations of the classical (Kantian) aesthetic ideals of truth and beauty into astrophysics. The use of such words as "beauty" and "creation" are abundant in the text, and the words "Idea," "Grand Mystery," and "Eternal truth" are capitalized throughout (Thuan 2011, 152–53).

But even when astronomers do not openly refer to aesthetics as a guiding principle, the final results may nevertheless be aesthetically informed. In their sociological study, Michael Lynch and Samuel Y. Edgerton Jr. examine the role of aesthetic considerations in contemporary astrophotography. They distinguish between work done for the general public and that which the

7   It is interesting to compare this with attempts to include categories from the natural sciences into the humanities, specifically, media studies. For instance, Jussi Parikka writes, "cultural heritage, cultural memory, and social memory are increasingly debated in relation to the planetary, the geological, and the Anthropocene-scenarios involving chemical, geological, and biological processes that displace the concepts and frameworks that are normally associated with 'the social'" (2016, 145).

8   Trinh Xuan Thuan is referring to similar notions employed by the physicist Werner Heisenberg, who preceded him. Hossenfelder also points to the long tradition of physicists who view their work as a quest for beauty (2011, 22). On the history of thinking about the cosmos in terms of harmony and beauty within the discipline of astronomy, see also Herrmann (2017).

astronomers described as being part of an image-processing
routine with no aesthetic intent (such as reconstitutions of "noisy pictures"). Nevertheless, Lynch and Edgerton observe that even these latter practices were guided by aesthetic principles: "what aesthetics means here is not a domain of beauty or expression. Instead, it is the very fabric of realism: the work of composing visible coherences, discriminating differences, consolidating entities, and establishing evident relations" (1987, 212).

They conclude:

> What we now call science sustains an ancient art: a crafting of natural resemblances; an 'art' which is practiced as *mere technique* without 'aesthetic' pretensions (in the modern sense). … [E]xamination of the detailed production of visual displays in science suggests to us that science may have taken over the original sense of *techne*, while professional art has become dissociated from traditional representational concerns. (1987, 214–15)

Cinema as an aesthetic medium has particularly strong historical ties to the notion of "mere technique." The discourses on cinema in the early 20th century dismissed the new medium's potential for aesthetic expression precisely on the grounds that it was deemed "mere technique." Consequently, it became a trope of classical film theory of the first half of the 20th century to defend cinema's potential as a medium that allows for authorial intervention and creative choices.[9]

We can identify in both astronomy (in its observational and visual form) and cinema a shared affinity for a particular manner of crafting reality. By connecting Canales' recognition of the 'cinematographic turn' in astronomy with Thomas S. Kuhn's notion of "paradigm shifts" in science, we may ask what kind of a new world view or *Weltanschauung* results from the emergence

9   Important examples of this trope include the seminal works on film by Arnheim (1974), Kracauer (1973), or Bazin (1975).

 of a cinematographic paradigm in astronomy. Kuhn, who in his seminal book often draws on astronomy to exemplify paradigm shifts in the history of science, asks in one such case: "[c]an it conceivably be an accident, for example, that Western astronomers first saw change in the previously *immutable* heavens during the half-century after Copernicus' new paradigm was first proposed?" (Kuhn 2012, 11; italics added)

Would cinematographically chartable heavens then signify skies that are not only mutable, but skies made visible—or existent—as a highly *transmutable image*? Can the processual change of the image be ascribed to a technical operation as well as an aesthetic or a "magical" gesture? In the case of the Hubble Space Telescope, Sean Cubitt goes as far as to suggest that "[t]hough built for the tremendous reasons of science, Hubble is a special effects movie" (1998, 65).[10] With regard to digital images more generally, he points out that an indexical relation to the photographed subject is neither an inherent feature of analog cameras nor digital ones, and that the products of both are always translations of photon-scale events into visualizations (Cubitt 2014, 245). This observation recalls Vilém Flusser's (2001) notion of technical images that are less indexes of the actual physical phenomena they depict than references to the apparatuses that bring those images about. However, the astronomical movies of the Sun discussed in this essay are particularly interesting in that they seem to refer to *a different apparatus* than the one that actually generates them—namely, to the (historical) dipositive of cinematographic technology. The references to "the movie theater," the film strip, and film frames on the SOHO website are readily apparent examples of this phenomenon. But in addition to these references (that I earlier termed as paratextual), and on a more ontological level, the specific use of time-lapse and heterogenous editing techniques suggest that a part of the

10   See also Elizabeth Kessler's (2012) study of the relation between Hubble's images and the aesthetics of the sublime.

epistemic repertoire at work here is not only the technical
knowledge of movement synthesis—of the succession of singular
frames suggested by the vocabulary on the website—but, more
importantly, of aesthetic cinematic knowledge, in which the
malleability of the passage of time as a visual phenomenon
is never solely technical, but rather a subjective, aesthetic
process of crafting reality. The result thus reveals a double
phantasm at work. On the one hand, there is the phantasm of the
cinematographic *dispostif* as imitated by astronomic technology,
and on the other, there is the purported visibility of celestial
phenomena that ultimately lie beyond the phenomenological
scope of our senses and can only be experienced as images.

Literature

Albera, François. 2002. "Pour une épistémographie du montage: préalables."
    Cinémas /Revue d'études cinématographiques 13 (1–2): 11–32.
Arnheim, Rudolf. 1974 [1932]. *Film als Kunst*. München: Hanser.
Bazin, André. 1975 [1958–62]. *Was ist Kino? Bausteine zu einer Theorie des Films*. Köln:
    DuMont Schauberg.
Balázs, Béla. 2001 [1924]. *Der sichtbare Mensch oder die Kultur des Films*. Frankfurt am
    Main: Suhrkamp.
Benjamin, Walter. 1979 [1931]. "Kleine Geschichte der Fotografie." In *Theo-
    rie der Fotografie II, 1912–1945*, edited by Wolfgang Kemp, 200–13. München:
    Schirmer-Mosel.
Canales, Jimena. 2006. "Movement Before Cinematography: The High-Speed
    Qualities of Sentiment." *Journal of Visual Culture* 5 (3): 275–94.
———. 2002. "Photogenic Venus: The 'Cinematographic Turn' and Its Alternatives in
    Nineteenth-Century France." *Isis* 93 (4): 585–613.
Cubitt, Sean. 2014. *The Practice of Light: A Genealogy of Visual Technologies from Prints
    to Pixels*. Cambridge: The MIT Press.
———. 1998. *Digital Aesthetics*. London: Sage Publications.
Epstein, Jean. 2008 [1921]. "Bonjour cinema." In *Jean Epstein: Bonjour Cinéma und
    andere Schriften zum Kino*, edited by Nicole Brenez and Ralph Eue, 28–36. Trans-
    lated by Ralph Eue. Vienna: Synema.
Fisher, Andrew. 2016. "On the Scales of Photographic Abstraction." *Photographies* 9
    (2): 203–215.
Flusser, Vilém. 2001. *Für eine Philosophie der Fotografie*. Berlin: European Photograph
    (Edition Flusser; Vol. 3).
Herrmann, Dieter B. 2017. *Die Harmonie des Universums: Von der rätselhaften
    Schönheit der Naturgesetze*. Stuttgart: Kosmos.

200 Hopkins, Albert A. 1897. *Magic: Stage Illusions and Scientific Diversions, Including Trick Photography*. London: Sampson Low, Marston and Company.

Hossenfelder, Sabine. 2018. *Lost in Math: How Beauty Leads Physics Astray*. New York: Basic Books.

Kessler, Elizabeth A. 2012. *Picturing the Cosmos: Hubble Space Telescope and the Astronomical Sublime*. Minneapolis: University of Minnesota Press.

Kracauer, Siegfried. 1977 [1927]. "Die Photographie." In *Das Ornament der Masse. Essays*, 21–39. Frankfurt: Suhrkamp.

———. 1973 (1960). *Theorie des Films*. Frankfurt: Suhrkamp.

Kuhn, S. Thomas. 2012. *The Structure of Scientific Revolutions*. Chicago: University of Chicago Press.

Lynch, Michael, and Samuel Y. Edgerton Jr. 1987. "Aesthetics and Digital Image Processing: Representational Craft in Contemporary Astronomy." In *Picturing Power: Visual Depiction and Social Relations, Sociological Review Monograph 35*, edited by Gordon Fyfe and John Law, 184–220. London and New York: Routledge.

Nead, Lynda. 2007. *The Haunted Gallery: Painting, Photography, Film, c. 1900*. New Haven: Yale University Press.

Parikka, Jussi. 2016. "Planetary Goodbyes: Post-History and Future Memories of an Ecological Past." In *Memory in Motion: Archives, Technology and the Social*, edited by Ina Blom, Trond Lundemo, and Eivind Røssaak, 129–51. Amsterdam: Amsterdam University Press.

Seeber, Guido. 1979 [1927]. *Der Trickfilm in seinen grundsätzlichen Möglichkeiten: Eine praktische und theoretische Darstellung der photographischen Filmtricks*. Frankfurt: Deutsches Filmmuseum.

Sobel, Dava. 2016. *The Glass Universe: How Ladies of the Harvard Observatory Took the Measure of the Stars*. New York: Viking.

Soojung-Kim Pang, Alex. 2016. "Technologie und Ästhetik der Astrofotografie." In *Ordnungen der Sichtbarkeit: Fotografie in Wissenschaft, Kunst und Technologie*, edited by Peter Geimer, 100–41. Frankfurt: Suhrkamp.

Trinh, Xuan Thuan. 2011. *Le cosmos et le lotus: confessions d'un astrophysicien*. Paris: Albin Michel.

Trouvelot, Étienne Léopold. 1882. *The Trouvelot Astronomical Drawings Manual*. New York: C. Scribner's sons.

(Audio)Visual Material

Australian Centre for the Moving Image. 2021. "Phenakistiscope disc (shooting star), France, c. 1833." *ACMI*. Accessed June 29, 2021. https://www.acmi.net.au/works/120070--phenakistiscope-disc-shooting-star/

Library of the Paris Observatory. 2021. "Passage artificiel de Vénus devant le Soleil." *L'Observatoire de Paris: Bibliothèque / PSL*. Accessed June 29, 2021. https://cosmos. obspm.fr/index.php/Detail/objects/30684.

National Aeronautics and Space Administration. 2021a. "2012 Venus Transit Data." *SDO Solar Dynamics Observatory.* Accessed June 29, 2021. https://sdo.gsfc.nasa.gov/epo/venustransit/.

———. 2021b. "SDO Instruments." *SDO: Solar Dynamics Observatory.* Accessed June 29, 2021. https://sdo.gsfc.nasa.gov/mission/instruments.php.

———. 2021c. "SOHO Movie theater." *SOHO: Solar and Heliospheric Observatory.* Accessed June 29, 2021. https://soho.nascom.nasa.gov/data/Theater/.

———. 2021d. "SDO Data." *SDO: Solar Dynamics Observatory.* Accessed June 29, 2021. https://sdo.gsfc.nasa.gov/data/aiahmi/.

———. 2021e. "The Sun now." *SDO: Solar Dynamics Observatory.* Accessed June 29, 2021. https://sdo.gsfc.nasa.gov/data/.

EPHEMERA

MEDIA MATERIALITY

TACIT KNOWLEDGE

FILM

CINEPHILIA

Crafty Cinephilia:
The Scrapbook and
Film History as Media
Anamorphosis

Andrea Mariani

This essay focuses on a collection of scrapbooks
of a cinemagoer from Udine, Italy, who recorded
and collected visual materials about every
screening he attended from 1926 to 1999, day
by day. I will discuss the scrapbook as a place
where the materiality of film is re-configured
in a complex way, arguing that the scrapbook
is not just a mere "archive" but a potentially
"active" cultural object where non-explicit
cinematic knowledge is passed on through
interactions with and among the layers of
material accumulated on each page. On the
one hand, I will excavate the scrapbook not
just as a product of social and cultural practice
but also as an object that informs and shapes a

 particular cinematic knowledge (of film). On the other hand, I want to question how the gestures of the scrapbook maker incorporate a peculiar form of cinematic technicity.

This essay analyzes how films are reconfigured in scrapbooks, stressing how the media's materiality elicits forms of reflexive performativity through these objects. My observations bear on a twofold and intertwined inspiration: on the one hand, they are rooted in some elements of Dieter Mersch's negative media theory (2013; 2015), and, on the other hand, they take up a dialectic proposed by Michael Polanyi in his theory of the tacit dimension of knowledge: the *proximal* and the *distal* (2009, 10).[1] Scrapbooks and scrapbooking, as objects and as a mediating process informed by specific technological operations, respectively, allow me to discuss how films and filmic knowledge are passed on through forms of *apperception* that go beyond the mere memory of viewing or experiencing a film.

Relying on Mersch's (2016) emphasis on the *medial* (ger. *das Mediale*), as a "structure" that "shows what 'media' create, represent, transfer or mediate" (Mersch 2013, 208), I will contend that attending to the materiality underlying the functions and operations of a given media object undermines clear-cut formulations of media boundaries and media concepts. Furthermore, the shift in perspective that I propose here aims to overcome exclusive discourse-driven approaches to media cultures and practices by offering a more nuanced and, at the same time, more radical understanding of what a media process can really "do,"

1   Polanyi defines these terms in the following passage: "The two terms of tacit knowing, the proximal, which includes the particulars, and the distal, which is their comprehensive meaning, would then be seen as two levels of reality, controlled by distinctive principles. The upper one relies for its operations on the laws governing the elements of the lower one in themselves, but these operations of it are not explicable by the laws of the lower level" (2009, 34).

albeit tacitly. To do that, I look at minor media formations and the elemental structures of objects operating according to techno-logics that refer to a major and broader media system. Ephemeral film-related/film objects open an extraordinary field of inquiry and theoretical speculation that has yet to be fully explored.

Ephemera and scrapbooks have already received attention in cultural studies and recent histories of cinema. Todd Gernes defines the scrapbook as "a popular medium of expression shaped by the human impulse to collect material objects and invest them with meaning, producing, in many cases, what Krzysztof Pomian has called a 'semiosphere'" (2001, 109). His account is part of a significant literature about scrapbooks that stresses their discursive value as a practice and a technology of cultural memory (Anselmo 2019; Gruber Garvey 2003; Wickham 2010). The symbolic, discursive, declarative, and signifying modes dominate cultural histories of these objects and related practices. These characteristics are undeniably crucial features of scrapbooks. Nevertheless, this essay will instead insist on the nature of the "medial"[2] (Mersch 2016) in the scrapbook, inves-tigating the "underlying materialities, dispositives and perform-ances that accompany medial processes" (Mersch 2013, 208). To emphasize the "medial" in scrapbooks requires us to understand such objects as *not yet* media proper, but, instead, as material formations where cultural practices and technological operations transition from one media configuration (film)[3] to what we could identify as an *ur*-medium where film's material remains are reconfigured as (potentially) endless circulation of data).

With such a definition, I insist on an open, transitory state of media and implicitly draw upon Niklas Luhmann's (1995) notion

---

2   Mersch argues that the "medial" allows for a different mode of reflection, distinguishing the material from the symbolic (2013, 208–09).

3   The term *configuration* recalls the state of cinema as a medium "in per-manent transformation," as formulated by Vinzenz Hediger and Miriam De Rosa (2017).

 of *form*[4] and Fritz Heider's (1927) differentiation between medium and thing. More precisely, in the scrapbook, I highlight the co-presence of a definite formal configuration (the structure and functionality of the album, the order and distribution of the clippings) and an environment in which the film's dispersed remains (material and technological) are conveyed and actively transformed. In particular, I show how multiple materialities—the film's, the paper album's, or the makers' gestures—are drawn into specific knowledge performances: an epistemology informed by a sub-conceptual integration of cinematic technicity. As Katerina Krtilova writes: "Mersch stresses … [that] materiality cannot and must not be described as something situated *in* the symbolic order, forced into a discourse, logic, or reasonable order of things, forced to mean something" (2015, 36). Accordingly, I will discuss media reflexivity that proceeds "across" the opposition of symbolic/material (Krtilova 2015, 39). In doing so, this essay will interrogate the performative mode of the materiality of the scrapbook, against or across the discursive strategies implemented through it, as a tacit, non-explicit (non-discursive) dimension of a particular cinematic knowledge (of the film). To do so, I will excavate the scrapbooks crafted by an Italian film fan who connoted his albums with a sophisticated historiographical and encyclopedic character.

Framedness

The scrapbooks I will discuss here show a complex relationship between the film and the spectators'/scrapbook maker's gestures. The scrapbook maker's gestures take part in the process of disassembling the film and its *dispositif* by retaining parts of its remains, whether in the form of a visual trace (i.e., a still or a film-related picture), or in the form of material detritus or remediation of a technical element of the cinematic apparatus (i.e., the

---

4   Contrary to Luhmann's conception of *form* as purely structural and systemic, I will focus on the role of matter and materiality in shaping the medial.

framing, the projection). In the next section, I will detail these dynamics as forms of participation in tacit cinematic knowledge. However, before doing that, I will reflect on the quality of framedness of these scrapbooks.

I understand framedness as the quintessential material quality of the scrapbook and divide it into three operative stages: the *mark*, the *erasure,* and the *increase.* The *mark* stands for a chain of gestures that isolate the clipping from the source (by cutting it out), transfer its profile into an *unmarked space* (by pasting it into the album's folio), trace its contours (often using a color pastel as a re-marker), and differentiate between that clipping and the rest of the empty page (or other clippings) by creating physical distance.[5]

The second operative stage, the *erasure,* is structurally linked to the *mark,* although it opens itself up to a complex medial state. The clipping into the scrapbook page is obtained by eliminating everything beyond the figure's outline (the background). This action privileges the detail—the one, single element—and opens it to fundamentally new combinations in the scrapbook. As we will see, the erasure strongly impacts the definition of tacit knowledge of film and creates the most controversial intermedial effects with cinema. In fact, on the one hand, the rotogravure technique that produces most film magazines—the source of the clippings—allows for sensory continuity with the screened film frame (Beegan 2017). It facilitates *an effect of transientness,* as to say traces of the transition of film material elements into the paper: this results in a materialization of debris from the dis-assemblage of the film as a medium (i.e., a "grain effect" or the persistence of halftone colours). On the other hand, this process erases the link to the film source to which the clipping refers. The clipping does not *automatically* refer to the original film. Hence, the clipping is often self-evident with regards to what

5   This feature is the closest to the elementary operations that shape a *form* in George Spencer-Brown's (2008) and Luhmann's (1993) writings.

 it represents but it is "mute" in relation to its origins. As I will discuss below, taking the memory of a film for granted is misleading. This is because the implicit cinematic knowledge captured in the scrapbook is primarily produced through the removal of the film's medial and narrative specificity.

The *increase* is mainly related to the gesture of pasting and accumulating clippings into the scrapbook folio. Nevertheless, the *increase* is not the same as montage. The *increase* still pertains to the framedness of the scrapbook: it is three-dimensional and vertical rather than sequential and linear; it is material rather than narrative. The increase enhances the frame's appearance and its three-dimensionality; it elucidates the frame as a transitional infrastructure characterized by the juxtaposition of clippings over the same spot or their distribution over the surface of the same folio. There is no temporal progression in the increase; there is only spatial growth. The increase is a scrapbook-specific feature that builds upon the gesture of marking and the erasure of the source. Accordingly, it expands the combinatory potentialities of the scrapbook as an environment for reassembling and transforming the medium of film and *grounds* the scrapbooks medial process. In the next section, I will examine the case of an Italian fan's scrapbooks, stressing how these features inform film-related knowledge. Specifically, this case study will help me discuss how tacit cinematic knowledge of film captured in the scrapbook impacts the film spectator's understanding of cinema history and mediality on an epistemic level.

Limits of the Discourse

Walter Faglioni was an Italian cinephile and a film lover. From 1926 to 1999, across 35 diaries, he took note of every film he watched in movie theatres, cine clubs, or on television. In the 1980s, he started organizing these data and related ephemera into six scrapbooks, in which, over decades and decades, he accumulated layers on layers of clippings. He produced albums one after the other and continuously overwrote them while articulating increasingly sophisticated critical and self-referential conceptions of his viewing and scrapbooking work.

Within this expressive domain, I can distinguish several discursive and generic regimes:

1) Chronicle. Every album is organized by decade and follows a linear chronology. Every screening is reported chronologically year by year, day by day, and some albums are even organized in alphabetical order, title by title, year by year. He also articulated a symbolic order within this literary regime, choosing different colors to indicate repeat viewings and to underline favorites or uncertain pleasures. He even specified the screening locations: cinema theatres, cine clubs, or television.

2) Insights into film history: handwritten notes about film genres, actors, and trivia, as well as academic sources of inspiration.

3) Personal memories. He includes handwritten pages describing memories of his own cinemagoing experience that also work retrospectively. For example, he attempts to re-contextualize some film screenings which he attended during the fascist period by overwriting the earlier albums.

4) Criticism. Alternating his own handwritten essays with clippings from professional film critics that he disputed with or approved of, he tried his hand at film criticism.[6]

These rationalizing efforts form an all-encompassing order. We could even speak of a *panoramic knowledge*, which strives to grasp and control a broad field—spanning more than 70 years—putting what Christian Keathley calls a "panoramic perception" (2006,

6   These discursive regimes have been extensively discussed from a cultural history perspective in Bernabei and Mariani (2022).

30) of each picture[7] into a productive discursive relation with an all-encompassing understanding of film history. Accordingly, *montage* has a crucial function within this discursive operation: it puts a series of fragments into a meaningful sequence, embracing decades upon decades of major film directors' filmographies, actors' performances, and trivia. It creates "a sequential viewing experience" (Levin 1993, 75) that is also open to a film historiography both bespoke (relying on Faglioni's own cinema viewing experience) and perfected (according to Faglioni's personal critical opinions).[8] In scrapbook after scrapbook, temporality is meticulously and obsessively punctuated and recorded through expressive and informative writing and a montage of clippings. To a certain extent, these scrapbooks' discursive and symbolic fluctuations tend to the pole of the *distal* in Polanyi's dialectics of tacit knowledge (2009, 10).

Discursive strategies operate as a constant, an *all-embracing background, fostering* unity, coherence, and evolution. Through forms of discursive montage, Faglioni creates recursive "jumps" that connect contemporary screenings to memories of past viewing experiences of the same film (merging decades into one fragment) and relate a single film fragment to a film director's entire oeuvre or to a film genre (situating a film into a chronological sequence that intended to demonstrate artistic progression or decay). He also shows how his personal critical viewpoint has changed over time and re-connects it to a period in the past or, for instance, when he connects a picture of Louise Brooks in *Pandora's Box (Pabst 1929)* to her portrait at the age of 83 (scrapbook no. 1). Thus, montage dominates the scrapbook's composition from this discursive perspective. Forming a distant lens ordering each fragment into a temporal sequence, it embodies

---

7   The cinephile's "defining mode of vision" *scrutinizes* the surface of the magnified fragment as she or he layers it onto the scrapbook's folio.

8   In a certain way, this is also a form of "utopian" film history, based on a complex balance between an institutional canon (attested by the film criticism Faglioni explicitly mentions) and his personal taste.

what Polanyi calls the second term of a tacit knowledge, the *distal,* in the context of film.

Materiality

With regard to their representational content, clippings are directly related to the discursive laws that the cinephile tries to regulate: they are *illustrative*, serving to represent the film references. Nevertheless, the materiality of the scrapbook, suggests a new perspective on the logic underpinning the process of cutting-out the clippings and the way they are pasted in. However, even speaking of "logic" threatens to take us back to a discursive impulse. On the contrary, it is the material side of these clippings that I want to emphasize by focusing on the principles of framedness discussed above. First of all, these pictures have *already been experienced* by the gaze of the cinephile. They have already been seen (every fragment derives from an *already-watched* film), and they have already been printed (in film and later paper, usually through rotogravure). This peculiar redundancy accentuates the *mark* of the fragment and—according to Mersch—is a condition for the "perception of a frame" (2015, 3). It turns the fragment into an actual *iconic* element.[9] In Mersch's words, these fragments "are not so much disposed to impart something to the observer, instead, they rather *show*" (2015, 2); they "epitomize an act of exhibition,"[10] indicating a way to view, and so make patent the visual *per se,*

9   I rely here on Mersch's definition of the "iconic": "It is, however, the framing dispositif that initially turns the image-like into an image and produces the duplicity of 'viewing something as an image' and 'observing something in the image.' Every border is marked with a difference, and it constitutes itself along this difference. Here, it can be designated as 'iconic'" (2015, 3).

10   I often refer to this expression by Francesco Casetti and Andrea Pinotti, used to question Vilem Flusser's technical images. I am stressing a pre-cursive affinity between technical images as "mosaics assembled from particles" (Flusser 2011, 31), and the material quality of the scrapbook's framedness: accordingly, technical images, as the scrapbook's framedness, "literally 'design' our sensibility and our action" (Casetti and Pinotti 2020, 197).

[Figure 1] Spread folio from Scrapbook no. 1 (Source: Faglioni ca. 1980, courtesy of Centro Espressioni Cinematografiche, Udine–Walter Faglioni Collection)

rather than making (other) things visible. Stressing the materiality and mediality of clipping means that one perceives not just the things shown within the fragment (a visible reminder of a film or an isolated reference to an actor/actress) but instead sees the fragment "as" an image or, better, as a thing "that makes 'something' visible" (Mersch 2015, 2).

Furthermore, it is worth mentioning here how the simultaneous juxtaposition of clippings of multiple, different scales (even when pasted on different layers) make each fragment's content—often redundant and sometimes lost in vagueness without explicit captions or discursive contexts provided by Faglioni—*excessive.* For example, certain spreads—often without any explicit verbal statement—foreground the *mark* and the multi-scale format of the frames as *dispositifs* or "open windows": they manifest a substantial similarity with computer desktop boxes and windows while recalling an operational toolset where each single "window" discloses a potential for hyper-expansion (see fig. 1).

Accordingly, this first material feature of framedness opens a complex relationship with the cinematic apparatus. The clipping's operations resonate with Vilem Flusser's definition of *technical images*, which are "not mirrors but projectors" (2011, 51). More than expressions of content, these clippings or cut-ups are exhibitions of media operations: material displays of a

disassembled, re-mediated cinematic medium. This is the first
feature of the scrapbook's tacit cinematic power.

The fragments *do not automatically* refer to the film they
originated from or recover a particular film experience. This is
the second material feature of framedness. Suppose we stop
thinking about these fragments discursively and try to let them
speak as material formations. In that case, we realize, in Mersch's
words, that they do not refer to "that thing which surrounds the
image and separates its interior from the exterior" (2015, 3). This
is where the *erasure* operates: the *mark* intensifies the vacuum
around the fragment (the erasure of the graphic background)
and the void of the film it derives from. From this material perspective, the framedness of the scrapbook is working *against* the
memory of film, *stricto sensu.*

Nevertheless, this effect does not depend on the presence or
absence of a given caption or other explicit references to the
film in question: it is not just the lack of a description that blurs
the fragment's reference to the film it originated from. Roland
Barthes stressed this characteristic in his tentative theory of the
film still. His well-known text concerning "obtuse meaning" (1977)
is based on an in-depth analysis of film fragments from Sergei
Eisenstein's *Ivan the Terrible* (1944). Not surprisingly, he opens
his argument by declaring his absolute disregard for the exact
memory of a film, whether discursively—"it matters little if I am
unable to remember the details of the story exactly" (Barthes
1977, 52)—or materially, when he refers not to excerpts of the
film directly but to stills reproduced in the *Cahiers du cinéma*
(they were taken from magazines, precisely like the scrapbook's
fragments). Even more radically, Barthes assumes that framing
has an infrastructural function, explaining the nexus between a
film still and the film it comes from in terms of a palimpsest. The
erasure is so radical that it defers the reference of the fragment
towards a film that "has still to be born theoretically" (Barthes
1977, 67).

[Figure 2] Single folio from Scrapbook no. 3 (Source: Faglioni ca. 1980, courtesy of Centro Espressioni Cinematografiche, Udine–Walter Faglioni Collection).

The scrapbook's framedness relies on this same principle: the erasure accentuates the iconic value of the fragment, and, as Barthes was right to argue radically, it makes evident the infrastructural function of the frame, opening the door to a potentially infinite re-assemblage of the film. In an eloquent passage from the scrapbook Faglioni dedicated to the 1950s (Scrapbook no. 3), the cinephile assembled a multi-layered folio focused on Billy Wilder's *The Seven Year Itch* (1955) (see fig. 2). In this folio, one may distinguish among three overlapping layers. The first, on the outer surface, is a scene (a photogram) from the film, portraying Marilyn Monroe and Tom Ewell in a hilarious and seductive moment when she fell off of a piano bench; the second one, at a medium depth, is the iconic photograph of Monroe standing above a subway grate with her famous white "flying skirt" (a promotional image derived from the shot of a street photographer); the third layer—the deepest and the largest one, covering the entire background of the folio—is a "modern" advertisement from the 1980s in which a model is mimicking Marylin's iconic gesture, with a red dress and false blond hair (with brown eyebrows).

The reference to *The Seven Year Itch* is explicit (and even verbalized in the form of a caption). Nevertheless, the erasure operates progressively and profoundly towards a material betrayal of the original reference: the first layer is a black and white reproduction printed on low-cost newsprint paper (while the film was shot in Technicolor and with a CinemaScope lens). Thus, the effect of material transientness that rotogravure would have allowed for is missing. The second fragment does not even belong to the film: as we know, the subway's "delicious breeze" scene is astutely edited, alternating a low shot of Marylin's feet and legs (at knee height) and close-ups of Ewell's and Monroe's faces. That total shot is never shown in the film; finally, the last layer represents the absolute material detachment from the bodily presence of Marylin Monroe: the iconic value is transferred—for its formal function—and transubstantiated onto another body.

The third material feature of framedness relates to montage. In a pioneering text about the cultural value of the scrapbook, Maud Levin sees in the montage an integral *mechanism* that defines the scrapbook, and it even informs an intermedial relation with the cinematic medium: "the [scrap]book as a whole functions as a montage as well. As a sequential viewing experience, it could even be called filmic. Turning the pages, 'reading' the book, introduced the element of time" (Levin 1993, 75). I would call Levin's account of montage "discursive." On the one hand, temporality in the scrapbook is shaped by montage; therefore, as I discussed earlier, montage informs the "*distal*" level of tacit knowledge of film. On the other hand, I suggest that the *increase* is structurally

[Figure 3] Single folio from Scrapbook no. 2 (Source: Faglioni ca. 1980, courtesy of Centro Espressioni Cinematografiche, Udine–Walter Faglioni Collection).

linked to Polanyi's first term, or the *proximal* level of tacit cinematic knowledge.

As I wrote above, the increase is served by the mark and serves the erasure. The increase as a vertical, additive, spatial growth of the folio does not create explicit associations or temporal connections. It rather enhances the outline of the fragment within the space—that is, it enhances its *presentness* both in terms of a temporal break and in terms of an image that "ceases to be a re-presentation of a reality it refers to …, presenting itself directly as reality in the flesh" (Casetti and Pinotti 2020, 204). The increase shapes an environment where modes of visual apperception governed by material elements, such apertures and projections defined by the gestures of the mark that I have previously described, are revealed, and the material remains of the cinema

apparatus, more profoundly and subtly than the those described
by Levin, are incorporated. Accordingly, the increase reveals the
epistemic "tacit power" of the fragment.

Some of the most audacious, multi-layered folios of Faglioni's
scrapbooks (see fig. 3) render visible the erasure of the source
(the original films disappear in a "mute" iconic pulp of partial
frames and picture fragments), and, simultaneously, they allow
the film's transformations across media to survive in residual
material formations, wherein framedness opens to immersion as
a technical illusion and a way to access a form of non-symbolic,
non-expressive knowledge.

What Knowledge?

In these scrapbooks, the materiality of the cut-outs uncovers
epistemic frictions that conjoin the symbolic and discursive
structure of these cultural objects. Materiality puts forward the
detail, the fetishization of a particle. The *proximal*, which is a
magnified mode of viewing an ensemble of particularities, cannot
be bound by the laws and principles of the comprehensive entity
it originates from; that is, the detail cannot be governed by the
discourse of the film. Rather, what is primarily emerging here is
the framing of the particular. Moreover, the framing first refers
to the *dispositif*—the system of material and non-material conditions that mark a "border." Framing, as Mersch writes, "evolves
into a principle of reflexivity that draws attention to something
which is at the same time veiled by the image: the scene of its
visualization" (2015, 5).

Through the materiality of the clippings and the particularities
emerging through framedness, the scrapbook draws attention
to the *mediality* of film, and cinema as a medium in permanent
transformation. By focusing on framedness, the distal disappears: the film's discursive aspects dissolve in the incompress-
ible tangle of lines and angles in which any specific references
to the film are erased. The "comprehensive entity" is negated,

 as Mersch argues; instead, the pictorial and the iconic mark the peculiar material experience of the scrapbooks. He proposes the artistic technique of "anamorphosis," originating in the Renaissance, as a metaphor for such a material and speculative approach to the medial. Anamorphic techniques of representation "intervene in the construction of illusion by simultaneously revealing and confirming the secrets of their production" (Mersch 2013, 213), and again:

> [Anamorphosis] provides no recognisable representation; rather, it erases that which is represented and dissolves the figure in order to have it emerge in another place, namely at an extreme angle of almost 180° … The picture has to be negated, it has to be dissolved in an incomprehensible tangle of lines, in order to create a puzzle that the observer can experience, the solution to which he can only discover if he looks at it from the side. (Mersch 2013, 214)

And therefore, "[i]n this way anamorphosis creates a paradoxical figurality that by appearing to show nothing, shows the mediality of image construction" (Mersch 2013, 215). Accordingly, I argue that the materiality of the scrapbooks, their tacit cinematic dimension, opens up a similar paradox based on a rupture between the discursive and formal representation of film history and experience and a means to experience the history and materiality of the film by virtue of their deliberate material construction.

A *media anamorphosis* operates here. Structuring knowledge through the incorporation of cinema's material remains, the tacit cinematic knowledge materialized in these scrapbooks produces an implicit destabilization of the gaze that intersects with the discursive knowledge of film, producing a view "from the side."

This article has been conceived within the collaborative project PRIN2022 Cinephemera. Ephemeral materials for the study of Italian cinema between the 1930s and 1960s (Project Code 20228MRWL2 PI Mariapia Comand), funded by UE-PNRR of the Italian Ministry of University Research.

Literature

Anselmo, Diana W. 2009. "Bound by Paper: Girl Fans, Movie Scrapbooks, and Hollywood Reception during World War I." *Film History* 31 (3): 141–72.

Barthes, Roland. 1977 [1970]. "The Third Meaning: Research Notes on some Eisenstein Stills." In *Image, Music, Text, edited and translated by Stephen Heath, 52–68.* London: Fontana Press.

Beegan, Gerry. 2017. "The Picturegoer: Cinema, Rotogravure, and the Reshaping of the Female Face." In *Women's Periodicals and Print Culture in Britain, 1918–39: The Interwar Period,* edited by Catherine Clay, Maria DiCenzo, Barbera Green, and Fiona Hackney, 185–206. Edinburgh: Edinburgh University Press.

Bernabei, Maria Ida, and Andrea Mariani. 2022. "Story of a Cinema-Goer. Seventy Years of Film Viewing in the City of Udine as Seen Through Ephemera." *Participations: International Journal of Audience Research.* Accessed March 30, 2023. https://www.participations.org/18-02-23-bernabei.pdf.

Casetti, Francesco, and Andrea Pinotti. 2020. "Post-Cinema Ecology." In *Post-Cinema: Cinema in the Post-Art Era,* edited by Dominique Chateau and José Moure, 193–218. Amsterdam: Amsterdam University Press.

De Rosa, Miriam, and Vinzenz Hediger. 2017. "Post-What? Post-When? A Conversation on the 'Posts' of Post-Media and Post-Cinema." *Cinéma & Cie: International Film Studies Journal 16 (26–7): 9–18.*

Flusser, Vilém. 2011 [1985]. *Into the Universe of Technical Images.* Minneapolis: University of Minnesota Press.

Gernes, Toss. 2001. "Recasting the Culture of Ephemera." In *Popular Literacy: Studies in Cultural Practices and Poetics*, edited by John Trimbur, 107–27. Pittsburgh: University of Pittsburgh Press.

Gruber Garvey, Ellen. 2003. "Scissorizing and Scrapbooks: Nineteenth-Century: Reading, Remaking, and Recirculating." In *New Media 1740–1915*, edited by Lisa Gitelman and Geoffrey B. Pingree, 207–28. Cambridge: MIT Press.

Heider, Fritz. 1927. *Ding und Medium.* Dortmund: Weltkreis Verlag.

Keathley, Christian. 2006. *Cinephilia and History, or The Wind in the Trees*. Bloomington: Indiana University Press.

Krtilova, Katerina. 2015. "Media Matter: Materiality and Performativity in Media Theory." In *Media/Matter: The Materiality of Media/Matter as Medium*, edited by Bernd Herzogenrath, 28–43. London: Bloomsbury.

Levin, Maud. 1993. *Cut With the Kitchen Knife: The Weimar Photomontages of Hannah Hoch.* New Haven: Yale University Press.

Luhmann, Niklas. 1995. *Die Kunst der Gesellschaft.* Frankfurt am Main: Suhrkamp Verlag.

———. 1993. "Die Paradoxie der Form." In *Kalkül der Form,* edited by Dirk Baeker. Frankfurt am Main: Suhrkamp.

Mersch, Dieter. 2016. *Das mediale Als. Für einen epistemologischen Medienbegriff.* Köln: Universität zu Köln/Zentrum für Medienwissenschaften und Moderneforschung (Cologne Media Lectures, 32). DOI: https://doi.org/10.25969/mediarep/12600.

——. 2015. "The Image and the Gaze: On the 'Logic' of Iconic Structures." *Dieter Mersch*. Accessed March 30, 2023. http://www.dieter-mersch.de/.cm4all/iproc. php/Englische%20Texte/Mersch_image%20and%20gaze.pdf?cdp=a.

——. 2013. "Tertium Datur: Introduction to a Negative Media Theory Theory." *Matrizes* 7 (1): 207–22.

Polanyi, Michael. 2009 [1966]. *The Tacit Dimension.* Chicago and London: University of Chicago Press.

Spencer-Brown, George. 2008. *Laws of Form.* Leipzig: Bohmeier.

Wickham, Phil. 2010. "Scrapbooks, Soap Dishes and Screen Dreams: Ephemera, Everyday Life and Cinema History." *New Review of Film and Television* 8 (3): 315–30.

(Audio)Visual Material

Eisenstein, Sergei. 1944. *Ivan the Terrible (part 1).* Feature-length film, 99 min., Soviet Union.

Faglioni, Walter. ca. 1980. *Scrapbooks 1 to 6.* Collection, Centro Espressioni Cinematografiche, Udine.

Pabst, Georg Wilhelm. 1929. *Pandora's Box.* Feature-length film, 133 min., Germany.

Wilder, Billy. 1955. *The Seven Year Itch.* Feature-length film, 105 min., United States of America.

AUDIENCE

DIGITAL TECHNOLOGY

NEW MEDIA

MALAYALAM CINEMA

COLLECTIVE CULTURAL LABOR

New Media(tions): Audience's Engagement in Contemporary Malayalam Cinema

R. Haritha

In this essay, I look at some emerging patterns in the audience's engagement with Malayalam cinema—cinema produced in the south Indian state of Kerala—corresponding to the dissemination of digital technology and the popularity of new media. Correlating the new modes of film reception with the expansion of culture industries in the digital age, I read contemporary audience's engagements with cinema as a "collective cultural labor" (Terranova 2000), contributing to an ever-expanding repertoire of knowledge on Malayalam cinema on the internet.

With the spread of digital technology and the proliferation of new media, many online platforms have emerged for sharing and discussing cinema-related content. There are numerous social media pages, websites, blogs, and YouTube channels created by cinema enthusiasts, individually and collectively, in which they share opinions, information, reviews, memories, and observations about films. These platforms also offer opportunities for sharing songs from the films, trailers, behind-the-scenes footage, interviews with filmmakers and industry professionals, memes and troll videos, edited and compiled clips from films, and much more.

In this essay, I explore these emerging patterns in film reception as symptomatic of the transformations in cinema sparked by the emergence of new media. Correlating the new modes of film reception with the expansion of culture industries in the digital age, I read contemporary audiences' engagements with cinema as a "collective cultural labor" (Terranova 2000), contributing to an ever-expanding repertoire of knowledge on Malayalam cinema on the internet.

"Cinema In Detail": Looking into the Screen

When a digital copy of a film becomes available on the internet, the audience gets the chance to rewatch the film multiple times. There are options to pause, rewind, and repeat the film as many times as we want. We can also download the film, possess copies, and edit or repurpose them. A recent trend in the reception of Malayalam cinema indicates a newfound interest in scanning the screen for narrative and technical details, which we may overlook in a single viewing. People post in Malayalam about the details and mistakes they find in old and new Malayalam films on social media pages and YouTube channels and seek further interactions and discoveries from others in the comments section (see fig. 1).

[Figure 1] A screenshot showing the list of videos posted by different YouTube channels analyzing the hidden details in the Malayalam film *Kappela* (Musthafa 2020) (Source: R. Haritha and YouTube 2023a)

They extract frames from the films using readily available tools and mark the details and mistakes that they find.

In these online discussions, users scrutinize various aspects of a movie. These aspects include details in the background of a scene (such as the positioning of background actors, the use of props, or the significance of the background music), technical qualities (the use of visual effects, color grading, and computer-generated images, etc.), and cinematic and narrative elements (such as the development of the plot, narrative continuity, or locations selected). YouTube channels such as *Reeload Media* (2023), *DUO Media* (2023), and *Movie Mania Malayalam* (2023) are notable channels that focus on this method of reading films.

Malayalam Movie and Music DataBase (m3db), one of the largest online databases on Malayalam cinema, has started a separate section on their Facebook page, inviting cinema enthusiasts to share the details they discover from Malayalam films (m3db 2023a; 2023b) . The section, which is titled "Cinema In Detail" (CID), is introduced on the m3db Facebook page as follows:

> M3DB is starting a CID work. 'Cinema In Detail' (CID) is a place to document the overlooked or notable scenes and mistakes in every movie through pictures. Thanks to Mukesh, who suggested this witty and meaningful title. Let's hold the lens and look at each film like a CID. Let this give way to a new visual culture.[1] (Kiranz 2016)

The terms such as "CID" (a pun on the "Criminal Investigation Departments" in India and Britain) "evidence," "hidden," and "decoding" are often used in this Facebook page's discussions, comparing the act of finding details in a film to an act of investigation or a play of discovery. Like a treasure hunt, there seems to be an element of pleasure in scrutinizing and deciphering the screen for details. Laura Mulvey reads the newfound pleasure in scrutinizing the screen as symptomatic of the emergence of a curious spectator. She observes the emergence of "an alternative spectator who was driven, not by voyeurism, but by curiosity and the desire to decipher the screen," and adds:

> Curiosity, a drive to see but also to know, still marked a utopian space for a political, demanding visual culture, but also one in which the process of deciphering might respond to the human mind's longstanding interest and pleasure in solving puzzles and riddles. (Mulvey 2006, 191)

The curiosity that Mulvey observes among the audience in deciphering the film screen is not only a drive to see and to know informed by ideology but also something that responds to our innate interest in solving puzzles and riddles. According to

---

1   All translations by the author.

Mulvey, the prevalence of digital technology has made the close reading of a film text possible for everyone (2006, 144). The critic's special vision "has been generalized and is now democratically available to anyone sufficiently obsessed with cinema to fetishize some special moment that might be either of aesthetic interest or personally fascinating" (Mulvey 2002, 100). This enables anyone who has access to new technology to enjoy the pleasure of analyzing and interpreting films, expanding film interpretation beyond restricted academic domains (Mulvey 2006, 191 and 144).

The audience's detailed readings of Malayalam cinema indicate that viewers are not merely interested in the particularities of a specific shot or scene, but are inclined to scrutinize the significance of the details they identify in order to derive a deeper understanding of the film as a whole. These online exchanges often discuss the importance of certain details for building narrative coherence and verisimilitude throughout the film.[2] Mary Ann Doane states that "the detail and enormity are inextricable in cinema" (2003, 110) and substantiates her argument with the example of close-up shots in cinema. She observes that a close-up has a contradictory quality of being both a detail of a larger scene and a totality in its own right. According to her, the close-up is one of the ways in which cinema responds to the needs of its viewer, who "clings to the hope of simulacra of wholeness" when "faced with an accelerating rationalization, specialization, and disintegration of the sense of a social totality" (Doane 2003, 93). Doane proposes that the proliferation of screens of different magnitudes—from IMAX theatres to mobile screens—and the novel ways of viewing film in the digital age can be better

2   The discussions that investigate details in films became a trend after the release of the film *Maheshinte Prathikaram* (eng. *Mahesh's Revenge*) (Pothen 2016) on February 5, 2016. The film was released in digital format on DVD and VCD on May 10, 2016, after running successfully for more than 125 days in theatres. It was the highest grossing film in Kerala in the January-June box office records. After the film's digital release, the details in the film became a discussion on social media and the phrase "Pothettan's brilliance" was coined to praise the director Dileesh Pothan for the film's realism.

  understood by recognizing that cinema inherently employs paradoxes of detail and enormity, the miniature and the gigantic, as exemplified in the effect of close-up shots.

A Shift in Spectatorship?

31 years after the publication of her seminal article "Visual Pleasure and Narrative Cinema" (1975),[3] Mulvey revisited her theory of spectatorship in her book *Death 24x a Second: Stillness and the Moving Image* (2006), in which she identifies a transformation in spectatorship in the digital age. According to her, for the spectators who watch films on digital devices, the chances of completely surrendering to the narrative drive of the film weaken as they are "aided" by the options to pause, rewind, and repeat the scenes. Hence, the new spectator is driven not towards the voyeuristic pleasure achieved from a loss of ego and identification with the character on screen, but towards a "fetishistic" act of analyzing the scenes in a film (Mulvey 2006, 166). Although manners of film viewing have altered over the years alongside technological advancements, is there a transformation in spectatorship related to digital technology, as Mulvey observes? Were not the options to delay and repeat the scenes already present in the analog video recordings on cassettes such as the Video Home System or Super-8 film?

The shift that Mulvey observes in spectatorship is disputable in light of the genealogy of film viewing discussed by other scholars (Hansen 1991; Hoek 2010; hooks 1992). In her recent study of the cinema audience in Bangladesh, the media anthropologist Lotte Hoek (2010) notes that the narrative coherence of a film is

3   In this article, Mulvey notes that cinema is dominated by a voyeuristic scopophilic gaze that creates a binary of active male and passive female in relations of looking. According to her, the voyeuristic gaze can be broken down further into three different looks associated with cinema. First, "[the look] of the camera as it records the pro-filmic event, [second, the look] of the audience as it watches the final product, and [third, the look] of the characters at each other within the screen illusion" (Mulvey 1975, 17).

not always guaranteed when watched 24 frames per second in cinema halls. Hoek's study focuses on the inclusion and exclusion of "cut pieces"—illegal sexually explicit sequences—in films, which depend upon the practices and conditions of exhibition. She explores how such situations change the form and reception of films, observing that even before the advent of digital technology-aided film viewing, the audience was able to control the narrative coherence in different ways. She identifies that "when thinking about active audiences and their appropriation of mass media, the possibility must be considered that dialogic opportunities do not arise with new digital technologies but are present in cinema halls screening films on celluloid" (Hoek 2010).

However, I consider Mulvey's observation of the involvement of fetishistic behavior in the new modes of analyzing film text significant for my analysis, since it can further elaborate specific characteristic changes pertaining to new media interventions in the reception of cinema. New media is a form of accelerated capitalism (Chun 2016, 2), which functions on user-generated content in various forms, including the fetishistic, obsessive, and repeated activities of cinema enthusiasts. Although subjective and emotional impulses characterize these activities, a great deal of labor is involved in them. Collectively, they contribute to the production and expansion of knowledge about cinema.

Looking Behind the Screen

Today, there is a growing awareness of the technicalities at work behind a cinematic production. With a mobile phone and internet connectivity, anyone can learn the technicalities of using a video camera. In addition to analyzing film text and gathering knowledge on various aspects of cinema, the audience responds to cinema through creative expressions in memes, trolls, video tutorials, video essays. Readily available mobile applications make it easier today to recreate scenes from films or repurpose fragmented frames in the way one wants. These creative

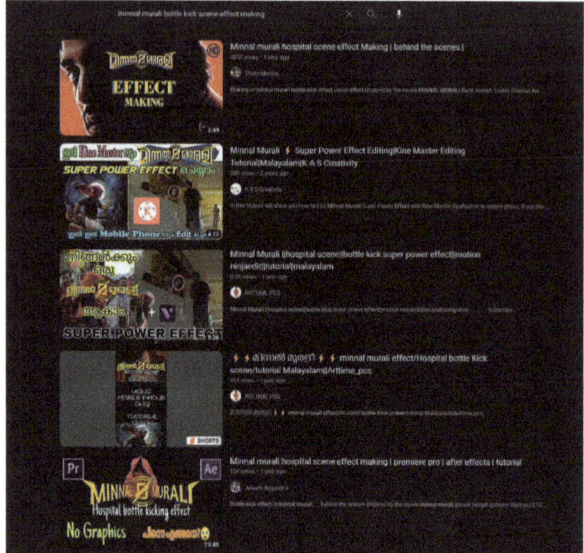

[Figure 2] A screenshot showing the list of videos posted by different YouTube channels demonstrating the making of the bottle kicking scene from *Minnal Murali* (Joseph 2021) (Source: R. Haritha and YouTube 2023b)

expressions are symptomatic of a trend in which viewers find pleasure not only in scanning for details on the screen but also in finding the details of the process at work behind the screen.

On YouTube, there are video tutorials in Malayalam that are shot and edited on mobile phones, which demonstrate the process behind the making of certain computer-generated visual effects in Malayalam cinema (see fig. 2). A YouTube video tutorial posted by *KAS Creativity* (KAS Creativity 2020) showcases the creation of a visual effect used in a scene from the movie *Minnal Murali* (eng. *Lightning Murali*; Joseph 2021). The scene depicts the protagonist gaining superpowers and reflexively kicking a fallen steel vessel back onto the table before it hits the ground. This scene and its creation sparked discussions even after the trailer's release. In the video tutorial, two children act out this scene in their local surroundings while demonstrating the process of creating the effect using the Kine Master—a video editing app—and sharing their mobile screens. Another video demonstration of the same scene posted by *Thakx Movies* features a young man and an older woman, who may be his grandmother, performing the vessel-kicking act within the interior of a house and portraying the creation of the effect (Thakx Movies 2021).

In these videos, the creators use their local surroundings to demonstrate visual effects used in cinema. With the prevalence of new media, people from different social backgrounds started making videos using their neighborhoods and personal spaces. New media applications such as TikTok have recently made notable changes in videomaking and sharing on the internet. On TikTok, one can create and share short videos of a maximum length of 15 minutes. All the shared videos will be displayed on the newsfeed and categorized according to one's tastes and interests. TikTok was India's most downloaded Android mobile application in 2019, with more than 150 million subscribers (Jhony 2023). In 2020, the Indian government banned TikTok along with around 300 Chinese apps, citing concerns about the exposure of user data (Jhony 2023). The short lifespan of TikTok in India seems to have influenced the visual culture in various ways. The different regional, class, and caste locations typically erased or ignored in mainstream media narratives gained visibility through TikTok and other similar new media platforms. These videos, captured first-hand from one's immediate surroundings, offer a distinct conception of realism, arguably influencing the audience in their consumption of verisimilitude in cinema. The interest in the technicalities at work behind the screen, as reflected in the above-mentioned YouTube videos and database websites, indicates audiences' tendency to focus not only on the film's portrayal of reality on screen but also on the technical elements employed to produce an impression of realism on screen. The prevalence of digital devices and the new media have made it easier for the audience to satisfy their long-held curiosity about cinematic technique.

"Collective Cultural Labor": Film Reception and Knowledge Work

The audience's engagements with cinema are symptomatic of an understanding that cinema is a "dispersed phenomenon manifested in various forms" (Mukherjee 2014, 49). Repetitive, obsessive, and laborious activities have always characterized a cinephile's engagements with cinema. Cinema enthusiasts used to collect film memorabilia such as ticket stubs, film posters, images of actors, newspaper cuttings, and the like. In his article tracing early Tamil film history through materials gathered by personal collectors of film memorabilia, Stephen Hughes refers to these collectors as "living archives" and describes their activities as knowledge production that involves a "labor of love" (2013, 74). In the digital age, the internet provides a collective form to the dispersed cinema enthusiasts and the knowledge they gather voluntarily out of their love for cinema.

As Hughes notes, a great deal of labor is involved in these subjective expressions of cinema lovers on the internet (2013, 74). The laborious activities—including extracting frames, researching details, compiling and editing fragmented scenes, gathering and classifying information, and creating videos—not only reproduce, recraft, and reimagine cinema but are also involved in knowledge production. Furthermore, Wendy Hui Kyong Chun suggests understanding new media in terms of "habitual repetition" (2016, 17), arguing that in the age of new media, information is a habit. The habits she describes include streaming, updating, linking, sharing, downloading, saving, mapping, and trolling (Chun 2016, 1). Through constant repetition of these activities, users produce knowledge voluntarily and freely, blurring the distinction between production and

consumption. Thus, these activities are significant aspects of the
digital economy.

Tiziana Terranova (2000) refers to the labor that is voluntarily, enjoyably done, and to time unwaged and exploited as "free labor" in the context of the digital economy. According to her, free labor on the internet includes the activities of "building websites, modifying software packages, reading and participating in mailing lists" (Terranova 2000, 34) as well as many tasks which we do not immediately recognize as labor, such as "chat, real-life stories, armature newsletters and so on" (Terranova 2000, 38). These forms of labor, as she notes, contribute to the emerging and expanding field of "digital economy" that indulges in "the process of economic experimentation with the creation of monetary value out of knowledge/culture/affect" (Terranova 2000, 35). In this sense, free labor is "a trait of the cultural economy at large and an important, yet undervalued, force in advanced capitalist societies" (Terranova 2000, 33). Although exploitation is undoubtedly present in these forms of labor in different ways, Terranova differentiates it from the Marxist conception of an alienated worker. She says:

> Cultural and technical work is central to the internet but is also a widespread activity throughout advanced capitalist societies. I argue that such labor is not exclusive to the so-called knowledge workers, but is also a pervasive feature of the post-industrial economy. The pervasiveness of such production questions the legitimacy of a fixed distinction between production and consumption, labor and culture. (Terranova 2000, 35)

Terranova differentiates free labor from the conception of work associated with "servitude, misery and subordination" (2000, 35). Free labor diminishes the distinction between work and cultural expression in the post-industrial economy. The knowledge work that the film audience voluntarily performs online out of their love for cinema can be understood as a form of such free labor.

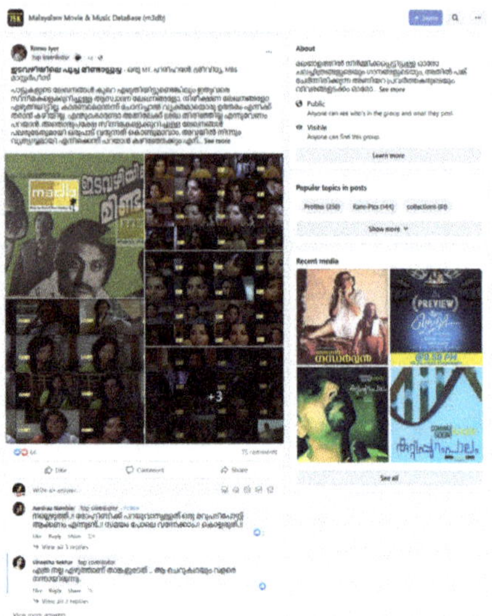

[Figure 3] Screenshot of the m3db Facebook group (Source: m3db 2023a)

Considering the collective nature of these activities of gathering and sharing information, the new forms of audience responses on the internet can be identified as "collective cultural labor" in Terranova's terms.

The internet provides a platform for film enthusiasts from different parts of the world to connect with each other, form collectives, and share and discuss information about cinema. For instance, m3db, Malayalasangeetham.info, and Malayalachalachi-thram.org are online databases on Malayalam cinema which are formed by collectives of Malayali film enthusiasts from different parts of the world. They function using user-generated content gathered from their social media pages and maintain Facebook pages where the members can share everything related to Malayalam cinema, ranging from extensive research on obscure and lesser-known details (such as unreleased films, lesser-known actors, and uncredited artists) to discussions on personal

memories and opinions about films and film-related matters (see
fig. 3).

The topics of the discussions cover nearly every aspect of film-making, from pre-production, to production, post-production, and distribution. The database websites are updated regularly from the information gathered from these discussions, and admin teams check the reliability of the information and give credit to the contributors. These database websites contain comprehensive knowledge about 6.000–8.000 Malayalam films, detailed profiles of more than 50.000 film professionals, and a vast collection of Malayalam films and soundtracks. Apart from that, they have the details of film award winners, a list of film studios, featured articles, collections of essays on cinema, and interviews with film professionals. This user-generated information is classified in these databases and made available for public access.

As Terranova notes, "knowledge labor is inherently collective" and gives form to a "collective intelligence" (2000, 46; 43). However, as she points out, these formations of collective intelligence are not to be romanticized like the "cyber drool of the digiterati" since all these feed into capitalism which "extract[s] as much value as possible out of this abundant, and yet slightly intractable, terrain" (Terranova 2000, 46). Although capitalism did not produce these types of cultural and technical labor as a response to its economic needs, she notes that they emerged in relation to the expansion of cultural industries and are a result of economic experimentation aimed at generating monetary value from knowledge, culture, and affect (Terranova 2000, 38).

Conclusion

In this essay, I have read the audience's engagements with Malayalam cinema in the contemporary as collective and voluntary activities of producing and sharing knowledge. I propose that these new modes of film reception can be understood as "collective cultural labor" (Terranova 2000), in light of the prevalence of new media and emerging forms of capitalism in the digital age.

My goal is not to jump into technological determinism but rather to focus on finding alterations and mutations in film reception at its juncture with emerging new-media forms. Marshal McLuhan argues that new forms of media "alter sense ratios or patterns of perception" (1994, 18), calling this change in perception the "ratio of the senses" and emphasizing that the way we perceive is constantly being altered by new technologies. As we adapt to these changes, our bodies and senses may also change and adapt to the new possibilities offered by these technologies (McLuhan 1994). In the 21st century, cinema is no longer cultural dominant as it has been "surpassed" by the new media and cinema's "core technologies of production and reception have become obsolete" (Shaviro 2016, 848). As Steven Shaviro points out "older media forms don't necessarily disappear; instead, they are repurposed" (ibid.). In this essay, I discussed some observations about cinema's current repurposing, focusing on audience's engagements in online platforms.

Literature

Chun, Wendy Hui Kyong. 2016. *Updating to Remain the Same: Habitual New Media*. London: The MIT Press, Cambridge.

Doane, Mary Ann. 2003. "The Close-Up: Scale and Detail in the Cinema." *Differences: A Journal of Feminist Cultural Studies* 14 (3): 89–111.

Hansen, Miriam. 1991. *Babel and Babylon: Spectatorship in American Silent Film*. Harvard University Press.

Hoek, Lotte. 2010. "Unstable Celluloid: Film Projection and the Cinema Audience in Bangladesh." *BioScope: South Asian Screen Studies* 1 (1): 49–66.

hooks, Bell. 1992. "The Oppositional Gaz: Black Female Spectators." In *Black Looks: Race and Representation*, 115–32. Boston: South End Press.

Hughes, Stephen Putnam. 2013. "The Production of the Past: Early Tamil Film History as a Living Archive." *BioScope: South Asian Screen Studies* 4 (1): 71–80.

Jhony, Ritu Maria. 2023. "TikTok Shuts India Office, Fires All Employees Three Years after Ban: Report." *Hindustan Times*. February 10. Accessed April 5, 2023. https://www.hindustantimes.com/business/

tiktok-shuts-india-office-fires-all-employees-three-years-after-ban-report-101676018194464.html.

McLuhan, Marshall. 1994. *Understanding Media: The Extensions of Man*. London: The MIT Press, Cambridge.

Mukherjee, Debashree. 2014. "Folding a World into Itself." In *Filmi Jagat: A Scrapbook: Shared Universe of Early Hindi Cinema*, edited by Kaushik Bhaumik, Debashree Mukherjee, and Rahaab Allana, 35–64. Delhi: Niyogi Books.

Mulvey, Laura. 2006. *Death 24x a Second: Stillness and the Moving Image*. London: Reaktion Books Ltd.

———. 2002. "Detail, Digression, Death: The Movies in Chris Petit's Film Negative Space." *Afterall: A Journal of Art, Context and Enquiry* 5 (January): 98–105.

———. 1975. "Visual Pleasure and Narrative Cinema." *Screen* 16 (3): 6–18.

Shaviro, Steven. 2016. "The Post-Cinematic in Paranormal Activity and Paranormal Activity 2." In *Post-Cinema: Theorising 21st-Century Film*, edited by Shane Denson and Julia Leyda Denson, 841–78. Falmer: Reframe books.

Terranova, Tiziana. 2000. "Free Labor: Producing Culture for the Digital Economy." *Social Text* 18 (2): 33–58.

(Audio)Visual Material

DUO Media. 2023. "DUO media: about." *YouTube*. Accessed April 6, 2023. https://www.youtube.com/@DUOmedia0/about.

Joseph, Basil. 2021. *Minnal Murali*. Feature-length film, 159 min., India.

Kiranz. 2016. "Cinema In Detail." *m3db.com*. Accessed April 5, 2023. https://m3db.com/cid/mp.

KAS Creativity. 2020. "Minnal Murali Super Power Effect Editing|Kine Master Editing Tutorial|Malayalam|K A S Creativity." *YouTube*, September 20. Accessed April 5, 2023. https://www.youtube.com/watch?v=8z3gol hy1BU.

M3db. 2023a. "Facebook Group: Malayalam Movie & Music DataBase (m3db)." *Facebook*. Accessed April 6, 2023. https://www.facebook.com/groups/m3dbgroup/.

m3db. 2023b. "Malayalam Movie & Music DataBase (m3db)." *m3db.com*. Accessed April 6, 2023. https://m3db.com/.

Movie Mania Malayalam. 2023. "Movie Mania Malayalam: about." *YouTube*. Accessed April 6, 2023. https://www.youtube.com/@MovieManiaMalayalam/about.

R. Haritha and YouTube. 2023a. "Results for the YouTube Search 'hidden details in the Malayalam film Kapeela.'" *YouTube*. Accessed April 6, 2023. https://www.youtube.com/results?search_query=hidden+details+in+Malayalam+film+kappela.

R. Haritha and YouTube. 2023b. "Results for the YouTube Search 'minnal murali bottle kick scene effect making.'" *YouTube*. Accessed April 6, 2023. https://www.youtube.com/results?search_query=minnal+murali+bottle+kick+scene+effect+making.

Reeload Media. 2023. "REELOAD MEDIA: about." *YouTube*. Accessed April 6, 2023. https://www.youtube.com/@REELOADMEDIA/about.

Thakx Movies. 2021. "Minnal Murali Hospital Scene Effect Making | Behind the Scenes |." *YouTube*. May 21. Accessed April 5, 2023. https://www.youtube.com/watch?v=4huUAqpmoso.

Musthafa, Muhammad. 2019. *Kappela*. Feature-length film, 113 min., India.

Pothen, Dileesh. 2016. *Maheshinte Prathikaram*. Feature-length film, 120 min., India.

POLITICAL THEORY

MARKETING

DEMOCRACY

PROPAGANDA

FILM THEORY

USER-GENERATED CONTENT

DIGITAL PLATFORMS

Unauthorized Fictions: Political Conflict as Spectacle and the Question of Trust in the Age of Trump

Vinzenz Hediger and Felix M. Simon

Why do supporters of former US president Donald Trump make short tribute videos which resemble mainstream action film trailers with their idol as the protagonist? And why does the Trump campaign use a similar trailer template for video of rallies and campaign spots? This contribution traces the increasing use of cinematic storytelling templates in the digital media environment, particularly for Trump's right-wing authoritarian politics. We focus on tribute and campaign videos which appeal to the viewer's tacit knowledge of the trailer format to make political conflicts legible as dramatic confrontations. We argue that their stylization of political conflict as spectacle

should be understood as an example of "ocular democracy" (Green 2011), in which the gaze, rather than the voice, is the source of popular empowerment. To the extent that these films signal a threat to liberal democracy, it lies not in the narrativization of conflict in cinematic terms, but in the propagation of generalized distrust in combination with particularized trust in the figure of the demagogue.

Ocular Democracy and the Rise of the Trump Tribute Trailer

In the run up to the 2016 US presidential election, short video tributes to Donald Trump appeared on YouTube, attracting thousands and sometimes hundreds of thousands of views (Montreux 2017a; 2017b; Chapman 2019; Guardian News 2018). Made by supporters, these films emulate the style and tone of contemporary action film trailers. They use news footage to build a narrative of Trump as the strident outsider who takes on the dark forces of the establishment in the name of the people and ends up winning against all odds. The model was taken up by the Trump campaign itself, which used the trailer template for warm-up videos at rallies and in the all-important "closing argument" final spot of the campaign (The Telegraph 2022; Trump White House Archived 2020). In the 2020 election cycle, supporter-made tribute trailers appeared again (MateyProductions 2019; 2020a; 2020b). A trailer video whipped up the crowd on the mall on January 6, 2021, and a trailer-style video announced Trump's 2024 presidential bid on "Truth Social" (Liberty South Media 2022).

These videos appeal to a "knowledge the viewers don't realize they have," a tacit knowledge of the trailer as a generic form, acquired in passing through their exposure to contemporary audiovisual culture (Gregersen and Lankjær 2017, 76).[1] Contemporary trailers simulate a film by providing a condensed summary which ends in a cliffhanger, but suggests that the protagonist will prevail. In a seeming paradox, trailers anticipate the coming attraction by creating an incomplete sense of something that has already happened, and leaving one desiring to fill in the gaps (Hediger 2011, especially chapter 7). If "horse-race coverage" casts politics in terms of sports, trailer videos cast political conflict in terms of immersive fiction with as-yet-open but largely pre-ordained outcomes.

Julian Sanchez, a conservative pundit who made a name for himself decrying the "epistemic closure" on the right, has criticized the encroachment of cinematic templates on politics as a "cinematic epistemology": voters see themselves as actors in quasi-fictional plots and crowd out rational argument (Sanchez 2022). If we define democracy with Adam Przeworski (2019) as a system of governance in which parties lose elections and accept defeat, and consider that the Trump tribute trailers express allegiance to a movement which led to the attempted overthrow of the duly elected government of the US on January 6, 2021, Sanchez would seem to have a point. Democratic deliberation usually requires propositional knowledge and openness.[2] By contrast, a framing of politics anchored in tacit knowledge of immersive fiction with seemingly preordained outcomes undermines this standard, which could explain the delusions of power which drove the insurgency of January 6.

1   The concept of "tacit knowledge," which stipulates that "we can know more than we can tell," was introduced by Michael Polanyi (2009; 2015). For a discussion of tacit knowledge and corporeality in film experience see Christiane Voss' article "Film Experience and the Formation of Illusion: The Spectator as 'Surrogate Body' for the Cinema" (2011).
2   "Our knowledge has propositional structure; beliefs can be represented in the form of statements," is the opening statement of Jürgen Habermas' "Theory of Communicative Action," which provides a framework for his theory of democratic deliberation (Habermas 1984, 8).

Going one step further, and following a pattern of "Weimar analogies" which cast Trumpism as the second coming of fascism (Bessner 2017), philosopher Jason Stanley (2021) marshalled an impressive visual lexicon to read the rally video/trailer shown on January 6, 2021 as a reiteration of 1930s propaganda. However, fascism can be defined as the defense of the state against perceived internal enemies—in the case of Nazi Germany, Jews, Sinti, Roma, homosexuals, communists, etc. (Nolte 2008). Trump videos tell the opposite story: that of the state, in the guise of the current government, as the enemy. A line from one of Trump's speeches, often used in the trailer videos, summarizes the plot: "Our movement is about replacing a failed and corrupt political establishment with a new government controlled by you, the American People"(Montreux 2017a). Far from a harbinger of imminent fascism, systematic distrust of government and the state is a key marker of a functioning modern democracy (Rosanvallon 2008). As a matter of fact, the story of the leader who reclaims democratic rule from a corrupt elite in the name of the people is as old as democracy itself. The figure of the *demagogos* installed by the masses to challenge the nobility is central to Aristotle's—deeply skeptical—assessment of democracy in his "Politics" (Canfora 2008, 9). What is more, left-wing versions of this story also exist (Mouffe 2018).

The tribute trailers should thus not be relegated to a fringe area outside of democratic politics, nor should they be too quickly read as a devious misappropriation of democratic tropes, as Stanley warns in his earlier work on propaganda (2016). Rather, the story they tell is part and parcel of the "democratic political imaginary" (Trautmann 2020), and their form and mode of production are inherently democratic. In his classic study on the emergence of popular sovereignty, Edmund S. Morgan speaks of the "necessary fictions" which are required for governance:

> Make believe that the king is divine, make believe that he can do no wrong or make believe that the voice of the people is the voice of god. Make believe that the people *have* a voice or

> make believe that the representatives of the people *are* the people. (1988, 13f.)

The tools of make-believe in both modern representative systems of governance and totalitarian ones include a set of authorized stories and symbols that legitimate claims to power and define a space of governance (Frank 2021). The Trump tribute trailers emerge in a more equitable and democratic media ecology. As fan art and user-generated content, they are unauthorized fictions of popular sovereignty. They exemplify what Philipp Manow (2020) calls "the (de)democratization of democracy", a surplus of popular democracy which poses a challenge to established, liberal democracy. In the fiction of the tribute trailers, distrust is warranted by the people's sense of dispossession, and trust is restored through the capture of democratic processes by the populist insurgency under the leadership of the *demagogos,* who serves as the conduit of popular sovereignty. As such, the tribute trailers propose a solution, however imaginary, for a core problem of democratic governance: namely, how trust in government can be maintained and, if necessary, restored in complex societies ridden by conflicts which threaten to erode that trust.

In this contribution, we focus on how the Trump videos dramatize the dynamics of trust and conflict using the trailer template, and what that dramatization entails. The trailer videos warrant an empirical study concerning their reach and impact, but our focus in the current essay is theoretical. By framing insurgent democratic politics as a spectacular drama, the videos participate in what Jeffrey Edward Green has called "ocular democracy," a configuration of popular sovereignty in which not the voice, but the eyes of the people function "as a site ... of popular empowerment," and in which power over politicians is exerted through the "disciplinary force of the People's gaze" (Green 2011, 3 and 107). Distrust and the emergence of trust in ocular democracy, then, is a matter of spectatorial affect, and of the power of the spectatorial gaze, trained on both the protagonist and their antagonists in the drama of political conflict. This also means that spectatorial affect and the tacit knowledge of cinematic templates are inherent to democratic deliberation, and not just noise to be filtered out on the way to a rational theory of deliberation focused on propositional knowledge (Chambers 2012).

Trump Tribute Videos as Trailers and Political Cinema

The term "trailer" initially designated a black strip attached to a film print for protection. In serials from the 1910s, this strip was used to announce the week's episode. With the advent of the feature film, the term "trailer" carried over to short films consisting of clips which advertised the coming attractions. Cinematic trailers are still considered to be the most effective advertising for films, because they address a captive audience of moviegoers.

For a century now, the industry has been counting on the audience's tacit knowledge of the trailer's form to facilitate communication. Based on an extensive empirical study, Ed Tan and Valentijn Visch argue that viewers recognize film genres not through story events but by processing of what they call "filmic realization cues" (Tan and Visch 2008, 301). These cues include what David Bordwell (1985) in his neo-formalist theory of film narration calls "style," i.e. filmic surface parameters such as color, light, sound, music, or editing, which he opposes to "deep" features such as "syuzhet" (or plot) and "fabula" (or story world). "Filmic realization cues" can also be described as elements of style which the viewer has learned to classify as typical for, and thus indicative of, specific genres of film. In Hollywood's classical sound era, trailers used voice-overs, roll-on titles, and a wide variety of wipes (i.e., image transitions), regardless of the genre of the advertised film. Audiences would instantly know that they were watching a trailer and process the information accordingly.

Wipes and titles vanished around 1960, and since the mid-1980s North American mainstream movie trailers have been built from the soundtrack up. Now, the beginning of a trailer is marked by an element of sound—usually a fragment of dialogue—paired with a segment of black film. Continuity is established through dialogue and music, and visuals are added in an editing pattern which is unique to trailers and which trailer makers describe as "the grid." In this pattern images from a scene with dialogue are interspersed with other images which add information and perspective. This editing technique allows trailers to condense the narrative of a two-hour feature film into a two-minute summary.

Viewers often complain that trailers give away too much of the film, but this is done by design. In a saturated media market with highly specific target groups, moviegoers rely on trailers for information first, but they trust word of mouth the most. Trailers are designed to reach the intended core audience of the film, but they are also designed to keep everyone for whom the film is not intended away from the cinemas, to minimize negative impressions spread by word of mouth (Hediger 2001). Trump tribute trailers, TV spots, and campaign videos carefully emulate this stylistic template. However, they are not advertisements for films, but tools of affective mobilization. They tell the story of the Trump movement as a popular insurgency to help the viewer justify and feel good about their voting preference. They address viewers not simply as citizens and voters, but as members of a protest movement and participants in a conflict of historical proportions, and just as contemporary trailers do, they deliberately exclude part of the audience as well.

However, if the Trump tribute videos are trailers in form, but not function, and if they are also not simply campaign spots, then what, exactly, are they?

From a media studies point of view, the tribute trailers are UGC or "user-generated content" (Cunningham and Craig 2019). Trump tribute trailers, some of which were made by film-industry

[Figure 1] A screenshot of Donna Gail's commentary and the responses it generated (Source: Montreux 2017a).

professionals, may also be described as a semi-professional form of fan art (Barnes 2022; Hediger 2020). For the fan, political allegiance is not primarily a matter of rational calculation and material interest, like union or party membership. In fact, and despite the many suggestions to the contrary, the driving force of the Trump movement is not the often-quoted "economic anxiety." In 2016, Trump voters on average had twice the income of voters for Hilary Clinton (Silver 2017), and they typically were among the wealthiest in poor districts (Blum 2017). Trump voters eat cake every day, and the solace which MAGA-supporter Donna Gail finds in Brandos Montreux' tribute video may well be described as a form of political wellness for the relatively affluent.[3] Much in that spirit, in the comments section of Montreux' "Trump: The Great Victory" (2017a) tribute video , Donna Gail writes: "Whenever I feel a little down in the dumps, I watch this video. It always makes me feel good! MAGA!" (see fig. 1).

From a film studies point of view, the tribute trailers can be seen as amateur films. The TV spots are advertising, and the rally videos are non-artistic utility films. They are also found-footage

3   A recent study in experimental economics shows that partisan group identity was a better predictor of political positioning and polarization than assumptions about rational choice and material interests (Bauer et al. 2022).

films composed of documentary and stock footage. Incidentally, **249**
this classificatory fuzziness proves an important point: like other
types of tacit knowledge, cinematic knowledge has "a sweeping
presence in the world" but "cannot be easily formalized and put
into exact words" (Sen 2009, x). This can explain why even in the
new digital media environment, which is sometimes called the
"post-cinema condition" (De Rosa and Hediger 2017), "cinema"
has proven to be remarkable resilient as an umbrella term for
audiovisual formats. The persistence of the term "cinema" can
be seen as an indicator that "cinema" circumscribes a distinctive
realm of knowledge, rather than a specific medium, technology,
or art form. It is, perhaps first and foremost, a name for what we
know about, and through, cinema, but cannot say.

So, if Trump tribute trailers are "cinema," can we also treat Trump
videos as "political cinema"?

If cinema were political by default, we would not need a category
like "political cinema" to designate when and where cinema is,
in fact, political. But if cinema were apolitical by default it would
not be the quintessential modern art it has often been hailed
to be, let alone a "democratic emblem" (Badiou 2009). Jacques
Rancière (2013) has argued that in the transition to modernity a
"regime of representation" makes way for an "aesthetic regime"
of art. In the first, art is directly subservient to power and serves
to represent and legitimate the established order. In the second,
art acquires the freedom to concern itself with the play of form,
while the privilege of artistic representation is accorded not just
to the king, but to anyone. This also means that in the "aesthetic
regime," art has to negotiate its relationship with power, which
is why modern art incessantly oscillates between the poles of
autonomy and engagement, i.e. between setting its own rules
apart from politics, and taking a stance by shaping political
causes into an aesthetic experience.

By virtue of its popular resonance and its strong purchase on
social reality (which is usually theorized under the rubric of

 "realism") cinema is perhaps more strongly entangled with power than any other art. Narrative films translate complex social issues into accessible and memorable emotional experiences, shaping what audiences perceive as relevant, representable, and socially feasible. Cinematic representation, in other words, is also a form of political representation. Political representation is the approximative procedural solution for the problem of self-governance in modern societies (Möllers 2021; Stasavage 2020). Through elections, the governed consent to be governed by delegates for a limited period of time. For cinematic representation, the ballot box is the box office. Stars express and represent the desires and aspirations of their fans, ruling by charisma, but they serve at the mercy of the audience (Dyer 2019). Struggles about cinematic representation, like the recent award show controversies (e.g. #OscarsSoWhite, addressing the non-nomination of Greta Gerwig for Barbie), are actually political struggles about who belongs to a polity and who does not.

In Hollywood, the standard response to cinema's entanglement with politics has been to avoid overt political statements whenever possible. Studios operate with an ethos of neutrality not unlike that of a professional bureaucracy in the Weberian sense. Until the 1960s, Hollywood studios used the Motion Picture Production Code to make films inoffensive and palatable to the broadest possible audience on a global scale (Black 1996). More recently, Hollywood has engaged in what Thomas Elsaesser (2011, 247) calls "structured ambiguity," offering narratives which accommodate multiple perspectives and ideological positions, rather than endorsing a rigid ideology. However, even an innocuous format like the trailer is embedded in politics. The Trump tribute trailers make this inherent connection explicit by taking a clear side. They break with Hollywood's cardinal rule of neutrality and enlist one of cinema's most recognizable formats, the trailer, for a partisan cause. These trailers project a particular view and partisan notion of the democratic polity not as the inclusive unity of "we, the people" but as a community bound by a systematic distrust in government and the particularized trust in a single leader. In this dynamic, as we will see, structured ambiguity remains in play.

Cinematic Epistemology, Ocular Democracy, and the Question of Trust

In his Twitter thread from January 2022, Sanchez observes that QAnon followers and other conspiracy theorists on the right were increasingly using cinema as a frame of reference (Sanchez 2022). Conspiracy theories have, of course, been a constant element of democratic politics since the French revolution, with a decisive uptick since the 1950s, particularly in the US (Hofstadter 2016). Yet the "mistake" embedded in what Sanchez calls "cinematic epistemology" is to believe that outsiders are right simply because they are outsiders. As a defender of the Enlightenment, Sanchez sets out to undermine the epistemic authority which the conspiracy theorists accord to such cinematic templates. In the Enlightenment tradition, the democratic subject is a rational actor. As Jason Frank writes, quoting John Locke, "If the king's passive subjects were an 'image doting rabble,' democracy's active citizens were a ratio-critical public" (Frank 2021, 2). In order to become rational, the members of this public have to first become iconoclasts and emancipate themselves from the thrall of images, a task which is never fully completed. In Sanchez' *Kulturkritik* view, though, the adherents of cinematic epistemology fall prey to the "movie logic" and regress to the state of "image doting rabble."

However, the Trump tribute trailer creators are not so much part of an "image-doting rabble" as they are of an "image-making rabble." Rather than dismissing them as "low-information voters," defenders of liberal democracy would be well advised to assume that the image-making rabble know what they are doing. Empowered by easy-to-access and easy-to-use digital resources—including online repositories, recording devices, and editing software—they use the trailer template to make a spectacle of politics, but it is a spectacle of their own making. It is the gaze of the filmmaker and their implied audience, starting with themselves in the imagined position of the spectator, which casts the protagonist in a quasi-fictional conflict and endows him with the power to resolve it.

Rather than a victim of "cinematic epistemology," the bearer of this gaze resembles the inaugural figure of "ocular democracy." Since antiquity, spectatorship has been associated with ignorance and dependence: looking, viewing an illusion (on stage, or on screen) is the opposite of knowing, and of action. By contrast, the "emancipated spectator" (in the words of Jacques Rancière) has been freed from the restrictions of a hierarchical social order: free to see what they see, know what to think of it, and to do what they think needs to be done about it (Rancière 2021). The spectator of the tribute trailer assumes the position of an emancipated spectator and endows it with the "disciplinary force of the People's Gaze" (Green 2011, 107): they know they cannot trust government, and they act accordingly.

As a form of holding the governing to account, distrust is indispensable for democratic governance. But so is trust—"for the simple reason that trust expands the domain of democratic self-rule," as Mark Warren (2010, 310–45) argues. For Warren, distrust in liberal democracy needs to be confined to a narrow section of government. In the US voters channel their systematic distrust towards the legislative branch and, to a lesser extent, to the executive, which explains the constantly low approval ratings of both Congress and the President, while the judicial branch of government and the electoral process have traditionally been a source and object of generalized trust, i.e. trust which generalizes "from family, clan, or congregation to extensive relationships among compatriots" (Warren 2018, 77). To this procedural optimism Claude Lefort (1981) opposes a more skeptical view when he argues that by making politics a separate domain of thought, modern democracies are predisposed to totalitarianism. Striking the right balance between distrust of certain parts of the

system and generalized trust in the institutional arrangements
and representatives of government is thus key to democratic governance.

A trusting relationship is established, as Warren writes, "when trust judgments are met with *trustworthy* responses by those who are trusted" (Warren 2018, 75). But in mass democracy, those responses are almost always mediated, and very few people know or have met their elected representatives. To build trust in such a mediated environment, politicians and other figures purporting to govern with the consent of the governed must be responsive to their constituents' expectations of trustworthiness and regularly display responses which are public, generalized, and verifiable. Mass democracy requires "infrastructures of political address," as Ravi Vasudevan (2022, 360) calls them, which project an image of leadership that enables and sustains systems of governance. Long and grueling electoral campaigns are one of the most important trust-building exercises in liberal democracy. To build trust, politicians must subject themselves to public scrutiny and pass a series of character tests which are largely unrelated to their policies, with journalists acting as the steward of the public's interest (Albalat-Mascarell and Carrió-Pastor 2019). The personalization of politics, then, is a feature, not a bug: not a sign of decay of the public sphere and of democratic governance, but indispensable to a mediated, ocular mass democracy (McAllister 2007). This also means that the governed are, ineluctably, spectators of the self-presentations of the governing, and as such, their primary role is to be judges of character.

In a mediated, ocular democracy the governed are in a spectatorial relationship (Smith 2022) to a public figure appearing by virtue of the "infrastructures of political address," and the trust judgment is primarily one of allegiance or non-allegiance. Images of voters interacting with the candidate in political advertisements dramatize this trust relationship. In film studies terms, such images show a diegetic audience, much like the audience reaction shots in "backstage" musicals from the classical Hollywood period, which serve as indicators of the artistic success (or failure) of the protagonist-performers. Trump differed from traditional candidates in that he failed every character test in every way, but nevertheless persevered. Studies show allegiance is subject to confirmation bias, and that constituents will tend to stay loyal to a leader they trust for longer than is warranted by the available information (Brader and Ryan 2017). One could argue that character judgments in ocular democracy constitute a kind of tacit knowledge, and that tacit knowledge is slower to change than explicit, propositional knowledge. But we argue that a key to understanding Trump's resilience is that the "disciplinary force of the People's gaze" (Green 2011, 107) lies not just in the power to pass judgments, but also in the power to redeem. The emancipated spectators of the Trump tribute trailers wield their power as fans to judge. Granting forgiveness for the transgressions of their idols is one of the many pleasures of fandom. It gives fans a sense of agency and power, as their act of forgiveness mimetically replicates the act of transgression by defying the existing normative order. In this mimetic transgression, the emancipated spectators affirm themselves as the unbound subject of popular sovereignty. The "People's gaze" is always potentially an insurgent gaze, and the sense of lawlessness is part of Trump's appeal.

But exactly how democratic—or anti-democratic—is the emancipated spectator's gaze in the Trump tribute trailers?

In the Trump storyline, the viewer's (and voter's) distrust extends to the entirety of the government apparatus, including the electoral process, upon which Trump started to cast aspersions even during his successful first campaign for president. These tactics aim to undermine what Warren describes as "second-order trust" in institutions (Warren 2018, 34). This is a case of distrust extending beyond the narrow confines envisioned as productive by Warren and threatening to undermine trust in the system of governance as a whole. During such a conflict, the candidate, much like the hero in an action film fighting a corrupt bureaucracy or large-scale conspiracy, is the only trustworthy actor—aside, of course, from the viewers themselves. As Rainer Forst writes, "trust in charismatic leaders and in 'taking back control' or aggressive demarcations (both internally and externally) are also a response to social and political insecurity and it challenges democratic forms of conflict, compromise, and social pluralism" (Forst 2022). Trump would obviously represent such a challenge. But eventually, in the course of the storyline and the resolution of the conflict, trust in government is restored through the candidate's success at the ballot box. The storyline, then, would seem to be one of a crisis of trust, in which generalized trust in the institutional arrangements of liberal democracy is drowned out by systematic distrust, and ultimately replaced by what Forst and others describe as "authoritarian trust," i.e. trust based on exclusionary criteria (us vs. them) or unquestioning allegiance. To authoritarian trust, Forst opposes the normative notion of justified trust, i.e. trust for which reasons are given. Justified trust can be achieved through partial or impartial justification, i.e. idiosyncratic justifications based on personal (and potentially exclusionary) reasons and motivations and justifications which are based on commitments to fairness or moral norms.

In the case of Trump, the partial justification is, at first sight, strongly exclusionary. Much of Trump's political appeal seems to be based on racial animus (Breunig, De Neve, and Fabian 2020[4]). Trump cut his teeth in right-wing politics by mainstreaming the "birther" conspiracy theory, according to which then-President Barack Obama was ineligible for his office (Carew and Kelley-Romano 2017–8). Trump also put a portrait of Andrew Jackson in the Oval Office, the 7th president and populist champion of racial democracy for whites, at the exclusion of non-whites. There is evidence that racially motivated epistemic overconfidence

---

4   This study confirms our previous claim that the economic roots of Trump's success are overstated.

affects beliefs in all areas of politics, including trust or distrust in scientific research, and other positions typically held by loyal Trump supporters (Benegal and Motta 2022). Trust in Trump would thus seem to strongly be rooted in racists attitudes. However, in the history of American presidential politics, other candidates have tried, and failed, to win the highest office with campaigns centered around racial animus, from Strom Thurmond in 1948 and George Wallace in 1968 to Pat Buchanan in 1988. To win the presidency, a candidate has to build a coalition. In the case of Trump the coalition included neo-Nazis and white supremacists alongside evangelicals (a non-trivial share of which admittedly, are and have been white supremacists (Hawkins 2021)), right-wing Jews and supporters of Israel (Cavari 2021), as well as a surprising number of Hispanics and even a smattering of conservative African Americans (in particular celebrities like Kanye West or Candace Owens). The tribute trailers and clips always include shots of African Americans and other minorities in the diegetic audience. This may be dismissed as empty rhetoric, but there may be more to Trump's persona and the composition of his audience. "Very fine people on both sides," his statement after the 2017 Neo-Nazi riots in Charlottesville, VA, (Drobnic Holan 2019), points to the core of his public persona: transgressive, but strategically ambiguous.

Victims of Condescension and a Champion of Fairness

As indicated previously, Trump is not the candidate of economic anxiety. His voters are on average twice as wealthy as those of Clinton. Rather, Trump is the candidate of status elevation, and more specifically, status elevation through consumption. In Trump's case, name recognition is luxury brand recognition. In a 2013 financial statement he claimed that $4 billion of his $9 billion net worth alone were attributable to his brand value, and while that number may be vastly overstated, the excessive nature of

[Figure 2] An image of justified trust: Trump posing in front of Lincoln with fast food for the Clemson Tigers, January 14, 2019 (Source: X and The White House 2019).

the estimate itself is part of the brand (Nguyen 2020, 85). Trump's promise is not so such much that of welfare for all, but of self-indulgence for all (including, and starting with, himself).[5]

This is also the political meaning of Trump's performative pre-dilection for fast food. "Practices with food," as Sheila Bock (2021) writes, "send powerful messages". In early 2019, Trump hosted the Clemson Tigers basketball and the North Dakota State Bison football teams in the White House (see fig. 2). "We could have had chefs. But we got fast food," Trump said at the North Dakota State Bison reception, "I know you people very well" (ABC News 2019).

The note of condescension in the (racially coded) remark "you people"—which refers both to the teams and the broader audience—matters. There is a longstanding trope of white people referring to African-Americans as "you people," and the majority of the basketball players are African-Americans. Trump here embodies and performs a core dynamic of Jacksonian racial democracy: The equality of whites implies that even the lowliest

5   For Trump's affinity with the world of home shopping see Hediger (2020).

 of whites still have non-whites to look down on. At the same time, the remark comes from someone who himself has been, and continues to be, the object of condescension. It may or may not have been a coincidence that Trump posed with fast food in front of a portrait of Abraham Lincoln. But by doing so Trump, in an apparent paradox and departure from Jacksonian racial democracy, aligns himself with those who he himself treats with condescension.

The tribute trailers tell a story of overcoming condescension as a matter of political principle. Trump was treated unfairly by the establishment, the story goes, but he managed to get back at those who despised and mocked him (including Obama, who mercilessly roasted Trump at the 2016 White House Correspondents' Dinner). Trump's stated mission throughout his presidential campaign was avenging himself and others like him who have been allegedly treated unfairly, including all of the US, who have been taken advantage of by Europe, China, NATO, and others. Trump the politician and protagonist of tribute trailers is a (self-proclaimed) fighter against the humiliation of unfairness and for the universal principle of fairness. In that sense, trust in Trump is not actually authoritarian, but justified, both partially—through the idiosyncratic motif of a shared interest in self-indulgence—and impartially—by reference to the principle of fairness. The spectatorial subject interpellated by the protagonist of a Trump tribute trailer is thus indeed firmly anchored in the democratic political imaginary, and in ocular democracy. Any threat to democracy Trump might pose comes from within. Or, to put it differently: Trump tribute trailers develop their greatest value as a lesson in democracy if we read them not as fascist action spectaculars but as Haunted White House horror films.

Conclusion: Boring is the New Unfair

According to political scientist Tom Nichols (2021) and geographer Ben Anderson (2021), populism thrives in wealthy societies because citizens are bored. There is, writes Nichols (2021, 31), "no more reliable indicator of a society's ripeness for a mass movement than unrelieved boredom." In an interview in 2019, comedian Norm McDonald, who famously parodied presidential candidate Bob Dole on Saturday Night Live and never spared politicians in his work, discussed why he chose not to make jokes about Trump (CTV News 2018): Trump was too easy to laugh at and impossible to laugh with. Most importantly, however, Trump was himself an entertainer: he played a version of himself in wrestling shows (Moon 2022; O'Brien 2020), and his free-flowing presentational style at rallies worked more like a variation of stand-up comedy than like a conventional political speech.[6] Television executives like CBS' Les Moonves, since retired because of a #metoo scandal and his long history of sexual abuse in the workplace, understood this perfectly. Trump the candidate may not be good for America, Moonves famously stated, but he brought in advertising money and made for good television (Bond 2016). This, rather than an alignment in political convictions, was the reason that Trump was given so much free airtime in live broadcasts of his rallies during the 2016 campaign: His ratings were high. His entertainment value made Trump the perfect protagonist for political conflict as spectacle. Trump "The Entertainer" was the leader that contemporary ocular democracy needed: a leader not of the unemployed, but of the underemployed and restless. Trump thrives in the unauthorized fictions of tribute trailers because he is, after all, the enemy not so much of unfairness but of boredom

---

6   On the aesthetics of the Trump rally see also Johannes Voelz's paper "Towards an Aesthetics of Populism, Part I: The Populist Space of Appearance" (2018).

Literature

Albalat-Mascarell, Ana, and María Luisa Carrió-Pastor. 2019. "Self-Representation in Political Campaign Talk: A Functional Metadiscourse Approach to Self-Mentions in Televised Presidential Debates." *Journal of Pragmatics* 147: 86–99.

Anderson, Ben. 2021. "Affect and Critique: A Politics of Boredom." *EPD Society and Space* 39 (2): 197–217.

Aumont, Jacques. 2007. "Der Point of View." *Montage AV* 16 (1): 13–44.

Badiou, Alain. 2009 (2008). "Cinema as Democratic Emblem." *Parrhesia*, 6: 1–6. Translated by Alex Ling and Aurélien Mondon.

Barnes, Renée. 2022. *Fandom and Polarization in Online Political Discussion: From Pop Culture to Politics.* Basingstoke: Palgrave Macmillan.

Bauer, Kevin, Yan Chen, Florian Hett, and Michael Kosfeld. 2022. "Partisan Group Identity Predicts Politics" (working paper). Goethe University Frankfurt.

Benegal, Salil, and Mark Motta. 2022. "Overconfident, Resentful, and Misinformed: How Racial Animus Motivates Confidence in False Beliefs." *Social Science Quarterly* 1: 1–24.

Bessner, David. 2017. "The Ghosts of Weimar: The Weimar Analogy in American Thought." *Social Research* 84 (4): 831–55.

Black, Gregory S. 1996. *Hollywood Censored: Morality, Codes, Catholics, and the Movies.* Cambridge: Cambridge University Press.

Bock, Sheila. 2021. "Fast Food at the White House." *Western Folklore* 80 (1): 15–44.

Bond, Paul. 2016. "Les Moonves on Donald Trump: 'It may not be good for America, but it's damn good for CBS.'" *Hollywood Reporter*, February 29. Accessed June 21, 2023. https://www.hollywoodreporter.com/news/general-news/leslie-moonves-donald-trump-may-871464/.

Bordwell, David. 1985. *Narration in the Fiction Film.* London and New York: Routledge.

Bow O'Brien, Shannon. 2020. *Donald Trump and the Kayfabe Presidency: Professional Wrestling Rhetoric in the White House.* Basingstoke: Palgrave Macmillan.

Bump, Philip. 2017. "Places That Backed Trump Skewed Poor; Voters Who Backed Trump Skewed Wealthier." *Washington Post, December 29.* Accessed July 18, 2020. https://www.washingtonpost.com/news/politics/wp/2017/12/29/places-that-backed-trump-skewed-poor-voters-who-backed-trump-skewed-wealthier/.

Canfora, Luciano. 2008. *La democrazia: Storia di un'ideologia.* Bari: Laterza.

Cavari, Amnon. 2021. "Trump, Israel, and the Shifting Support for a Traditional Ally." In *The Trump Doctrine and the Emerging International System*, edited by Stanley A. Renshon and Peter Suedfeld, 281–315. Basingstoke: Palgrave Macmillan.

Chambers, Simon. 2012. "Deliberation and Mass Democracy." In *Deliberative Systems. Deliberative Democracy at the Large Scale*, edited by John Parkinsonan and Jane Mansbridge, 52–71. Cambridge: Cambridge University Press.

Chapman, Matthew. 2019. "Internet Ruthlessly Mocks Trump for Tweeting 'Very Cool Trailer' about Democrats' Impeachment Inquiry." *Rawstory, September* 24. Accessed February 8, 2023. https://www.rawstory.com/2019/09/

internet-ruthlessly-mocks-trump-for-tweeting-very-cool-trailer-about-democrats-impeachment-inquiry.

Cunningham, Stuart, and David Craig. 2019. *Social Media Entertainment: The New Intersection of Hollywood and Silicon Valley.* New York: New York University Press.

De Rosa, Miriam, and Vinzenz Hediger. 2017."Post-what? Post-when? A Conversation on the 'Posts' of Post-media and Post-cinema." *Cinéma & Cie: International Film Studies Journal* 26/27 (XVI): 9–20.

Drobnic Holan, Angie. 2019. "In Context: Trump's 'Very Fine People on Both Sides' Remark in Context (Transcript)." *Politifact*, April 26. Accessed June 21, 2023. https://www.politifact.com/article/2019/apr/26/context-trumps-very-fine-people-both-sides-remarks/.

Dyer, Richard. 2019 (1979). *Stars.* London: BFI/Bloomsbury.

Elsaesser, Thomas. 2011. "James Cameron's *Avatar:* Access for All." *New Review of Film and Television Studies* 9 (3): 247–64.

Fabian, Mark, Robert Breunig, and Jan-Emmanuel De Neve. 2020. "Bowling with Trump. Economic Anxiety, Racial Identification, and Well-Being in the 2016 Election." *IZA Discussion Papers* 13022. Bonn: Institute of Labor Economics (IZA).

Forst, Rainer. 2022. "The Justification of Trust in Conflict. Conceptual and Normative Groundwork." *ConTrust Workingpaper Series 1.* Frankfurt: ContTrust 2022. Accessed June 13, 2023. https://www.econstor.eu/handle/10419/265103.

Frank, Jason. 2021. *The Democratic Sublime: On Aesthetics and Popular Assembly.* Oxford: Oxford University Press.

Green, Jeffrey Edward. 2011. *The Eyes of the People: Democracy in the Age of Spectatorship.* Oxford and New York: Oxford University Press.

Gregersen, Andreas, and Birger Lankjær. 2017. "Cognitive Film Theory: A Personal Status—Interview with Professor Ed Tan." *Journal of Media, Cognition, and Communication* 5 (2): 70–80.

Habermas, Jürgen. 1981. *Theory of Communicative Action. Vol 1: Reason and the Rationalization of Society.* Boston: Beacon Press

Hawkins, J. Russell. 2021. *The Bible Told Them So: How Southern Evangelicals Fought to Preserve White Supremacy.* Oxford, New York: Oxford University Press.

Hediger, Vinzenz. 2020. "Warum lieben ihn so viele? Trump als Idol." *Frankfurter Allgemeine Zeitung*, October 7. Accessed June 21, 2023. https://www.faz.net/aktuell/feuilleton/trump-als-idol-warum-ihn-so-viele-lieben-16988988.html.

———. 2020. "How to Fight a Pandemic with Status Elevation: The Home Shopping Governance of Donald J. Trump." In *Pandemic Media: Preliminary Notes towards an Inventory*, edited by Laliv Melamed, Philipp Dominik Keidl, Vinzenz Hediger, and Antonio Somaini, 343–52. Lüneburg: meson press.

———. 2001. *Verführung zum Film: Der amerikanische Kinotrailer seit 1912.* Marburg: Schüren.

Hofstadter, Richard. 2012. *The Paranoid Style in American Politics.* New York: Knopf.

Kelley-Romano, Stephanie, and Kathryn L. Carew. 2018. "Make America Hate Again: Donald Trump and the Birther Conspiracy." *Journal of Hate Studies* 14 (1): 33–52.

Lefort, Claude. 1981. *L'invention démocratique: Les limites de la domination totalitaire.* Paris: Fayard.

262   Manow, Philipp. 2020. *(Ent)Demokratisierung der Demokratie*. Berlin: Suhrkamp.

McAllister, Ian. 2007. "The Personalization of Politics." In *The Oxford Handbook of Political Behavior*, edited by Russell Dalton and Hans-Dieter Klingemann, 571–88. Oxford, New York: Oxford University Press.

Möllers, Christoph. 2021. *Freiheitsgrade: Elemente einer liberalen politischen Mechanik*. Berlin: Suhrkamp.

Moon, David S. 2022. "Kayfabe, Smartdom and Making Out: Can Pro-Wrestling Help Us Understand Donald Trump?" *Political Studies Review* 20 (1): 47–61.

Moore, Alfred. 2016. "Conspiracy and Conspiracy Theories in Democratic Politics." *Critical Review* 28 (1): 1–23.

Morgan, Edmund S. 1988. *Inventing the People: The Rise of Popular Sovereignty in England and America*. New York: W.W. Norton.

Mouffe, Chantal. 2018. *For a Left Populism*. London: Verso.

Nguyen, Xuan-Thao. 2020. "Unpacking Trump's Brand Value: The Cost to Secured Creditors." *Cardozo Arts & Entertainment Law Journal* 38 (1): 85–99.

Nichols, Tom. 2021. *Our Own Worst Enemy: The Assault from within Modern Democracy*. Oxford: Oxford University Press.

Nolte, Ernst. 1965. *The Three Faces of Fascism*. London: Weidenfeld & Nicholson.

Polanyi, Michael. 2015 (1958). *Personal Knowledge: Towards a Post-Critical Philosophy*. Chicago: University of Chicago Press.

———. 2009 (1966). *The Tacit Dimension*. Chicago: University of Chicago Press.

Przeworski, Adam. 2019. *Crises of Democracy*. Cambridge and New York: Cambridge University Press.

Rancière, Jacques. 2021. *The Emancipated Spectator*. London: Verso.

———. 2013. *The Politics of Aesthetics: The Distribution of the Sensible*. Translated by Gabriel Rockhill. London: Bloomsbury.

Rosanvallon, Pierre. 2008. *Counter-Democracy: Politics in an Age of Distrust*. Cambridge: Cambridge University Press.

Ryan, Timothy R., and Ted Brader. 2017. "Gaffe Appeal. A Field Experiment on Partisan Selective Exposure to Election Messages." *Political Science Research and Methods* 5 (4): 667–87.

Sen, Amartya. 2009. "Foreword." In *The Tacit Dimension by* Michael Polanyi, vii–xvi. Chicago: University of Chicago Press.

Silver, Nate. 2016. "The Mythology of Trump's Working Class Support." *FiveThirtyEight, May 3*. Accessed February 12, 2023. https://fivethirtyeight.com/features/the-mythology-of-trumps-working-class-support/.

Smith, Murray. 2022. *Engaging Characters: Fiction, Emotion, and the Cinema*. Oxford and New York: Oxford University Press.

Stanley, Jason. 2021. "Movie at the Ellipse: A Study in Fascist Propaganda." *Just Security*, May 4. Accessed February 9, 2023. https://www.justsecurity.org/74504/movie-at-the-ellipse-a-study-in-fascist-propaganda/.

———. 2016. *How Propaganda Works*. Princeton: Princeton University Press.

Stasavage, David. 2020. *The Decline and Rise of Democracy: A Global History from Antiquity to Today*. Princeton: Princeton University Press.

Sternhell, Zeev. 2008. "How to Think about Fascism and its Ideology." *Constellations* 15 (3): 280–90.

Trautmann, Felix. 2020. *Das Imaginäre der Demokratie: Politische Befreiung und das Rätsel der freiwiligen Knechtschaft.* Göttingen: Wallstein.

Vasudevan, Ravi. 2022. "Infrastructures of Political Address: The Film and Media Archive." In *A Companion to Indian Cinema*, edited by Neepa Majumdar and Ranjani Mazumdar, 360–85. Hoboken NJ: Wiley Blackwell.

Visch, Valentijn, and Ed S. Tan. 2008. "Narrative Versus Style: Effect of Genre-Typical Events Versus Genre-Typical Filmic Realizations on Film Viewers' Genre Recognition." *Poetics* 36: 301–15.

Voelz, Johannes. 2018. "Towards an Aesthetics of Populism, Part I: The Populist Space of Appearance." *Yearbook of Research in English and American Literature (REAL)* 34: 203–28.

Voss, Christiane. 2011. "Film Experience and the Formation of Illusion: The Spectator as 'Surrogate Body' for the Cinema." Translated by Inga Pollman. *Cinema Journal* 50 (4): 136–50.

Warren, Mark E. 2018. "Trust and Democracy." In *The Oxford Handbook of Social and Political Trust*, edited by Eric M. Uslaner, 75–94. Oxford, New York: Oxford University Press.

———. 2010. "Democratic Theory and Trust." In *Democracy and Trust*, 310–45. Cambridge, New York: Cambridge University Press.

(Audio)Visual Material

ABC News. 2019. "Pres. Trump Hosts NCAA Champion North Dakota State Bison at the White House." Accessed February 17, 2023. https://www.youtube.com/watch?v=V7SyczyMKG0.

CTV News. 2018. "Norm Macdonald Talks Trump, Trudeau and the Secrets to Political Comedy." Accessed February 17, 2023. https://youtu.be/olkgPzlh5A8.

Guardian News. 2018. "The Action-Movie Style Trailer Trump Says He Played to Kim Jong-un." Accessed June 13, 2023. https://youtu.be/aYsaC2CADs0.

Liberty South Media. 2022. "A Nation In Decline." Accessed June 21, 2023. https://youtu.be/RsOXP-HrNWc.

MateyProductions. 2020a. "President Trump 2020 Trailer #2." Accessed June 13, 2023. https://youtu.be/xWJ1eblKQTQ.

———. 2020b. "We Love You President Donald J Trump." Accessed February 8, 2023. https://youtu.be/qpMfOUp_2Qs.

———. 2019. "President Donald Trump Inspirational Tribute (America First)." Accessed June 13, 2023. https://youtu.be/NQXjlJgIT64.

Montreux, Brandos. 2017a. "Trump: The Great Victory." Accessed February 8, 2023. https://youtu.be/7HDCn3gE-Dk.

———. 2017b. "Trump—American Badass." Accessed February 8, 2023. https://youtu.be/Zaqvc-0XDMM.

264 Sanchez, Julian 2022. "Tweeter Thread." January 23. Accessed February 2, 2023. https://twitter.com/normative/status/1485313085321719813.

The Telegraph. 2022. "Donald Trump Hints at Running for President Again with Campaign-Style Video." Accessed June 13, 2023. https://www.youtube.com/watch?v=TztxwKfud-k.

Trump White House Archived. 2020. "President Donald J. Trump: 'Our Best Days Are Yet to Come.'" Accessed June 13, 2023. https://youtu.be/enJwnRjkE9g.

X, and The White House. 2019. "Trump posing in front of Lincoln with fast food for the Clemson Tigers." January, 14.

Authors

Rebecca Boguska is a Film and Media Studies scholar. She was a recipient of the Postdoc.Mobility fellowship from the Swiss National Science Foundation (Brown University and University of Passau), and is a former member of the Graduate Research Training Program "Configurations of Film" at Goethe University Frankfurt.

Larissa Fischer is a PhD candidate and research fellow at the Institute of Sociology at the RWTH Aachen University. She currently works on the project "Sociotechnical Systems of Anticipatory Truth Verification in the Field of Airport Security," funded by the German Research Foundation. Her research interests include cultural sociology, qualitative methods, science and technology studies, visual culture, and science fiction.

Veena Hariharan is associate professor of Cinema Studies at the School of Arts and Aesthetics, Jawaharlal Nehru University. She is currently Alexander von Humboldt Fellow at Goethe University Frankfurt, where she is working on her project on non-human-human entanglements in cinema and new media. Her research focuses on documentary, non-fiction cinema, and the environment.

Vinzenz Hediger is professor of Cinema Studies at Goethe University Frankfurt where he directs the Graduate Research Training Program "Configurations of Film." He is a principal investigator at the Forschungszentrum Normative Orders and co-director of the research project "ConTrust – Conflict and Trust in Political Life." His research interests include marginal film forms, utility films, and the film trailer format.

Guilherme Machado holds a doctorate in Film and Media Studies. He is a former member of the Graduate Research Training Program "Configurations of Film" at Goethe University Frankfurt (2019–21). His research deals with the visual culture of labor and the epistemological implications of visual techniques and technologies used to control the production and circulation of labor-related knowledge.

Andrea Mariani is assistant professor in Film Studies at the University of Udine. He is a member of the Material Archival Studies Network and of the SSHRC project "International Amateur Cinema Between the Wars (1919–39)." His research and teaching focus on media theory, film philology, Italian amateur and experimental cinema, and media archaeology.

Bettina Paul is a senior researcher and lecturer in Criminology at the Department of Social Science at Hamburg University. Her current research is inspired by the intersection of science and technology and cultural animal studies. It centres around interspecies awareness, multispecies knowledge production, sociotechnical imaginations, and the polychronicity of technologies as in the case of truth technologies.

Rebecca Puchta is a PhD candidate in Film and Media Studies and a former member of the Graduate Research Training Program "Configurations of Film" at Goethe University Frankfurt (2017–20). Situated at the intersection of film and cultural studies, her doctoral research project investigates representations of big data and surveillance in documentary filmmaking in the post-Snowden era.

Jelena Rakin is a senior researcher and lecturer in Cinema Studies at the University of Zurich. She is currently working on her second book on the aesthetics of images of the cosmos, examining the convergence of scientific and magical visual repertoires in these images. Her research and artistic practices deal with imaging techniques and visual epistemologies. She is a member of the University of Zurich Space Hub.

R. Haritha is a PhD candidate at the Centre for Comparative Literature at the University of Hyderabad. She is currently working on a research project tentatively entitled *Digital Turn in Cinema:*

Reconfigurations in Cinemas of Kerala Post-2000. Her research focuses on digital cinephilia, minor cinema, and intermediality.

Marin Reljić holds a doctorate in Musicology and Film Studies and is a former member of the Graduate Research Training Program "Configurations of Film" at Goethe University Frankfurt (2017–20). He was the first recipient of the Gisela and Peter W. Schatt Foundation's scholarship. His postdoctoral project focuses on the interface between music/musicology and ecology.

Claire Salles holds a doctorate in Film and Media Studies (Sorbonne Nouvelle University). She works on feminist ecocriticism of moving images. Her research focuses on the imaginaries of telecommunication and pregnancy. She is part of the feminist research collective Les Jaseuses, where she explores alternative entanglements.

Henning Schmidgen is professor of Media Theory and History of Science at Bauhaus University Weimar. He has worked extensively on the machines of Félix Guattari, the concepts of Georges Canguilhem, and the problem of time in laboratory psychology.

Felix M. Simon is a communication researcher and doctoral student at the Oxford Internet Institute (OII), Knight Fellow at Columbia University's Tow Center for Digital Journalism, and an affiliate at the Center for Information, Technology, and Public Life (CITAP) at the University of North Carolina at Chapel Hill. He also works as a research assistant at the Reuters Institute for the Study of Journalism (RISJ) and regularly writes and comments on technology, media, and politics for various international outlets.

(Luiz) Felipe Soares is professor of Cinema Studies at the Federal University of Santa Catarina. His research deals with film music, literary theory, and image theory. After a sabbatical researching Sergei Eisenstein at King's College London (2015), he is now conducting his second doctoral research project in Music at Santa Catarina State University, dealing with Sergei Prokofiev's music for Sergei Eisenstein's *Ivan the Terrible*.

268   **Benoît Turquety** is professor in Film Studies at the University
Paris 8. He is working on the history and geography of media
technology, from a perspective informed by Gilbert Simondon
and historical epistemology.